Class in the New Millenni

CW00833420

Class in the New Millennium paints a fresh and comprehensive picture of social class in Britain today. Anchored in a broad repertoire of methods and pursuing a distinctive theoretical agenda, it not only painstakingly maps the structure, transformation and effects of the UK's key fault lines but goes behind closed doors to see how they play out in everyday family life.

Throughout the book Atkinson throws new light on a diverse array of themes, including: the continued effects of deindustrialisation, educational expansion, feminisation of the workforce and surging employment insecurity; the persistence of lifestyle cleavages despite cultural and technological change; the growth of political disengagement, the transformation of the Labour Party and the rise of nationalism; the entwinement of class with space, place and physical movement; and the way in which class interacts with intimate relations to shape not just the way we decorate our walls or talk over the dining table but the very reproduction of the class structure itself.

This innovative title will appeal to scholars as well as advanced undergraduate and postgraduate students interested in the fields of sociology, politics and political science, cultural studies, cultural geography, social policy and social work.

Will Atkinson is Reader in Sociology in the School of Sociology, Politics and International Studies at the University of Bristol, UK.

This book is essential reading for all those concerned about the state of social class in Britain. It builds on the work of Pierre Bourdieu to paint a nuanced and sophisticated picture of class in the new millennium. Richly theorised and beautifully written, it combines intensive ethnographic analyses with powerful conceptual insights which deepen and enrich readers' understandings of class structure, effects and place in the UK today.

Diane Reay, *Professor of Education, University of Cambridge, UK*

The vision of class captured by Will Atkinson in this book advances in an essential way our understanding of how everyday life is constituted of multidimensional structures of differentiation. The significance and interrelation of national, local and domestic spaces are presented via attentive exploration of rich data from the Ordinary Lives Project. The wealth of skilfully produced empirical material is particularly well used in the attention to the subtle drama about possible futures entailed in expectations of class mobility.

Elizabeth B. Silva, *Professor of Sociology, The Open University, UK*

Based on extensive and finely analysed evidence, Atkinson takes a further impressive step in consolidating his distinctive sociological interpretation of the effects of class on the reproduction of British culture.

Alan Warde, *Professor of Sociology, University of Manchester, UK*

Class in the New Millennium

The Structure, Homologies and
Experience of the British Social Space

Will Atkinson

LONDON AND NEW YORK

First published 2017 by Routledge

2 Park Square, Milton Park, Abingdon, Oxfordshire OX14 4RN
52 Vanderbilt Avenue, New York, NY 10017

Routledge is an imprint of the Taylor & Francis Group, an informa business.

First issued in paperback 2019

Copyright © 2017 Will Atkinson

The right of Will Atkinson to be identified as author of this work has
been asserted by him in accordance with sections 77 and 78 of the Copyright,
Designs and Patents Act 1988.

All rights reserved. No part of this book may be reprinted or reproduced
or utilised in any form or by any electronic, mechanical, or other means,
now known or hereafter invented, including photocopying and recording,
or in any information storage or retrieval system, without permission in
writing from the publishers.

Notice:
Product or corporate names may be trademarks or registered trademarks,
and are used only for identification and explanation without intent to
infringe.

British Library Cataloguing-in-Publication Data
A catalogue record for this book is available from the British Library.

Library of Congress Cataloging in Publication Data
A catalog record for this book has been requested

ISBN: 978-1-138-64472-4 (hbk)
ISBN: 978-0-367-87697-5 (pbk)

Typeset in Bembo
by Out of House Publishing

Table of contents

List of figures and box

Figures

Box

List of tables

Acknowledgements

I have accumulated many debts of gratitude in the years it has taken to complete this book: to the British Academy and the ESRC (project no. RES-062-23-2477), of course, for funding the underpinning research projects; to staff at the Office for National Statistics; to Roger Stafford at NatCen; to my colleagues on the Ordinary Lives project, Harriet Bradley and Adam Sales; to all the many people who tried to assist with recruitment; and to the various audiences at conferences and workshops where early versions of some of the analyses contained herein were presented.

1   Introduction

What is the state of class in Britain today? What – to give this somewhat abstract query more concrete form – is the shape of the nation's class structure, and how has it changed since the economic upheavals of the 1980s? How does it feed into our most apparently private of desires and tastes in music, sports, books, what we do to our bodies, watch on television and so on – not only setting us apart from others but setting up an order of worth in which some tastes are distinguished as 'legitimate' and others as 'vulgar'? In what ways has this mutated with entry into a new century supposedly characterised by choice, reflexivity and individualism? How does class orient our values and ethics, playing out in political attitudes, but also the degree to which we feel we even have a point of view worth articulating? And how has the neoliberal revolution that swept the world in the 1970s and 1980s played into that? How does class shape – but also how is it shaped by – the quotidian experience of space and place at the national, local and household level? How does it entwine with that specific bundle of relations we call 'family' in so doing? How, finally, are children's nascent and evolving class positions worked at through the most routine and prosaic, yet emotionally charged, objects and events of domestic life?

This avalanche of questions – vexations to countless scholars before me – I endeavour to answer in these pages, offering, as an end product, a novel vision of class, its effects and its place in everyday life in Britain for the new millennium. In so doing I mobilise the path-breaking and powerful view of what class is and how it works proffered by French sociologist Pierre Bourdieu in his *magnum opus*, *Distinction* (Bourdieu, 1984). Being rooted in a detailed analysis of his own country during *les Trente Glorieuses*, however, there have long been questions as to how far this perspective could be generalised to other Western nations and whether it still stood in 'the global age', 'the digital age', 'the age of the internet', 'late modernity', 'high modernity' or whatever other appellation one wants to foist on the last thirty or forty years. Thus set in motion was a rapidly accelerating train of scholarship aiming to test the applicability of Bourdieu's ideas in countries across the world. The UK was duly targeted as part of this, but in a way which, regrettably, overlooked some of Bourdieu's core insights and, as a result, left far too many questions unanswered. Moreover, Bourdieu himself, for all his evident advances, neglected to situate class fully in relation to other social structures and influences shaping the mundane experience of the world, essential for making sense of how the determinations of class are actually perceived, felt and lived, so there is need for some further conceptual elaboration. All this will be expanded upon in what follows as a means of contextualising the analyses presented throughout this book, but let me first recount precisely how Bourdieu came to prominence in class analysis and challenged the conventional schools of thought.

From life chances to the misrecognition order

For a period in the later twentieth century most scholars of class – notwithstanding a few resolute intellectual dissidents – fell into one of two camps. Marxists, on the one hand, claimed that class is defined by one's position in the production process – specifically, whether one is an owner of the means of production or a propertyless worker – and that everything, from work pressures, consumer desires and political leanings to the organisation of space, family relations and education, come down to the property owners' desire to maintain or deepen exploitation or the workers' determination to fight back. This boils down to a simple philosophical starting point: we are inherently labouring beings, transforming nature in order to survive. This comes before all else, defining the human condition and grounding all social relations. Some, like Erik Olin Wright (1997), have fought long and hard to fit the mess and complexity of contemporary societies into this framework, mapping multiple class fractions on the basis of how much skill or authority they possess and turning them into categories for survey respondents to fall into; but even for him class, and the opposition between owners and non-owners, remains primary.

The Weberians, on the other hand, asserted that social classes should be distinguished on the basis of the major fault lines in life chances in capitalist society, with John Goldthorpe (1980), their foremost representative, cutting up the occupational structure of Britain – and of other western nations later – into a vertical stack of boxes topped by the 'service class' of professionals and managers. Though light on philosophical anthropology, the Nietzschean thesis that people are driven to dominate one another echoes in Weber's own formulations and perhaps seeps unbeknownst into the most seemingly technical of sociological researches otherwise enthralled by the economic view of people as utility maximisers. However, in contrast to the expansive explanatory power that Marxists ascribed to class – which has always tended to veer into outright reductionism – they opt for a more modest view of its place in society. Educational inequalities may well be explained by rational choices made in the face of different resources, and political views may be attuned to maintaining or improving one's advantages, but consumption is, strictly speaking, a question of status, with little to do with class, and the everyday experience of space or family is of virtually no interest.

The two traditions often came into open conflict. Who, asked many, offered the soundest, most robust and most useful approach to class? When compared side-by-side, what does one reveal that the other hides? A famous investigation of these questions by Marshall *et al.* (1988) in the UK effectively came down in favour of Goldthorpe. Wright's Marxist map of class relations was deemed too difficult to implement, too narrow in its scope and too driven by theoretical and political prejudices to be of much use to workaday sociologists seeking to chart patterns of inequality efficiently. The timing of this intervention was hardly convenient for Wright: at the same time Marxism was declining both as a political and intellectual force around the world and, though he continued to publish the results of his endeavours in the late 1990s, few have since taken up and used his measure of social class. Goldthorpe and his colleagues thus emerged the victors, and since then his class map – known as the 'EGP scheme' in recognition of the three researchers who worked on it together, Erikson, Goldthorpe and Portacarero – has been consecrated as the official governmental measure of class, both at the national level, in the form of the UK Office for National Statistics' Socio-economic Classification scheme (NS-SEC), and at the international level, in the form of the European Socio-economic Classification (E-SeC) (Rose and Harrison, 2010). This is not to say there were no dissenting voices: some analysts preferred – and still prefer – to define stratification in terms of network clustering (e.g. Stewart *et al.*, 1980; Bottero, 2005) or small occupational clusters (Grusky, 2005), while others have endeavoured to devise alternative maps of class akin to the EGP scheme but taking into account the mushrooming service sector in post-industrial nations (Esping-Andersen, 1993; Oesch, 2006). These perspectives have failed, however, to gather quite the same momentum as Goldthorpe's vision of class, leaving the latter in a position of 'industry standard'.

As a new millennium loomed and dawned, however, a revolution swept class analysis. Many were frustrated by the inability of the EGP scheme, and its founding logic, to reveal anything about the way in which class is perceived in daily life, entwined with a sense of worth and denigration and inscribed deep into mind and body, while feminists in particular took issue with the simplistic view of household relations – as simply being ruled by the primary earner's (read: man's) class interests and opportunities – and, by implication, gender underpinning it (see Atkinson, 2015). A search for fresh inspiration was sparked, and out of the scramble for different foundations emerged one body of work which, for all its problems, could provide the conceptual ammunition necessary for reinventing the oldest of sociological topics: that of Bourdieu.

For Bourdieu, class is not defined by exploitation or life chances, though both are still enveloped within his perspective. Instead, harking back to the pithy meditations of Blaise Pascal, but with distinct echoes of Hegel, class is defined by possession of certain properties securing *recognition* in a particular social order, that is, worth and value in the eyes of others. More accurately, since these properties are essentially arbitrary yet signal immense legitimacy in the eyes of their beholders, they secure *misrecognition* – the mistaken belief that someone is inherently superior by virtue of the fact they display a socially esteemed set of characteristics – and, with that, *symbolic power* – the power to have one's definition of reality accepted and even taken for granted (rendering it 'doxic').[1] In post-industrial capitalist societies with developed educational systems, the three key sources of misrecognition toward which libidos – in the sense of desire for worth – are channelled are economic capital (money and wealth), cultural capital (a certain way of knowing the world emphasising mastery of abstract symbol/sign systems and linked to educational level), and social capital (connections and networks), all of which can be described as symbolic capital insofar as they are misrecognised as legitimate. Moreover, the class structure does not consist of a set of neat boxes piled on top of one another, as for Marxists or Weberians, but takes the form of a multidimensional *social space*. Three axes are key: total volume of capital in all its forms, composition of capital (i.e. whether one's capital is primarily economic or cultural in character) and changes in these properties over time. Bourdieu thus distinguishes three clusters or clouds of individuals in these spaces which can be labelled 'classes' for analytical purposes: the dominant at the top, the dominated at the bottom and an intermediate class in between. Yet he also distinguishes class fractions *within* these three classes on the basis of whether they are richer in cultural capital or economic capital, pitting, for example, intellectuals against business leaders in the dominant class, with professionals in between, and cultural intermediaries (nurses, youth workers etc.) against small-business owners in the intermediate class.

Those possessing similar capital volumes and compositions are deemed to have similar conditions of existence, which in turn foster different dispositions, or habitus, among those subject to them and, thus, different aesthetic and ethical outlooks – or lifestyles and political attitudes. Insofar as these are associated in perception with being 'smart' or 'rich' or their maligned opposites in line with the misrecognition order and distribution of symbolic capital, some tastes and views are cast as elegant, desirable or authoritative on a wider scale while others are seen as 'trashy', 'ignorant' and so on. Indeed, if one maps out topographically the maximum differences and similarities of lifestyles – the 'symbolic space' – and attitudes – the space of political position-takings – and then examines where the different classes and class fractions sit within them, a remarkable (though not necessarily perfect) homology or correspondence between their dimensions and the dimensions of the social space emerges, thus converting statistical distances and directions into not only a guide to everyday perceptions of social distance but maps of power relations. Bourdieu himself demonstrated all this not through linear statistical techniques of the kind familiar to anglophone sociologists of class but through the innovative method of simple correspondence analysis (CA) and, later, multiple correspondence analysis (MCA), both forms of factor analysis designed to uncover correspondences between variables or categories of variables and project them geometrically (see Le Roux and Rouanet, 2004, 2010).

The immediate difference from the EGP scheme is obvious: occupations which the latter rolls together in the service class or the intermediate class, or even within their constituent subcategories (lower versus higher professionals and managers, for example), would be distinguished according to Bourdieu's logic on account of the type of capital at their disposal. Several substantive advances follow from this. First, Bourdieu's scheme allows a more nuanced approach to the puzzle of educational reproduction by distinguishing the primary resource at a parent's or family's disposal. Rather than being a debate over whether economic advantage, social connections or familial transmission of cultural capital is the key, in other words, it is likely to differ by class fraction within the dominant class. Second, when it comes to studying lifestyles, the NS-SEC, in rolling together class fractions, also rolls together what are likely to be different classed aesthetics with different associated tastes and practices. Perhaps this is one reason why Chan and Goldthorpe (2007) fail to find any significant connection between class and lifestyle differences while recognising the distinguishing power of education (see Atkinson, 2011). Finally, Bourdieu's approach can throw fresh light on an issue which has plagued even Nuffield-sympathisers: the fact that, far from conforming to the hypothesis that the service class should be generally conservative in political outlook in order to protect their interests, the top class is fractured into an economically wealthy right-leaning faction and a highly educated left-leaning faction (see debates and contributions in Evans, 1999), which might again be hypothesised to flow from the different sources of their dominance. There have been all kinds of efforts to modify the EGP scheme to account for this (e.g. Güveli *et al.*, 2007), but they begin to depart from, and perhaps even undermine, the original neo-Weberian logical connection between class, life chances and political interests.

Mapping the British social space and its homologies

Many people, struck by the advances that Bourdieu's view offers, have endeavoured to apply his logic and methods to their own nations, mapping social spaces and their homologies in Norway, Denmark and more (Prieur *et al.* 2008; Rosenlund, 2009; see also Coulangeon and Duval, 2014). In the UK, however, reception of Bourdieu's ideas has traversed a rockier route. At first influential primarily among qualitative researchers and feminists interested in symbolic power and the experience of denigration, or 'symbolic violence', that it entails (e.g. Skeggs, 1997), latterly it has been taken up by scholars interested in charting broader national patterns of symbolic power. Bennett *et al.*'s (2009) analysis of the Cultural Capital and Social Exclusion (CCSE) survey undertaken in 2003 was the first move in this direction, though because they were more interested in the cultural landscape of Britain than class *per se* they dutifully constructed the symbolic space only to then stick to a slightly modified version of the NS-SEC as their definition of class for purposes of homology-checking.

More recently there has been the controversial effort of Savage *et al.* (2013) to use the BBC-sponsored 'Great British Class Survey' (GBCS) to construct a new map of the UK's class structure (see also Savage *et al.*, 2015). Based on a huge sample and deploying a plethora of analytical techniques, they identified seven classes characterised by varying levels and combinations of the three major capitals: the elite, the established middle class, the technical middle class, new affluent workers, emergent service workers, the traditional middle class and, at the bottom, the 'precariat'. Unfortunately, however, the logic of the GBCS analysis left something to be desired. The use of latent class analysis, which manages to obscure the relational nature of class – the topology defining it as a social space – by failing to unpick the relative distances and directions of class fractions *vis-à-vis* one another, is a small procedural niggle. More significantly – continuing an error displayed by the CCSE team (esp. Le Roux *et al.*, 2008) – by deciding to measure cultural capital in terms of lifestyle practices rather than measures of symbolic mastery (such as education), Savage *et al.* (2013) *conflated the social space and the space of lifestyles.* Let us be clear here: the social space and the symbolic space are two quite different types of epistemic space, or are of different 'orders' as Rosenlund (2009) puts it – the social space of class positions is what Bourdieu called a *field*, structured by possession of capital, while the symbolic space is a *space of position-takings* which are paired in perception with positions in the social space because of their correspondence and causal connection (see esp. Bourdieu, 1998: 6–7). Listening to Brahms is not 'distinguished' by itself but only when associated statistically and perceptually (albeit fuzzily) with being 'smart' or 'intelligent'. Degree of homology is, however, an empirical question, so if cultural capital is defined as certain lifestyle practices and read off directly from the symbolic space (which would be equivalent to taking political attitudes as directly constitutive of class), and class categories retroactively realigned in order to map more satisfactorily according to the researchers' preference, it becomes impossible to unpick or test empirically the nature and degree of homology between the spaces or the causal link. In short, the GBCS scheme is a disturbingly circular and descriptive model of class unable to distinguish cause and consequence, *explanans* and *explanandum*. Perhaps this fits the preference for 'descriptive theory' advocated by at least one leading member of the team (Savage, 2009), but it runs counter to Bourdieu's own logic as clearly witnessed in not only his causal model (1984: 171) but his warning that researchers should not 'confuse the symbolic structure with the social system which produces it' (1986: 816).

The upshot of all this, of course, is that no one has yet drawn up a map of the British social space and systematically checked its homologies with the symbolic space and the space of political position-takings. That, then, is what Part I of the present endeavour ventures to do, beginning first of all in Chapter 2 with the basic task of building and validating a new model of the British class structure *à la* Bourdieu – that is to say, identifying the key fault lines of the misrecognition order – and exploring its transformation in recent history. Chapter 3 goes on to chart the symbolic space in twenty-first-century Britain, using the CCSE team's own data, but departing from their manner of proceeding, to pull out the core dimensions of cultural difference. Checking the homology with the social space, it unearths the distinct continuities of class orientations despite the appearance of new media and forms of expression in the UK today. Chapter 4 then moves on to political attitudes, constructing the space of maximal differences and similarities in ethics and outlooks and then assessing the correspondence with class positions. A key finding, in line with Bourdieu's own analysis, is the distinct disenfranchisement of the dominated class in the UK today, so I spend a little bit of time digging further into the nature and genesis of this.

Field analysis and lifeworld analysis

There is still the question of the everyday experience of class. This is, to be sure, something which Bourdieu's perspective is often said to have brought back into the remit of class analysis after the Nuffield school effectively banished it. It allows us to grasp, after all, the way in which we perceive and judge the most mundane things and people we come across in the world, the common labels we use for them and the visceral responses they can elicit. Yet this still does not go quite far enough, for if we are to fully grasp the phenomenology of class experience we need to add in two extra steps. First of all we need to explore and conceptualise the *dialectical* relationship between, on the one hand, our class position and habitus and, on the other, those other things and people physically around us, raising the question of the socially structured location and movement of ourselves, and everything else, through space and time. In short, we need to pin the social space down in physical space and recognise that *place matters* in shaping class position, class habitus and perceptions of oneself and others just as class shapes positions in and perceptions of place.

Second, building on the theme of *multiplicity* increasingly flagged by critics and advocates of Bourdieu alike (e.g. McNay, 1999; Lahire, 2011; Decoteau, 2016; Ingram and Abrahams, 2016), we need to investigate the way in which class interplays in mundane experience with *other* struggles over (mis)recognition, i.e. other capitals and fields. These include the large-scale struggles to be recognised as a worthy artist, politician or business leader and so on studied by Bourdieu himself – with fields focussed on cultural, ideological and economic production themselves encased within a wider 'field of power' in which fractions of the dominant class struggle to impose their contrasting definitions of worth and the world as the truly legitimate one. We might also add the fields in which sexual worth and ethno-racial domination are forged (see Emirbayer and Desmond, 2015; Atkinson, 2016). At another level, however, there are all the 'micro-fields' identified by Bourdieu only later in his career (esp. 1998, 2000, 2005), employing organisations – themselves embedded within the wider field of power – and family relations – wherein *love* or *care* are forms of recognition and misrecognition struggled over (amongst others) – being perhaps the most important examples.

To articulate the difference in emphasis *vis-à-vis* Bourdieu a distinction can be drawn between field analysis and lifeworld analysis. The former is concerned with mapping the structure, homologies and associated experiences of a specific field – very much Bourdieu's own usual *modus operandi* and the *modus operandi* of Part I of this book. Lifeworld analysis, on the other hand, is an exploration of the way in which individuals' everyday worlds are structured by, first of all, multiple fields competing for their attention and desire and, on top of that, by the circuits of people and things produced by often far-removed others pursuing strategies in their own fields as well as within the social space.

It is only a change of perspective, led by different analytical interests and questions, and complements field analysis as much as vice versa. It does require a couple of new conceptual tools, though: *circuits of symbolic power*, rendering the differentiated and routinised movements of things, people and categories of thought across time and space generated by, but also facilitating, moves and counter-moves within various fields; and the *world horizon*, as the practical sense of what is possible and feasible across fields, e.g. of the effects that determinations and strategies related to one field are having or are likely to have on others, rather than within just one. If individuals have habitus in relation to class and specific fields, the world horizon binds them together to form what Bourdieu called a *social surface*, such that one's dispositions, schemes of perception and libidinal strivings are defined not just relative to the positions of others within each field defining one's world but relative to one another depending on which field they are pertinent to.

These notions have been elaborated more fully elsewhere (Atkinson, 2016), but here the point is to show them at work. Part II thus draws on the research project that first suggested their importance – an intensive qualitative study of family life in Bristol, deploying observational methods, interviews and diaries in a range of households across the city – to document the specific place of class within lifeworlds.[2] Chapters 5 and 6 deal with the two-way relationship between the social space and physical space in shaping mundane experience, but at different levels – one at the level of the nation and the city, the other at the level of the neighbourhood. Chapters 7 and 8 then move on to consider the structures underpinning the experience of domestic space and time, broaching the interplay of class, work and family – as so many fields with their own capitals – in directing consciousness and competing for libidinal investment. This theme is then taken further in Chapter 9, where I consider the interrelation of class and family in parent-child relations as they relate to educational performance and the acquisition, or not, of cultural capital. In so doing we will have come full circle, dissecting the daily activity, interactions, joys and frustrations through which the general structure of class relations anatomised in Part I is continuously reproduced and transformed from one generation to the next.

Notes

1 The distinction between recognition and misrecognition is important, however, for understanding the relationship between the human condition and the social relations through which it is realised. Human beings, in the face of finitude and equipped with the capacity for intersubjectivity, seek *recognition* in order to justify their existence, and this is first worked out in relation to the family (Bourdieu, 2000; Atkinson, 2016). They do not generally seek misrecognition directly, as if they were actively trying to dupe others while knowing that their properties are arbitrary. Misrecognition is, instead, the unintended consequence of the struggle for recognition from others. Whether it is an inevitable consequence is difficult to say. I am aware there is a philosophical debate over whether some sources of recognition are universally valid, which Bourdieu is accused of flip-flopping on (Lane, 2000), but I do not intend to engage with that here.

2 For full methodological details, see Appendix III. The project was spurred by an earlier study (Atkinson, 2010) which had revealed the importance of individual lifeworlds for gaining a fuller picture of class without being able to anatomise them comprehensively.

References

Atkinson, W. (2010) *Class, Individualization and Late Modernity: In Search of the Reflexive Worker*. Basingstoke: Palgrave Macmillan.

8   *Introduction*

Atkinson, W. (2011) 'The Context and Genesis of Musical Tastes: Omnivorousness Debunked, Bourdieu Buttressed' *Poetics*, 39(3): 169–186.

Atkinson, W. (2015) *Class*. Cambridge: Polity Press.

Atkinson, W. (2016) *Beyond Bourdieu*. Cambridge: Polity Press.

Bennett, T., Savage, M., Silva, E., Warde, A., Gayo-Cal, M. and Wright, D. (2009) *Culture, Class, Distinction*. London: Routledge.

Bottero, W. (2005) *Stratification*. London: Routledge.

Bourdieu, P. (1984) *Distinction*. London: Routledge.

Bourdieu, P. (1986) 'The Force of Law' *Hastings Law Journal*, 38: 814–53.

Bourdieu, P. (1998) *Practical Reason*. Cambridge: Polity Press.

Bourdieu, P. (2000) *Pascalian Meditations*. Cambridge: Polity Press.

Bourdieu, P. (2005) *The Social Structures of the Economy*. Cambridge: Polity Press.

Chan, T. W. and Goldthorpe, J. H. (2007) 'Social Stratification and Cultural Consumption: Music in England' *European Sociological Review*, 23(1): 1–19.

Coulangeon, P. and Duval, J. (eds.) (2014) *The Routledge Companion to Bourdieu's Distinction*. London: Routledge.

Decoteau, C. L. (2016) 'The Reflexive *Habitus*' *European Journal of Social Theory*, 19(3): 313–21.

Emirbayer, M. and Desmond, M. (2015) *The Racial Order*. Chicago: University of Chicago Press.

Esping-Andersen, G. (ed.) (1993) *Changing Classes*. London: Sage.

Evans, G. (ed.) (1999) *The End of Class Politics?* Oxford: Oxford University Press.

Goldthorpe, J. H. (1980) *Social Mobility and Class Structure in Modern Britain*. Oxford: Clarendon Press.

Grusky, D. (2005) 'Foundations of a Neo-Durkheimian Class Analysis' in E. O. Wright (ed.) *Approaches to Class Analysis*. Cambridge: Cambridge University Press, pp. 51–81.

Güveli, A., Need, A. and De Graaf, N. (2007) 'The Rise of 'New' Social Classes within the Service Class in The Netherlands' *Acta Sociologica*, 50(2): 129–46.

Ingram, N. and Abrahams, J. (2016) 'Stepping Outside of Oneself' in J. Thatcher, N. Ingram, C. Burke and J. Abrahams (eds.) *Bourdieu: The Next Generation*. London: Routledge, pp. 140–56.

Lahire, B. (2011) *The Plural Actor*. Cambridge: Polity Press.

Lane, J. (2000) *Pierre Bourdieu*. London: Pluto Press.

Le Roux, B. and Rouanet, H. (2004) *Geometric Data Analysis*. Dordrecht: Kluwer.

Le Roux, B. and Rouanet, H. (2010) *Multiple Correspondence Analysis*. London: Sage.

Le Roux, B., Rouanet, H., Savage, M. and Warde, A. (2008) 'Class and Cultural Division in the UK' *Sociology*, 42(6): 1049–71.

Marshall, G., Rose, D., Newby, H. and Vogler, C. (1988) *Social Class in Modern Britain*. London: Routledge.

McNay, L. (1999) 'Gender, Habitus and the Field' *Theory, Culture and Society*, 16(1): 95–117.

Oesch, D. (2006) *Redrawing the Class Map*. Basingstoke: Palgrave Macmillan.

Prieur, A., Rosenlund, L. and Skjott-Larsen, J. (2008) 'Cultural Capital Today: A Case Study from Denmark' *Poetics*, 36(1): 45–71.

Rose, D. and Harrison, E. (eds.) (2010) *Social Class in Europe*. London: Routledge.

Rosenlund, L. (2009) *Exploring the City with Bourdieu*. Saarbrücken: VDM Verlag Dr Müller.

Savage, M. (2009) 'Contemporary Sociology and the Challenge of Descriptive Assemblage' *European Journal of Social Theory*, 12(1): 155–74.

Savage, M. *et al.* (2013) 'A New Model of Social Class?' *Sociology*, 47(2): 219–50.

Savage, M. *et al.* (2015) *Social Class in the 21st Century*. London: Pelican.

Stewart, A., Prandy, K. and Blackburn, R. (1980) *Social Stratification and Occupations*. Basingstoke: Macmillan.

Wright, E. O. (1997) *Class Counts*. Cambridge: Cambridge University Press.

Part I

Field analysis: the British social space and its homologies

2 The social space and its transformations

For years Britain's class structure has been depicted as a one-dimensional hierarchy. At first there was the Registrar-General's map of occupational classes, dreamt up by a medical statistician in the early twentieth century to tap into birth, death and fertility rates (Rose, 1995). Built on the assumption that there was an upper, middle and lower class defined in terms of their degree of prestige in society, and later by their level of skill, it stacked professionals on top of managers, who were in turn on top of skilled workers and, below them, unskilled workers. Then came the scales. Influenced by the vogue sweeping US sociology, the argument in mid-twentieth-century sociology was that society could not be cut up into boxes but rather consists of a gradational ladder ordering occupations according to their 'desirability' (among men) – as with the Goldthorpe-Hope scale – or interaction distance – as with the Cambridge scale (Goldthorpe and Hope, 1974; Stewart *et al.*, 1980). Unlike in the US, however, they never got so far as to recognise there may be more than one scale that matters, and that social stratification may be defined by people's positioning in relation to multiple resources. Then again the interest in scales did not last all that long in the UK before the EGP scheme was born, claiming to incorporate anything of value that the scales might have measured at the same time as fending off threats from Marxism. Thus established was the dominant map of class in Britain, with the 'service class' of professionals and managers sitting atop a new unidimensional stack of boxes, the intermediate class of clerical and technical occupations and the working class of varying skill levels wedged beneath (Goldthorpe and Hope, 1974; Erikson and Goldthorpe, 1992). If there are other sources of prestige or power around, these are a question of status, not class, say its advocates (Chan and Goldthorpe, 2010).

Now, thanks to Bourdieu, we know that class is *multidimensional* – that while there may well be three major classes in society the internal variation within each is fundamental for grasping struggles to define the legitimate way to be. We know that classes are distributed not in a scalar or gradational way, with even rankings, but are defined *relationally*, with the gaps between class fractions being as important as the distances and the directions. And we know that struggles over prestige and esteem are not distinct and separate from class or material conditions of life but *part and parcel* of them. Yet our tools for measuring and studying class lag behind our knowledge. As we have seen, even Bourdieu-sympathisers often stick with the EGP scheme or else, like the GBCS team, produce maps of the class structure which cannot actually be put to any real use. The premier undertaking, before all else, therefore, is to draw up a map of the contemporary British social space and derive from it a scheme which can be easily mobilised across datasets. This is a question of constructing what Bourdieu called 'objective classes', 'analytical classes' or 'classes on paper', defined by maximum internal homogeneity and opposition to one another in relation to conditions of existence and, underpinning that, possession of the properties commanding misrecognition in advanced capitalist societies.

A two-step process

Bourdieusian research in other nations has practised two methods of constructing analytical classes. On the one hand, Hansen *et al.* (2009) in Norway have produced a matrix of classes and class fractions via a careful recoding of the occupational variable available in the country's datasets in line with theoretical logic as much as empirical indicators of capital, shedding useful light on, among other things, educational inequalities (Andersen and Hansen, 2012). On the other hand, Prieur *et al.* (2008) and Skjott-Larsen (2012) in Denmark and Rosenlund 2009) in Norway have opted to construct a social space of capital possession via an MCA of various relevant indicators and then map the homology with lifestyles and political stances, using existing occupational classifications as rough proxy measures. The most satisfactory and rigorous solution, it seems to me, is to combine both methods, starting with the assembly of a scheme of classes based on existing occupational codes – this way the scheme can be recreated in a wide range of datasets – but then *validating* it by means of MCA.

To the first step, then. And in much the same way as Bourdieu had to content himself with the categories available from his nation's official statistical agency, INSEE, so existing measures produced by the UK Office for National Statistics (ONS) have had to suffice for this endeavour, namely, the unit-level Standard Occupational Classification (SOC) codes. This is the most differentiated measure of occupation generally available in government datasets, with over 350 categories running from chief executives and senior officials to bar staff and theme park attendants. It is, in fact, the basis of the NS-SEC, which is essentially an aggregation of the SOC codes following a standardised procedure in accordance with its own conceptual logic. The SOC codes are not themselves free from preconstruction – they do not offer a sort of 'blank slate' from which one can start again – since decisions have already been made by their creators as to how to define and bound occupational categories (skill level and function are the key factors), but they are nevertheless differentiated enough to offer a practical starting point.

The initial map of the social space was constructed by aggregating the SOC codes according to systematic exploration of several criteria. First, distribution of economic capital was examined, at this preliminary stage, by exploring the mean net income of the unit-level occupations, controlling for remuneration rhythms, in the Labour Force Surveys (second quarter) for 2011, supplemented by comparison with the equivalent datasets for 2010 and 2009 to neutralise anomalies.[1] Even in a survey with a sample size as large as the LFS, however, the large number of SOC code categories meant a few codes yielded inadequate income data and decisions rested more on other criteria, though in some instances other credible publicly available sources, such as industry sources, were consulted to reinforce decisions. Second, the distribution of cultural capital, in the form of highest educational qualifications possessed, was investigated at the unit level. The resultant categories were then calibrated against multiple further, rather more robust, measures of economic, cultural and social capital, occupational effects and trajectory drawn from a variety of available surveys, in some cases resulting in re-exploration and repositioning of unit categories. The construction of the classes and class fractions and the mapping of their relative positions and dispersion are therefore informed by a considerable labour of analysis, though it should be stressed that it remains a conceptual model premised on a series of theoretical decisions.

The second step is confirmation of this construction of the object via more advanced statistical analysis. Elsewhere, with Lennart Rosenlund, this has been achieved by creating a map of the social space via MCA of a variety of measures of economic and cultural capital in the CCSE dataset and then projecting, as a supplementary variable, the categories of the class scheme into it to validate their correspondence (Atkinson and Rosenlund, 2014). As can be seen from Figure 2.1, summarising the outputs of that work, the fundamental structure of the UK social space in the twenty-first century closely resembles that of 1960s–1970s France, as well as 1990s Norway (Rosenlund, 2009), contemporary Denmark (Prieur *et al.*, 2008) and many other Western capitalist societies. There is a dominant class, an intermediate class and a dominated class, but within each there are distinct class fractions on the basis of capital composition. More recent data confirms this (Tables 2.1 to 2.3).

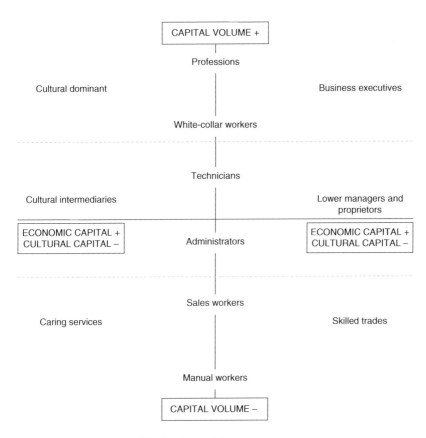

Figure 2.1 The structure of the British social space

Table 2.1 Some indicators of economic capital and demographics

Class fraction	Sex (%)★		White British (%)★	Per cent of working population★	Net weekly income (£)★	Received inheritance over £10k (%)★★	Mean total household wealth (£)★★★
	Male	Female					
Business executives	73.9	26.1	84.0	6.1	706	26.4	736,700
Professions	61.8	38.2	75.0	4.4	630	17.2	698,800
White-collar	61.6	38.4	79.3	9.7	493	16.4	521,200
Cultural dominant	39.7	60.3	81.6	10.2	434	18.4	694,358
LMPs	61.7	38.3	81.5	4.8	430	3.5	469,200
Technicians	80.4	19.6	86.2	4.0	477	10.0	407,800
Administrators	24.6	75.4	84.6	10.8	281	17.0	442,305
Cultural intermediaries	25.7	74.3	79.2	4.7	369	11.2	465,100
Skilled trades	90.3	9.7	84.5	10.9	339	4.4	280,200
Sales workers	36.8	63.2	81.1	7.6	205	5.7	279,800
Manual workers	66.1	33.9	72.2	17.3	240	2.9	194,500
Caring services	17.9	82.1	79.2	9.4	217	6.3	281,300

★ Source: LFS 2015. For details on all datasets see Appendix II.

★★ Source: CCSE 2003

★★★ Source: WAS 2006–8

Table 2.2 Some indicators of cultural and technical capital (row%)

Class fraction	Mother has a degree*	Highest qualification**							
		Higher degree	Degree	Higher vocational	A level or equiv.	Apprenticeship	GCSE and below	Other/don't know	No qualifications
Business executives	8.7	16.0	32.6	17.8	14.3	2.9	11.4	2.4	1.8
Professions	21.9	31.0	44.0	12.7	6.3	1.1	3.6	1.2	0.2
White–collar	11.8	13.3	35.8	17.4	16.1	1.7	12.0	2.2	1.3
Cultural dominant	22.9	42.6	35.9	10.4	5.0	0.6	3.3	1.4	0.3
LMPs	6.9	7.0	19.9	19.3	17.3	3.2	19.8	7.2	5.7
Technicians	5.7	10.4	25.6	22.0	17.6	5.4	14.1	3.9	1.2
Administrators	6.4	5.0	17.8	18.4	23.2	1.8	27.2	3.8	3.1
Cultural intermediaries	7.9	10.8	37.2	33.5	9.1	0.9	6.1	1.9	0.5
Skilled trades	3.0	1.4	5.2	18.9	23.4	14.4	17.7	9.6	9.0
Sales workers	3.7	2.0	12.2	12.9	28.9	2.1	28.9	5.1	8.4
Manual workers	2.2	1.1	5.7	10.0	20.7	4.8	26.8	16.1	14.6
Caring services	7.5	2.9	12.3	32.3	23.1	3.6	15.1	6.4	4.4

* Source: BCS 2012
** Source: LFS 2015

Table 2.3 Some indicators of social capital: proportion of class fraction knowing people in selected occupations (row%)

Class	Solicitor				Civil servant				Bank manager				Lecturer			
	Know?	Family	Friend	Acq.*	Know?	Family	Friend	Acq.	Know?	Family	Friend	Acq.	Know?	Family	Friend	Aq.
Business executives	52.1	9.6	23.3	19.2	38.9	9.7	19.4	9.7	26.4	2.8	11.1	12.5	37.0	9.6	16.4	10.9
Professions	70.6	5.9	52.9	11.7	55.6	5.6	30.6	19.5	37.1	5.8	22.9	8.6	54.3	8.6	37.1	8.7
White-collar	42.0	5.0	24.7	12.3	33.7	5.1	20.0	8.8	27.2	8.6	11.1	7.4	39.2	10.1	16.5	12.7
Cultural dominant.	44.3	5.2	31.3	7.8	38.6	6.2	24.6	7.9	27.0	4.3	14.8	7.9	63.2	11.4	45.6	6.2
LMPs	32.2	10.2	20.3	1.7	35.6	17.0	15.3	3.4	16.7	3.4	10.0	3.3	31.1	4.9	21.3	4.9
Technicians	36.5	3.8	25.0	7.7	33.3	7.9	21.6	3.9	13.7	3.9	7.8	2.0	40.4	7.6	13.5	19.3
Administrators	26.8	2.4	17.2	7.2	37.3	10.1	23.0	4.4	17.8	2.9	10.1	4.8	23.1	7.2	11.5	4.4
Cultural intermediaries	37.0	6.8	23.3	6.8	24.3	4.1	18.9	1.4	14.9	4.1	9.5	1.4	40.3	7.0	25.0	8.4
Skilled trades	21.3	2.4	11.8	7.1	25.1	8.4	13.2	3.6	17.9	2.4	8.3	7.1	23.2	5.4	11.9	6.0
Sales worker	19.3	5.5	9.0	4.8	22.1	8.2	11.7	2.1	14.5	4.9	7.6	2.1	26.4	7.7	11.8	7.0
Manual workers	21.7	2.4	9.3	9.9	21.0	9.1	8.6	3.3	17.7	2.5	9.7	5.6	18.7	4.9	8.2	5.4
Caring services	23.0	6.5	9.2	7.3	24.3	11.2	7.9	5.3	6.6	2.0	3.9	0.7	22.2	7.2	11.1	4.0

Source: CCSE 2003

* Acq.: acquaintance, including neighbour, work colleague etc.

The dominant class

Positioned at the right-hand side of the dominant class, rich in economic capital but less well endowed with cultural capital, are the business executives, i.e. managers and directors in production, finance and business operations (public relations, human resources, marketing, IT strategy management, etc.), as well as brokers. A highly masculine class fraction and one of the least diverse ethnically, these masters of the economic field have a high average weekly income after tax, and are also highly likely to be in possession of significant savings and investments and expensive homes. Their average total wealth possession – covering all financial assets, including pension wealth and property – is second only to that of the professions, and the total value of their household goods is highest of all. Of this fraction, 14.9 per cent are self-employed and 7 per cent are employers, i.e. the classical 'bourgeoisie', according to the 2015 LFS.[2] The CCSE data reveals they are also the class fraction most likely to have received an inheritance over £10,000 and to have had a senior manager as a primary-earning parent when they were young – 11.6 per cent as opposed to 6.3 per cent of professionals, 2.5 per cent of the cultural dominant and 2.6 per cent of white-collar workers – while less than half have attained higher education and few have parents possessing post-18 education (9.3 per cent of fathers, 7.1 per cent of mothers), suggesting a degree of closure and a mode of reproduction based on the intergenerational transmission of economic capital rather than cultural capital.

In direct opposition to the masculine economic fraction of the dominant class, across the social space, is the fraction richest in cultural capital but more modestly endowed with economic capital. Dubbed 'the cultural dominant' as a shorthand for 'the cultural fraction of the dominant class', included here are a number of subcategories which were initially distinguished but subsequently deemed to be too underpopulated to allow robust analysis in most cases and sufficiently close in terms of capital possession to be taken together. In analyses with large sample sizes it is possible to disaggregate them, and potentially interesting to do so too since they do possess different levels of capital, but they are sufficiently homogenous to be taken together as a 'class fraction on paper', to paraphrase Bourdieu – and indeed Bourdieu himself rolled his own categories together for some analyses where necessary. In relation to those in this zone of social space, for example, he referred to them collectively as the 'new bourgeoisie' – a term which, while more appealing to common discourse, is less analytically precise than 'cultural dominant'.

The first subcategory is intellectuals, i.e. HE teachers and scientists of all disciplines, the primary producers and professors of 'legitimate' knowledge premised on symbolic mastery and thus the most likely to be stamped with the markers of that knowledge in the form of certificates of higher education, including at postgraduate level. They might be considered more or less coterminous with (at least a large section of) the technical-intellectual field in the UK, including those parts which, insofar as members' employers are in the private or third sectors, are *heteronomous*, i.e. aligned with outside interests, such as product development (cf. Bourdieu, 1993). Of course, this points to the inevitable fact of internal dispersion, and the opposition within the field between powers spiritual (restricted production, specific symbolic capital, autonomy) and powers temporal (mass production, economic capital, heteronomy), but such dispersion is nevertheless oriented around a central point within the social space. Cultural producers/mediators – artists, writers, musicians and curators, or, in other words, members of the fields of cultural production and mediation, to whom the same caveat on internal dispersion just registered applies – form the second subcategory. They also possess very high levels of cultural capital compared to their middling economic capital, though not necessarily institutionalised in the easily measurable form of credentials, as for the intellectuals, so much as embodied as symbolic mastery and objectified in the form of cultural works (see Bourdieu, 1997).

The third and fourth subcategories are sociomedical services and teachers. Both are highly feminised and concentrated in the welfare and educational arm of the bureaucratic field. The sociomedical workers (physiotherapists, radiographers, clergy, social workers, etc.) are not lacking in economic capital, especially when the high numbers of part-time workers are filtered out, but their primary resource is their cultural capital in the form of certified symbolic mastery of humanity – i.e. a certain (classed) notion of human wellbeing and the abstract natural and social forces bearing upon it guiding application to concrete lives in daily practice. Teachers generally have slightly lower economic capital than other subcategories of the cultural dominant but possess ample cultural capital, even if their higher degrees are generally PGCEs rather than strictly academic qualifications. In field terms they are positioned outside of (i.e. they do not contribute to the struggles within), even if they are fundamental guardians of (and links in the chains of symbolic power emanating from) the fields of intellectual and cultural production. They are a diverse category in themselves, covering private- and state-school teachers, further-education teachers and special-needs teachers and educators in different subject areas, from the arts to physical education, but there is still enough homogeneity to warrant agglomeration for analytical purposes. Interestingly, Bourdieu (1984) himself separated primary teachers (*instituteurs*) from secondary teachers (*professeurs*) and placed the former in the intermediate class, but they are conflated and defined as dominant in some of his analyses.

The final subcategory of the cultural dominant is public-service executives, covering national and local politicians, senior officers in the protective services, managers in health and social services and educational inspectors and registrars. The division between business executives and public-service executives is highly homologous with the split between private- and public-sector employment, i.e. positioning within the economic and bureaucratic fields, but not – especially in light of deepening privatisation – strictly identical with it. It may be hypothesised that the private/public-sector division *per se* would more accurately approximate differences in capital possession than occupational title amongst executives, as well as capture more precisely the contrast between the public-service ethos and the profit motive. In order to test the former conjecture, all unit categories comprising the business executives and public-service executives were coded together and then the resultant 'higher executive' category split by sector and capital profiles explored. The differences in capital possession between private- and public-sector executives and between business and public-service executives were, in fact, virtually identical. Moreover, the public-service and profit-oriented ethics are, in reality, mixed to different degrees within the bureaucratic and economic fields depending on the state of the field and position within it (for example, the left and right hands of the state as discussed by Bourdieu, 1998a). Distinguishing by occupational title rather than sector was thus favoured partly for these theoretical reasons and partly because it can incorporate any pertinent public-private division when a specific variable for the latter is not available, as was the case for some of the analyses of wealth, anyway.

Between the two extremes of capital composition, nestled in the middle of the dominant class with high levels of both economic and cultural capital, are the professions: dominant positions in medicine, law and architecture (which are fields in their own right) but also finance professionals, civil engineers, pilots and captains. They sit, on average, at the apex of the social space, with a typical income comparable to that of the typical business executive and significant savings, investments, inheritance, house values and property ownership, even if the top earners among the business executives are likely to possess much more economic capital.[3] The professionals are also disproportionately in possession of ample institutionalised cultural capital, in the form of degree-level education, and the embodied cultural capital delivered through private education. Of these, 22 per cent are employers or self-employed (in other words, partners or owners of practices, etc.), and they appear to have a high probability of originating within the dominant class, inheriting economic and cultural capital from both parents, but also social capital – knowing the right people to get internships, build a clientele and so on. Perhaps this is part of the reason why they are among the more ethnically diverse sections of the social space, with Indians and the Chinese being notably over-represented, since a certain form of ethnicity-based social capital, or affiliation within the space of ethnic differences, may help. This is not, it should be stressed, the same definition of social capital used to explain the educational successes of Indians and the Chinese by Modood (2004), which essentially refers to the inculcation of particular aspirations by migrant families. However, Modood's interest in migration history does chime with Sayad's (2004) insistence that to make sense of a trajectory in one national social space one must situate it in the context of preceding intra- and intergenerational trajectories within other ('home') national social spaces and the historical political-economic-symbolic relations of domination between the different systems (e.g. between the UK and India and the UK and Pakistan). Migrants arrive with certain capitals (money, credentials, mastery of language) and certain strategies (the search for a 'better life'), forged in certain material and cultural circumstances, and those capitals are then recognised or not within the receiving social space, and those strategies of investment and conversion – or compensation through social capital – more or less successful as a result. Doubtless another reason why professions are disproportionate targets of migrant family strategies is because, constituting the most symbolically consecrated fraction of all in most Western societies, they are the safest guarantees of capital and the surest signs of having attained 'success'.

Finally, opposed to the professions in terms of volume of capital yet possessing a relative balance between economic and cultural varieties are the white-collar workers. They encompass the vast array of specialised occupations within the bureaucratic field and economic field (quality control, legal assistants, finance workers, estate agents, buyers, instructors, trainers, IT workers, etc.) but, while diverse, are less diffuse than previous definitions of white-collar workers, such as C. Wright Mills' (1958) expansive use of the term to cover managers, professionals and technicians too. Among all the class fractions within the social space this is perhaps the closest to an analytical boundary, with many individual members even extending down into the intermediate class on account of age, region, industry, ethnicity or gender effecting their capital volume. This could be, as we will see, reflective of the fraction's recent trajectory, but it acts as a reminder that analytical boundaries cannot be drawn too definitively, that they are only rough-and-ready proxies for the shifting dispersions of the social space (see Bourdieu, 1987) and that awareness of the composition of the fraction in any particular sample is important for making full sense of homologies.

The intermediate class

The intermediate class, a touch smaller than the dominant class, at least so far as the working population goes (25 per cent as opposed to 30 per cent), follows precisely the same chiastic structure as the dominant class. At one extreme are the lower managers and proprietors, or LMPs – lower in terms of capital compared to the managers and proprietors comprising the business executives, not function – who, while not especially rich in capital overall, are weighted toward the economic variety. Mostly men, they are players within the economic field, since they are almost all recorded as being in the private sector and almost a third are self-employed (the classic petite bourgeoisie), and their incomes and wealth levels are certainly relatively high for the class, but evidently they tend to occupy more dominated positions within the space of competing companies and businesses making up the economic system – perhaps due to their over-representation in the lower-pay commerce and service sectors (transport, retail, hotels, restaurants, pubs, salons, garages, travel agencies, etc.) rather than finance and manufacturing – and/or within their employing organisation as a field. In any case, they are relatively unlikely to have completed higher education.

In direct contrast, relatively high in cultural capital but low in economic capital and with a high degree of feminisation, are the cultural intermediaries, including nurses, paramedics, youth workers, counsellors, fitness instructors, conservationists and such like. Very much the equivalent of Bourdieu's 'new petite bourgeoisie', they often mediate and apply ideas and practices generated by members of the dominant class, but their appellation ultimately derives from their position within the distribution of capital rather than their function. Journalists and associated media positions are also put here, which might seem counter to common notions of high-flying and 'old-boy' journalists and editors with considerable power over political and popular discourse. However, while some journalists and editors – the very top slice of the journalistic field – may well be positioned within the field of power, the majority, on the basis of capital possession, evidently are not and, indeed, are also better thought of as 'intermediaries' rather than producers of doxa and orthodoxy (remembering that many editors relay the views of the newspaper's owners, who sit within the business executive class fraction).

In between the LMPs and cultural intermediaries are two class fractions with more balanced capital compositions, one more masculine, the other more feminised. The former have been called 'technicians' to reflect the relative equilibrium not just between economic and cultural capital but between technical capital and cultural capital, indicating a mastery of certain forms of 'technique', that is, the practical operationalisation and daily realisation of abstract principles pronounced upon by members of the dominant class, not unlike sections of the cultural intermediaries but as applied to the 'hard', masculine forms of knowing and being rather than the 'soft', feminine ones. Included here are medical, scientific and IT technicians, but also protective services (such as security workers, fire-fighters and low-ranking police officers) and engineers. Despite steady efforts to turn engineering into a graduate-entry occupation in the second half of the twentieth century, it remains very much open to those with higher vocational qualifications or even an apprenticeship, as demonstrated by the relatively low numbers possessing the most obvious indicator of cultural capital, a degree, and higher numbers possessing markers of technical capital. Since they also have a high probability of originating within the dominated class (54 per cent according to the 2009 BCS), engineers share notable family resemblances with the latter, especially the skilled trades, in terms of their dispositions – a certain 'practical ideology' clashing with 'gentlemanly' visions of legitimate culture, for example (Smith and Whalley, 1995) – though they remain distinct from them at a statistical level by their relative affluence and, therefore, distinct field of possibles. Civil engineers, on the other hand, are so dissimilar from the rest of the engineering categories – having significantly higher incomes than the rest as well as being dependent on cultural capital to a greater degree – and so sit among the professions instead.

Administrators, a majority female category, are less likely to possess higher certified forms of cultural capital than much of the intermediate class but are markedly more likely to do so than the dominated class. They tend to be fairly poorly paid, and are disproportionately likely to be part-time, but score relatively highly on other, wealth-related measures of economic capital (savings, home ownership, etc.). This is perhaps an effect of social capital, since administrators are relatively likely to have partners in higher regions of social space, though the direction of partnering differs by gender: according to the BCS, female administrators (the majority) are more likely to pair up with economically richer sections of the social space – 16 per cent are partnered with business executives, 12 per cent with LMPs and 21 per cent with affluent skilled workers – while male administrators are far more likely to connect with members of the cultural dominant (17 per cent) and caring services (20 per cent) or fellow administrators (27 per cent). Historically, it may well be that the white-collar workers and administrators separated and stretched apart vertically in the social space with the increased feminisation of the latter (since the former remains largely masculine) in the post-war period, with women being allotted the routinised clerical tasks in low-pay, poor-prospect jobs while men pursued career advancement and specialisation premised on higher education or training and returning greater economic and symbolic rewards (Crompton and Jones, 1984; Savage, 2000: 131).

The dominated class

In *Distinction* the only distinctions identified within the dominated class were vertical, opposing unskilled workers and small farmers possessing least capital overall and foremen possessing most, and little analysis of internal differences was done primarily due to inadequate numbers in Bourdieu's survey.[4] The wealth of data available for contemporary Britain, however, allows a somewhat closer analysis and, in fact, reveals that the dominated class is internally polarised not only vertically, in accordance with volume of capital, but horizontally too, with fractions pulled apart depending on whether economic or cultural capital is the primary resource at their disposal. True enough, analysis (esp. in Atkinson and Rosenlund, 2014) indicates that lateral dispersion is less pronounced than in other classes, despite the size of the class as a whole (at 45 per cent of the working population it is the largest class), yielding a funnel shape to the overall class structure, but that does not stop it possessing exactly the same internal structure as the dominant and intermediate classes. Moreover, the capital composition axis, just as in the other classes, reflects gendered dispositions and divisions, but to a much greater degree, one consequence of which is that, insofar as the structure of social space is premised on individual rather than household positions, the two horizontal poles of the dominated class have an increased likelihood of co-existing within dominated-class families.

At the top of right of the dominated class are the skilled trades – from gardeners and sheet-metal workers through mechanics and electricians to the building and textile trades. They are overwhelmingly male, fairly highly paid and self-employed in 36 per cent of cases, but their rate of cultural capital possession is the lowest of all within the social space, with higher vocational training and apprenticeships – the acquisition of technical capital, in other words – their usual pathways into work. Opposite them, displaying all the contrasting properties, are the caring and personal-service workers (nursery nurses, teaching assistants, veterinary nurses, care workers, hairdressers, etc.): they are mostly female, relatively highly educated for the class but fairly poorly remunerated. Sales workers, who display a balanced capital composition and middling position in terms of volume of capital within the class, are also mostly women and dependent upon particularly feminine caring, communicative and self-presentational dispositions (Gallie *et al.*, 1998; Hochschild, 2012). Research shows, however, that when men do undertake caring or sales work they deploy several strategies to protect their masculinity and manage to assume dominant positions (Simpson, 2004; Huppatz, 2012). Manual workers, from factory workers and drivers to cleaners and bar staff, constitute the largest class fraction of all, comprising over a sixth of the whole working population. Two-thirds male, they have low rates of all forms of pertinent capital and sit very much at the bottom of the class structure – though that is not to say they have no localised sources of recognition and misrecognition. Pakistanis, Bangladeshis and other Asian ethnic minority groups are disproportionately clustered here, though they do not form a significantly large proportion of the fraction altogether, dampening far-fetched claims about the 'super-diversity' of classes in an era of increased migration (Beck, 2007).

Theoretically speaking, it is likely that the manual workers sit above, and probably blend into, even more impoverished fractions in the social space characterised by long-term unemployment and, at the limit, destitution and homelessness – those who, in various stages of the symbolic struggle, have been labelled the 'lumpenproletariat', the 'underclass', the 'socially excluded' or, most recently, the 'precariat' by politicians, the media and other analysts. One can, of course, include the long-term unemployed in statistical analysis as a distinct category if one so wishes, the assumption being that they will display a particular variant of the dominated habitus – where necessity is extreme, accumulation of legitimate capitals particularly difficult and other sources of value (e.g. physical capital, local symbolic capital) sought instead. The same cannot be said for the short-term unemployed, or indeed those who do not have paid employment for other reasons (e.g. homemakers, students), who are far too heterogeneous in capital terms to be lumped together into a single useful category. Better to use other indicators of capital in analysis – household income, educational level, parental class, etc. – if one wants to make sense of the relative positions of individuals bearing that status.

Transformations over time

The social space is not static. Fractions rise and fall at different velocities with changes in capital possession over time – for example, certain occupations raising the educational barriers to entry, or others returning less economic capital than previously – or grow and shrink according to the shifting economic and industrial landscape of the country. Any two-dimensional map of the contemporary social space is therefore merely a snapshot – a freeze-frame of a moving picture – and that means it is necessary, if sense is to be made of current positions, experiences and strategies, to comprehend the recent past states of play. In the UK, as in other Western industrial capitalist nations to greater and lesser degrees, the major forces transforming the distribution of capital, and people, within the national social space over the last few decades have been progressive deindustrialisation, the rise of various services in its wake, including financial services anchored in the City of London, and expansion of the education system. The seeds of these changes lay at least sixty years back, with the rise of the state as an employer after the Second World War, steady automation in industry and so on, but the real spur came in the 1980s, when the Conservative government under Margaret Thatcher sought to reorder the balance of power within the economic field by assaulting the manufacturing and extractive industries, partly so as to weaken the strong trade unions attached to them (see chapter 4), and then deregulating financial markets with the intention of attracting foreign investment and fostering free market competition (the so-called 'Big Bang'). The resultant revolution in the national economic field, induced by the political field, was then consolidated in the early 1990s and subsequently, under the guise of 'third way' politics and propped up with appeals to maintaining global competitiveness, taken up by the 'New Labour' government from 1997–2010 (for reasons why, see Atkinson *et al.*, 2013). At the same time, however, since financial services were hardly going to offset the effects of deindustrialisation alone, there was a push to develop hi-tech and knowledge industries and an ambition, if this was to work, to 'up-skill' the workforce by increasing the proportion of the population obtaining degrees. The transformation of polytechnics into universities in 1992 was the first major move in this direction, followed by consistent efforts by New Labour to achieve its stated goal of sending 50 per cent of young people to university.

The shifting shape of the economic field can be glimpsed in the rise and fall of industries: manufacturing fell from employing 29 per cent of the workforce in 1978 to just 10 per cent in 2009; construction, agriculture and energy declined by smaller amounts; while financial services practically doubled from 11 per cent to 21 per cent in the same time period and public services (the various factions of the bureaucratic field) increased by 7 per cent to encompass almost a third of the workforce (ONS, 2010: 49). In terms of the structure of the social space, this has manifested in a marked decline in manual labour and, to a lesser degree, skilled trades, technicians and LMPs – in other words, much of the masculine right-hand side of the social space, though administrators have declined too – while white-collar workers, professions and caring and sales workers – the low-paid, feminine left-hand side of the social space, but also the higher centre, entwined with the swelling bureaucratic field – have grown (Table 2.4).[5]

This may be tied up with the degree of 'structural mobility' – or mobility spurred by the changing shape of the social space, altering the field of available positions – indicated by the BCS, which tracks a sample of children born in 1970, since far more people moved out of the dominated class than moved into it. All classes thus have a relatively high rate of being constituted by sons and daughters of members of the dominated class, though the rate by which the dominated class is comprised of people hailing from the dominated class is still vastly disproportionate (Table 2.5). However, if we compare outflow – the likelihood of arriving at a particular destination from a particular starting point – the disparity between the classes, and the difference by gender, is evident (Table 2.6). In short, men born into the dominant class are highly likely to stay in the dominant class and fairly unlikely to fall into the dominated, whereas children of the dominated class are most likely to end up in the dominated class *despite* its shrinking size. Strikingly, women of *all* class origins have tended to be drawn toward the intermediate zone of social space, where some highly feminised class fractions (administrators, cultural intermediaries) reside, at a high rate, and if one direction of travel might be explained partly by shrinkage of the dominated class – particularly manual work or the female-dominated skilled trades which have been decimated through global competition, such as textiles – the other can only be explained by a constrained field of possibles generated by certain gendered expectations and dispositions (see Atkinson, 2016).

Table 2.4 Morphology of the social space, 1991–2015 (%)

	Proportion of working population						Rate of feminisation					
	1991	1995	2000	2005	2010	2015	1991	1995	2000	2005	2010	2015
Business executives	6.5	8.3	8.9	8.1	8.7	6.1	24.1	29.0	30.6	23.7	25.7	26.1
Professions	2.8	2.9	3.3	3.6	4.2	4.4	20.5	22.2	28.1	28.7	34.5	38.2
White-collar	2.8	2.5	2.7	5.8	6.0	9.7	30.2	34.2	40.1	43.1	42.6	38.4
Cultural dominant	8.4	9.4	9.8	9.0	9.7	10.2	50.7	52.2	54.6	59.1	62.7	60.3
LMPs	6.5	6.2	5.8	5.6	5.8	4.8	31.9	31.4	34.4	38.7	38.5	38.3
Technicians	4.9	5.0	5.6	4.2	4.4	4.0	15.3	13.6	14.4	15.7	16.7	19.6
Administrators	15.3	14.5	14.1	13.3	11.9	10.8	79.9	81.4	80.7	79.4	77.8	75.4
Cultural intermediaries	2.5	2.7	2.9	4.2	4.5	4.7	86.7	87.6	86.6	71.6	71.7	74.3
Skilled trades	15.7	13.2	12.4	11.3	10.7	10.9	10.3	10.1	8.4	7.7	8.3	9.7
Manual workers	23.4	22.3	20.6	19.2	17.9	17.3	37.9	36.9	34.4	32.2	32.9	33.9
Sales workers	5.9	6.4	6.8	8.0	7.5	7.6	74.4	74.1	72.9	67.3	63.9	63.2
Caring services	5.4	6.7	7.1	7.8	8.8	9.4	82.7	83.9	85.1	83.8	83.1	82.1

Sources: GHS 1991–2; LFS 1995, 2000, 2005, 2010, 2015

Table 2.5 Social mobility: inflow

Class	Father's class							
	Men				Women			
	Dominant	Intermediate	Dominated	Total*	Dominant	Intermediate	Dominated	Total*
Dominant	30.2	23.7	46.2	100.1	28.0	24.3	47.7	100.0
Intermediate	20.9	17.8	61.3	100.0	18.8	18.3	63.0	100.1
Dominated	11.3	14.4	74.3	100.0	12.9	16.1	71.0	100.0

Source: BCS 2009

* Row totals do not always add up to 100 due to rounding.

Table 2.6 Social mobility: outflow

Class	Father's class					
	Men			Women		
	Dominant	Intermediate	Dominated	Dominant	Intermediate	Dominated
Dominant	53.9	46.7	28.0	42.8	37.8	23.7
Intermediate	25.2	23.7	25.1	37.2	36.8	40.5
Dominated	21.0	29.6	47.0	20.0	25.4	35.8
Total*	100.1	100.0	100.1	100.0	100.0	100.0

Source: BCS 2009

* Column totals do not always add up to 100 due to rounding.

As to the expansion of the higher education system, the principal effect has been to retranslate existing disparities between classes, and relocate the key sites of difference, in exactly the same way as Bourdieu (1984: 125–68) concluded of the growth of secondary schooling in post-war France (Table 2.7). So the first thing to note is that rates of acquiring higher education have risen across the whole social space, from manual workers to the professions, yet the gaps in possession of cultural capital between the various vertical layers of the social space remain as wide as ever. Consequently, at the same time as higher education has become ever more routinised as a means of reproducing social position within the dominant class, even among business executives who are otherwise still dependent to a greater extent on economic capital, it by no means guarantees exit from the intermediate or even the dominated class. This is no doubt in large part due to the fact that, rather than there being a rapid expansion of higher-level knowledge production jobs to absorb graduates, positions which used not to demand or expect higher education for entry are (since they are more able to) increasingly doing so. Comparison of relative possession of economic capital (at least as measured by ratio to the mean income) bolsters this interpretation: for the past twenty-five years most fractions have remained static on this front – except for the business executives who have stretched away at the top and manual workers, technicians and skilled trades who have declined.

Table 2.7 Changes in relative possession of capital over time, 1991–2015

	Possession of higher education (row%)						Income ratio to the mean*				
	1991	1995	2000	2005	2010	2015	1995	2000	2005	2010	2015
Business executives	21.0	28.3	31.6	39.2	45.1	50.8	1.68	1.76	1.89	1.90	1.88
Professions	64.2	72.1	72.4	70.4	74.1	79.3	1.85	1.85	1.82	1.89	1.68
White-collar	10.9	15.3	25.1	36.0	42.8	51.1	1.19	1.23	1.32	1.27	1.31
Cultural dominant	42.4	50.0	56.0	67.8	74.8	79.7	1.31	1.31	1.34	1.29	1.15
LMPs	4.0	8.0	11.7	17.2	21.3	27.7	1.21	1.20	1.22	1.18	1.14
Technicians	25.6	29.1	36.0	25.1	30.5	36.7	1.49	1.46	1.29	1.26	1.27
Administrators	2.3	6.0	8.7	12.3	16.4	23.7	0.79	0.76	0.77	0.75	0.75
Cultural intermediaries	7.0	13.4	22.3	30.4	37.3	49.7	0.98	1.03	1.00	1.00	0.98
Skilled trades	0.6	1.9	2.4	3.0	4.7	6.7	1.07	1.01	1.00	0.93	0.90
Sales workers	1.2	1.8	2.9	5.9	10.0	14.5	0.43	0.43	0.51	0.50	0.55
Manual workers	0.8	1.2	1.5	2.4	4.7	6.9	0.76	0.71	0.70	0.66	0.64
Caring services	2.2	2.1	3.3	6.4	11.0	15.6	0.56	0.53	0.59	0.60	0.58

Sources: GHS 1991–2, LFS 1995, 2000, 2005, 2010, 2015

* The GHS 1991–2 does not have a comparable income variable, while the 1991 LFS does not contain a suitable variable for constructing the class scheme

This means, of course, that as the chances of access to higher education, and its perceived feasibility, increase lower down in social space, its chances of actually delivering hoped-for 'self-betterment', in the sense of improving position within the social space, have decreased, not only threatening to breed the kind of disenchantment of which Bourdieu (1984: 143ff) spoke but cementing self-exclusion among the cynical (Archer, 2003: 134–5). Meanwhile, those for whom university was always a natural destiny are increasingly relying on the resultant restratification within the higher-education field – the hierarchy of disciplines and institutions, differentials in access to expensive extracurricular activities and family-arranged internships and relative exclusivity of postgraduate study – to battle this credential inflation and ensure reproduction (cf. Reay *et al.*, 2005; Wakeling, 2005; Tomlinson, 2008; Boliver, 2015; Savage *et al.*, 2015; Wakeling and Savage, 2015). Postgraduate qualifications, for example, have become increasingly important within the dominant class to maintain relative standing. Only 14 per cent of professionals and 13 per cent of the cultural dominant were in possession of a higher degree (doctorate, master's degree, etc.) according to the 1995 LFS, compared with 31 per cent and 43 per cent in 2015.

The space of disciplines, moreover, structured by rate of upper-class enrolment and gender balance – here recorded as the rate of continued male predominance, in a context of gradual yet uneven feminisation of higher education, so as to better map it against capital composition, with which, as we know, gender dovetails – reveals two oppositions (Figure 2.2, cf. Bourdieu and Passeron, 1990: 77–8, 93ff).[6] The first, corresponding to class, is between, on the one hand, established or traditional disciplines demanding a high level of symbolic mastery, and indeed institutionalised cultural capital for entry, and routinely leading, in turn, to positions within the field of power, or at least the dominant class – physics/geology/economics often lead into business if not research, classics leads into business, civil service and politics as well as cultural mediation; languages to teaching as well as diplomatic service; history by topic (the most prominent example of which is history of art) leads into cultural mediation[7] – and, on the other, more or less vocational courses certifying either forms of practical or technical mastery or dispositions of care and expression (including of 'opinions'). Medicine, dentistry and veterinary medicine, though sometimes described as 'vocational', are, on the contrary, among the most highly monopolised by the top sections of the social space, whether as a direct reproduction of social position (as for children of professionals) or a small investment and reconversion of capital (as for business executives and the intellectuals) to attain a place at the acme of the social space, and certainly demand a very high degree of institutionalised cultural capital (100 per cent of accepted candidates have grades of ABB or higher on their A levels). The same cannot be said for law, however, which perhaps ranks lower in the system of professions. The second opposition, corresponding with gender and revealing the possible and the thinkable for men and women, as well as a potential cross-cutting principle of symbolic violence between men and women but also perhaps, since it is so closely associated, between the class fractions separated according to capital composition, distinguishes the 'hard' sciences and vocational courses oriented around economic and physical or technical mastery from the 'soft', 'people-centred' social sciences, languages, creative arts and education. Music is an exception here, perhaps because its underpinning notation and frequent comparison to mathematics appeals more to masculine tastes as a whole. Of course, men and women can and do study subjects overpopulated by the opposite sex, but they may well still apply their gendered dispositions (however less pronounced they may be) and recreate the polarity within the discipline – demonstrating the 'self-similarity', as Abbott (2001) would call it, of the space of disciplines and the disciplinary space.

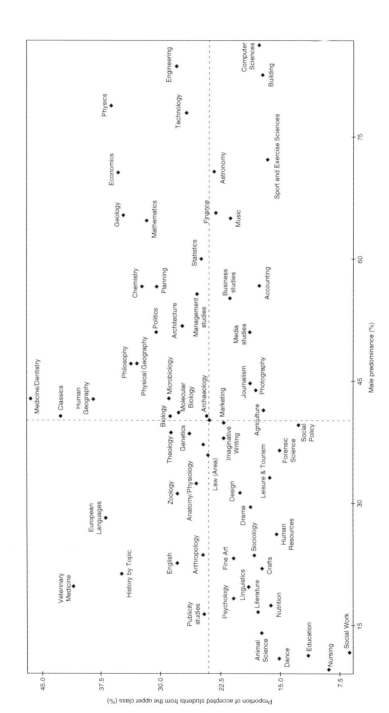

Figure 2.2 The space of disciplines

The expansion of higher education and shifting economic returns have also altered the internal structure of the classes. The dominated class, for example, has been stretched apart horizontally as the growing female-majority caring and sales fractions have increased their rate of possession of institutionalised cultural capital at a higher rate than the rest, perhaps in part due to credentialisation but also because of the overproduction of graduates for the labour market. Within the intermediate class, while all fractions have increased their cultural capital possession, the technicians, at one time the most highly educated, have done so at the slowest rate. They have been overtaken by the cultural intermediaries, whose north-westerly trajectory would appear to have been relatively rapid. Among LMPs, though they are still at the low end for the class as a whole, levels of cultural capital have increased rapidly at the same time as relative income and the rate of self-employment has declined, the latter from 47 per cent in 1995 to 31 per cent in 2015, indicating a 'proletarianisation' of the fraction and an increasing dependence on cultural capital rather than economic capital for social position. This is perhaps linked to compositional shifts within the group, particularly the decline of those in agriculture (from 13 per cent to 2 per cent between 1991 [GHS] and 2015 [LFS]) and an increase of those in finance (from 3 per cent to 15 per cent) and public and miscellaneous services (from 12 per cent to 18 per cent). Within the dominant class, finally, the cultural dominant have caught up with the professions in terms of cultural capital (with more having postgraduate qualifications) but declined a little in terms of economic capital, while the business executives and the white-collar workers have both surged in overall volume of capital. It may well be, in fact, that white-collar workers, as a whole, have only pulled closer to the other fractions of the dominant class than the intermediate class in the past thirty years or so.

Security of capital and stability of habitus

If the *shape* of the social space displays continuities through change, what of its *stability*? A familiar argument through the 1990s and beyond was that the rise of neoliberalism had extended employment flexibility, or insecurity, to greater sections of the populace, conservatives and the economically rich vociferously advocating it on the grounds that businesses – and governments – with greater control over the size and constitution of their workforces are better able to adapt to fluctuating demands and deliver the doxic goal of economic growth, while radicals construe it as merely one more strategy to sustain relations of domination as effectively as possible (Harvey, 2005). Relaxations of employment regulation, increases in temporary contracts, part-time work and self-employment, shifts between the different statuses and from one job type or skill-set to another were thus said to proliferate not only at the bottom of the class structure but across the whole social space (Bauman, 2000; Beck, 2000). Capital stocks and conditions of existence consequently fluctuate, individual trajectories in the social space are now erratic and dramatic and the likelihood of stable *class* habitus forming – as opposed to a widespread 'reflexive habitus' (Sweetman, 2003) – is diminished. Even Bourdieu (1998a) was of the view that objective chances of job loss, and with it subjective expectation of job loss, had surged, at least amongst the dominated and through the cultural fractions of the intermediate and dominant classes.

The pervasive idea that objective and subjective insecurity have levelled class differences on the grounds that capital possession acts as a reliable buffer against, and a safety net in times of, unemployment, has been challenged elsewhere (Atkinson, 2010a, 2010b, 2013), but we are now in a position to examine a few indicators of intragenerational

Table 2.8 Rates of part-time and temporary work by class and gender (row%)

| | Part-time work | | | | Temporary work | | | |
| | Men | | Women | | Men | | Women | |
	1995	2015	1995	2015	1995	2015	1995	2015
Business executives	2.3	4.9	16.0	22.9	1.9	1.3	4.2	2.2
Professions	6.0	7.8	25.0	26.0	11.7	4.4	17.4	7.0
White-collar	4.8	6.1	26.6	24.4	4.2	3.3	7.4	6.2
Cultural dominant	10.5	16.5	30.5	33.6	9.4	9.6	15.0	9.3
LMPs	5.3	8.4	23.7	25.8	1.4	1.2	2.0	0.7
Technicians	2.7	3.7	16.7	22.4	4.9	3.9	9.4	2.2
Administrators	9.4	15.0	36.0	41.5	9.8	8.5	6.8	5.2
Cultural interm.	4.7	15.5	40.7	36.8	4.3	9.2	6.7	6.2
Skilled trades	3.5	8.3	39.4	39.6	4.6	3.0	4.9	3.1
Sales workers	39.4	35.4	74.2	62.7	9.1	6.8	4.9	5.8
Manual workers	11.9	20.1	62.7	64.8	8.3	8.9	9.3	10.0
Caring services	17.0	24.3	55.1	45.6	9.0	8.7	9.5	7.7

Sources: LFS 1995 and 2015

stability of capital and habitus more comprehensively, starting with the changing distribution of 'non-standard' work forms through the social space. In fact, Table 2.8 reveals a striking pattern: the cultural fractions of all classes, along with manual workers and sales workers, generally occupy the most 'insecure' zones of social space of all, whether they be male or female, insofar as rates of temporary and part-time work are highest, whereas the economic fractions are much more secure.[8] Moreover, this pattern of impermanent and part-time work seems to have sharpened somewhat over the last twenty years. The overall rates may well follow the fortunes of the economy, with a peak in insecurity across the board in the late 1990s (Fevre, 2007) and then again in the aftermath of the economic crisis of the late 2000s, but the fact remains that it is the cultural fractions of each class, and manual workers and sales workers, among both sexes, who disproportionately work part-time or on temporary contracts.

On closer examination, however, a more complex picture emerges. First of all, 'temporary' work tends to be temporary to different degrees depending on possession of valued resources: 71 per cent of the dominated class in temporary work are on fixed-term contracts of less than a year, compared with 55 per cent of the intermediate class and 41 per cent of the dominant (LFS, 2015).[9] Moreover, everything would seem to indicate that the less likely a class fraction is to include part-time workers, the more likely it is that those within the class fraction who do work part-time have actively *chosen* to, signified by rates of agreement with the statement that they are working part-time because they did not want full-time work and signifying the effects of ample distance from necessity (Table 2.9). Thus, among men, the sections of social space richest in economic capital – the business executives, professionals and LMPs, as well as technicians – are opposed not only to manual workers and sales workers, but to the cultural dominant and cultural intermediaries too. Even within the dominated class the skilled workers are opposed to the fractions below it as well as the caring services. The same pattern holds

Table 2.9 Reasons for part-time work by class and gender (row%)

Class fraction	Did not want full-time work*		Reasons for not wanting full-time work**					
			Economically secure enough		Want to spend more time with family		Domestic commitments	
	Men	Women	Men	Women	Men	Women	Men	Women
Business executives	76.6	93.3	41.9	23.6	2.5	37.5	4.9	16.1
Professions	81.6	96.4	52.0	18.5	4.3	44.7	5.4	19.7
White-collar	54.9	85.9	37.2	11.4	4.2	42.9	3.0	17.6
Cultural dominant	54.6	80.6	26.6	19.4	7.0	34.6	3.5	12.5
LMPs	71.0	91.3	38.6	32.6	8.2	27.2	1.5	12.6
Technicians	74.0	89.4	43.8	12.3	6.7	43.8	2.9	25.5
Administrators	47.0	89.1	38.1	19.2	4.5	33.4	3.3	18.6
Cultural interm.	72.6	91.6	21.3	19.2	6.0	31.3	3.3	19.3
Skilled trades	39.2	82.7	20.9	21.7	2.0	22.4	4.1	17.3
Sales workers	13.3	65.9	10.2	10.7	1.8	19.6	2.4	15.8
Manual workers	25.5	75.8	13.7	9.3	3.1	17.6	2.8	18.2
Caring services	29.4	82.1	20.1	12.6	3.6	27.0	3.0	21.8

* Source: LFS 2015
** Source: LFS 2013. The question was not asked in 2015. Proportions are relative to total numbers choosing part-time work in 2013.

among women, albeit with considerably higher proportions opting for part-time work across the board. It also holds over time, as figures from twenty years previous, i.e. the 1995 LFS (undertaken when, as in 2015, a recession was recent history), show remarkably similar disparities, though men in all sections of social space seem to have been less likely to choose part-time employment. Hence business executives (77 per cent of men, 93 per cent of women) and professionals (82 per cent of men, 96 per cent of women) are still opposed to manual workers (26 per cent of men, 76 per cent of women) and sales workers (13 per cent of men, 66 per cent of women) but also the cultural dominant (55 per cent of men, 81 per cent of women).

When it comes to stated *reasons* for choosing part-time work, finally, it is notable that, among men, business executives and professionals are highly likely to report being (or rather perceiving themselves to be) economically secure enough – either because they earn enough from their jobs or because they have other sources of income (property, assets, etc.) – to work only because they want to, contrasting sharply not only with manual workers and sales workers but the cultural dominant and the cultural intermediaries. Women are much more likely to cite family and domestic life as reasons in all class fractions compared to men, revealing something of the continuing socialisation of the feminine libido towards the family field as well as the expectations and sense of the possible given by the power relations comprising the latter. Yet the likelihood of working part-time because one *wants* to spend more time with the family – more or less facilitated by distance from necessity – increases with volume of capital while the likelihood of domestic *commitments* enforcing part-time work, though relatively constant across classes, is lowest among the cultural dominant. Nor does it cancel out differences in distance from necessity, as those fractions richest in economic capital within their classes are still much more likely to plump for part-timing on the basis of financial conditions.

Recapitulation

To sum up, then, the UK social space, premised on distribution of the most significant capitals shaping conditions of existence and perceptions of worth and value in Western societies, displays exactly the same fundamental structure as revealed in a plethora of European nations. Total volume of capital is the primary axis, but the composition of capital opposes fractions within all classes, and the mark of time, manifest in the trajectories of class fractions and individuals within the social space (such as the decline of the old petite bourgeoisie and the ascent of the new petite bourgeoisie and the economically rich), layers them with further differences. The second axis of differentiation, moreover, is highly homologous with gender insofar as the cultural pole, especially in the middle and dominated sections, is statistically more 'feminine', and somewhat less integrated into the permanent, full-time workforce, whether male or female, though seemingly as much due to the channelling of the socialised libido away from paid employment – i.e. from the attendant fields and their internal struggles – as anything else.

As Bourdieu (1984: 169) noted, any model of the social space, as a constructed balance-sheet of power and recognition, offers a kind of 'bird's-eye view' on all the positions from which ordinary people view the world. Approximating its conditions of possibility, it underpins the phenomenological sense of feeling higher or lower than others, superior or inferior to them or socially near to or far from them present in each encounter insofar as any sign denoting, however roughly, a person's capital, or their place – a certain job, a certain level of qualification or whatever ('she's *only* a secretary', 'he's *only* got a degree', 'medicine is something to *aspire* to', 'he's made a *success* of himself', etc.) – is read and interpreted in relation to the reader's place. Yet direct symbols of capital are only half the story. Indirect symbols, in the form of stances, practices and goods *homologous* with the social space, because they flow from class habitus, serve to communicate difference and similarity, and inspire fellow-feeling or disgust, when no direct symbols of class position are visible and no thought of 'class' in mind. To these we shall now turn.

Notes

1 Net income, accounting for the tax regime, allows a more precise approximation of conditions of existence than gross income.
2 Since they constitute just 0.4 per cent of the working population, and 0.2 per cent of the whole population, therefore, it is not especially easy or useful to separate industrial and commercial employers for most analyses, as Bourdieu did, though they could be explored with the right variables and high enough numbers. One consequence of taking employers and executives together is a diminution of the mapping of the full dispersion of the right-hand zone of the dominant class, though one can well imagine how it might look.
3 See the figures marshalled by Sayer (2014) on the richest 1 per cent of the population, 0.1 per cent of the population and 0.01 per cent of the population, the vast majority of whom would fall into the business executive category.
4 It always seemed incongruous to me that farmers appeared lower down in the social space than farm labourers in Bourdieu's map in *Distinction*, though they were often taken together in any analysis he did. To confuse matters, in an earlier English-language presentation of the map (Bourdieu, 1980) the

two class fractions appear in the reverse – and more intuitively correct – positions, but then in later presentations (Bourdieu, 1998b: 5) they appear again in the incongruous positions. There is an extra layer of intrigue here because Bourdieu's own father was a sharecropper before he became a postman. In any case, in the contemporary British social space farmers are generally spread between the lower managers and proprietors and the skilled workers, depending on the precise classification of their position and, with that, their typical capital possession.

5 At least part of the reduction in business executives and concomitant increase in white-collar workers between 2010 and 2015 dovetails with changing SOC codes, as some job titles included in higher managerial classifications in the past were reallocated to 'business professional' and other classifications constituting the white-collar grouping to reflect changing status, and therefore trajectory. See Appendix I for more details.

6 Figures, which refer to all accepted university applicants in 2015, come from the Universities and Colleges Admissions Service. 'Upper class' here, unfortunately, refers to the 'higher managerial and professional' category of the NS-SEC – it was not possible to apply the measure of social space developed here. For how this category relates to the categories approximating the social space, see Appendix I. In a nutshell, it consists largely of business executives, professionals, certain white-collar workers and the top slice of the cultural dominant, i.e. intellectuals.

7 See the 'What Can I Do With My Degree?' page hosted by the Prospects agency (www.prospects. ac.uk/careers-advice/what-can-i-do-with-my-degree/), as well as the Higher Education Careers Services Unit's 'What do Graduates Do?' page (www.hecsu.ac.uk/current_projects_ what_do_graduates_do.htm), harnessing figures from the Higher Education Statistics Agency. There are also many who go into retail or bar work, but it is impossible from the figures to gauge whether that depends on class background (especially in the form of social capital), whether those jobs act as stop-gaps or more long-term moves, and whether even that latter difference is structured by class.

8 Fevre's (2007) point that a proportion of those who describe their work as impermanent in the LFS will actually be on permanent contracts but just *perceive* their job as transient has to be taken on board. The higher figures amongst those rich in cultural capital may thus be at least exacerbated by a disposition to perceive their work as less secure, whether for negative reasons (fear of changes in the sector) or positive ones (a sense of not being 'tied down'). Likelihood of having been with one's present employer for less than five years was also examined for the same time period by class and gender, but few significant differences surfaced, except that sales workers were by far the least likely to have been in the same job for more than five years, and no significant changes had occurred, except that professionals had become more likely to have been with their employers for less than five years.

9 Figures relate to those who know the length of their contract. There are no appreciable differences by gender, except that women in the intermediate class are slightly more likely to be on contracts of less than 12 months.

References

Abbott, A. (2001) *Chaos of Disciplines*. Chicago: University of Chicago Press.

Andersen, P.L. and Hansen, M.N. (2012) 'Class and Cultural Capital – the Case of Class Inequality in Educational performance' *European Sociological Review*, 28(5): 607–21.

Archer, L. (2003) 'The 'Value' of Higher Education' in L. Archer, M. Hutchings and A. Ross (eds.) *Higher Education and Social Class*. London: RoutledgeFalmer, pp. 119–36.

Atkinson, W. (2010a) *Class, Individualization and Late Modernity: In Search of the Reflexive Worker*. Basingstoke: Palgrave Macmillan.

Atkinson, W. (2010b) 'The Myth of the Reflexive Worker: Class and Work Histories in Neo-Liberal Times' *Work, Employment and Society*, 24(3): 413–29.

Atkinson, W. (2016) *Beyond Bourdieu*. Cambridge: Polity Press.

Atkinson, W. and Rosenlund, L. (2014) *Mapping the British Social Space: Toward a Bourdieusian Class Scheme*. SPAIS Working Paper No. 02–14, University of Bristol. Available at www.bristol.ac.uk/spais/research/workingpapers/.

Atkinson, W., Roberts, S. and Savage, M. (2013) 'Introduction: A Critical Sociology of the Age of Austerity' in W. Atkinson, S. Roberts and M. Savage (eds.) *Class Inequality in Austerity Britain: Power, Difference and Suffering*. Basingstoke: Palgrave Macmillan, pp. 1–12.

Bauman, Z. (2000) *Liquid Modernity*. Cambridge: Polity Press.

Beck, U. (2000) *The Brave New World of Work*. Cambridge: Polity Press.

Beck, U. (2007) 'Beyond Class and Nation: Reframing Inequalities in a Global World' *British Journal of Sociology*, 58(4): 679–705.

Boliver, V. (2015) 'Are There Distinctive Clusters of Higher and Lower Status Universities in the UK?' *Oxford Review of Education*, 41(5): 608–27.

Bourdieu, P. (1980) 'A Diagram of Social Position and Lifestyle' *Media, Culture and Society*, 2: 55–9.

Bourdieu, P. (1984) *Distinction*. London: Routledge.

Bourdieu, P. (1987) 'What Makes a Social Class?' *Berkeley Journal of Sociology*, 32: 1–17.

Bourdieu, P. (1993) *The Field of Cultural Production*. Cambridge: Polity Press.

Bourdieu, P. (1998a) *Acts of Resistance*. Cambridge: Polity Press.

Bourdieu, P. (1998b) *Practical Reason*. Cambridge: Polity Press.

Bourdieu, P. (1997) 'The Forms of Capital' in A.H. Halsey, H. Lauder, P. Brown and A. Wells (eds.) *Education: Culture, Economy and Society*. Oxford: Oxford University Press, pp. 46–58.

Bourdieu, P. and Passeron, J.-C. (1990) *Reproduction in Education, Society and Culture*, 2nd edition, London: Sage.

Chan, T.W. and Goldthorpe, J.H. (2010) 'Social Stratification of Cultural Consumption Across Three Domains' in T.W. Chan (ed.) *Social Status and Cultural Consumption*. Cambridge: Cambridge University Press, pp. 204–31.

Crompton, R. and Jones, G. (1984) *White-Collar Proletariat*. London: Macmillan.

Erikson, R. and Goldthorpe, J.H. (1992) *The Constant Flux*. Oxford: Clarendon Press.

Fevre, R. (2007) 'Employment Insecurity and Social Theory: The Power of Nightmares' *Work, Employment and Society*, 21(3): 517–35.

Gallie, D., White, M., Cheng, Y. and Tomlinson, M. (1998) *Restructuring the Employment Relationship*. Oxford: Oxford University Press.

Goldthorpe, J. H. (1980) *Social Mobility and Class Structure in Modern Britain*, 2nd edition, Oxford: Clarendon Press.

Goldthorpe, J. H. and Hope, K. (1974) *The Social Grading of Occupations*. Oxford: Clarendon Press.

Hansen, M.N., Flemmen, M. and Andersen, P.L. (2009) *The Oslo Register Data Class Scheme (ORDC)*. Memorandum No. 1, Department of Sociology and Human Geography, University of Oslo, Norway.

Harvey, D. (2005) *A Brief History of Neoliberalism*. Oxford: Oxford University Press.

Hochschild, A. (2012) *The Managed Heart*. Berkeley: University of California Press.

Huppatz, K. (2012) *Gender Capital at Work*. Basingstoke: Palgrave Macmillan.

Mills, C.W. (1958) *White Collar*. Oxford: Oxford University Press.

Modood, T. (2004) 'Capitals, Ethnic Identity and Educational Qualifications' *Cultural Trends*, 13(2): 87–105.

Office for National Statistics (2010) *Social Trends No. 40*. Basingstoke: Palgrave Macmillan.

Prieur, A., Rosenlund, L. and Skjott-Larsen, J. (2008) 'Cultural Capital Today: A Case Study from Denmark' *Poetics*, 36(1): 45–71.

Reay, D., David, M. E. and Ball, S. (2005) *Degrees of Choice*. Stoke on Trent: Trentham Books.

Rose, D. (1995) 'Official Social Classifications in the UK' *Social Research Update*, 9(1).

Rosenlund, L. (2009) *Exploring the City with Bourdieu*. Saarbrücken: VDM Verlag Dr Müller.

Savage, M. (2000) *Class Analysis and Social Transformation*. Buckingham: Open University Press.

Savage, M. et al. (2015) *Social Class in 21st Century Britain*. London: Pelican.

Sayad, A. (2004) *The Suffering of the Immigrant*. Cambridge: Polity Press.

Sayer, A. (2014) *Why We Can't Afford the Rich*. Bristol: Policy Press.

Simpson, R. (2004) 'Masculinity at Work: The Experiences of Men in Female Dominated Occupations' *Work, Employment and Society*, 18(2): 349–68.

Skjott-Larsen, J. (2012) 'Cultural and Moral Boundaries in a Nordic Context' *European Societies*, 14(5): 660–83.

Smith, C. and Whalley, P. (1995) 'Engineers in Britain: A Study in Persistence' in P. Meiksins and C. Smith (eds.) *Engineering Labour*. London: Verso.

Stewart, A., Prandy, K. and Blackburn, R. (1980) *Social Stratification and Occupations*. Basingstoke: Macmillan.

Sweetman, P. (2003) 'Twenty-First Century Dis-ease' *The Sociological Review*, 51(4): 528–49.

Tomlinson, M. (2008) "The Degree is Not Enough': Students' Perceptions of the Role of Higher Education Credentials for Graduate Work and Employability' *British Journal of Sociology of Education*, 29 (1): 49–61.

Wakeling, P. (2005) '*La noblesse d'état anglaise*? Social Class and Progression to Postgraduate Study' *British Journal of Sociology of Education*, 26(4): 505–22.

Wakeling, P. and Savage, M. (2015) 'Entry to Elite Positions and the Stratification of Higher Education in Britain' *The Sociological Review*, 63(2): 290–320.

3   The space of lifestyles

There is a long tradition of unravelling the linkages between class and culture in Britain, from the post-war community studies documenting the communal existence of the working class (e.g. Dennis *et al.*, 1969) and the privatism of the suburban middle classes (Willmott and Young, 1960) to the leading lights of cultural studies putting the various youth subcultures from the 1950s onwards – Teds, mods, rockers, punks, rastas – down to working-class resistance against the hegemonic bourgeois work ethic (Hebdige, 1979; Hall and Jefferson, 1999; Gilroy, 2000). Only with Bourdieu's view of class, however, do we get the means of tapping into the full mosaic of class cultures – the multidimensionality of symbolic domination and resistance, with each position defined against all others. Members of the dominated class may well define themselves against the dominant, but neither the dominant nor the dominated are all of a piece. Self-definition takes on multiple hues, varying according to relative distance and direction, and of course there is an intermediate class – which is not reducible to being simply a variation of the dominant class, as for most Marxists – struggling to assert their own way of being as worthy too.

This multidimensionality is, however, something which has often been fudged in recent research on class lifestyles in the UK, even among those purporting to test or update Bourdieu's proposition that there is a patent homology between the social space and the symbolic space. First there is the famous strand of work, originating in the US and kick-started by Richard Peterson (1992, 1997), which touts the evolution of symbolic domination. Dominant, legitimate culture, and therefore cultural capital, is no longer premised on exclusive, obscure cultural forms or knowledge as opposed to popular culture, the claim goes, but is a question of engagement, breadth, variety and openness – in other words, cultural 'omnivorousness' and cosmopolitanism – as opposed to disengagement or narrow interests. From its earliest airings to the most sophisticated later investigations, however, this thesis – which, as Coulangeon and Duval (2015) point out, was already accommodated by Bourdieu anyway – has rested on methods and variables which may well render it artefactual or, at the very least, which diverge so far from Bourdieu's own that no sure refutation or revision can be sensibly claimed. The use of extraordinarily broad 'genre' categories of the kind more or less absent in *Distinction*, for example, may well reveal the fairly superficial fact that some people consume or claim to like more than one arbitrarily defined cultural style of music, film or whatever, but they fail to reveal anything much of the underlying aesthetic dispositions or mode of consumption (Holt, 1997; Atkinson, 2011; Jarness, 2013).[1] Could it not be that familiar classed tastes premised on exclusivity – whether on account of symbolic mastery or economic capital – lead people to consume different cultural goods *within* the supposed genre, or to consume the same thing in different (more or less 'legitimate') *ways*?

Moreover, in most instances – especially in Chan and Goldthorpe's (e.g. 2007) research – defenders of the omnivore thesis mobilise measures of 'class' rooted in totally different traditions. Being premised on differences in life chances rather than symbolic power, and taking the form of unidimensional and economistic hierarchies rather than a multidimensional social space, they roll together class fractions (in the 'service class') with vastly different balances of economic and cultural capital – for example, higher-level business executives and intellectuals – and therefore different orientations toward symbolic goods (i.e. hedonistic versus ascetic orientations). It thus comes as little surprise that the consumption of the 'service class' might be internally variegated, or that when education, a key proxy for cultural capital and class fractions, is factored in it makes a substantial difference. This is exacerbated by reliance, in many cases, on linear statistical techniques of the kind Bourdieu avoided, rather than the MCA capable of revealing the hidden relational structures of correspondence he favoured (Wuggenig, 2007).[2]

Then there is the CCSE team mentioned in the Introduction. They did deploy MCA to construct a space of lifestyles, covering tastes in music, television, visual arts and more, and they did uncover several dimensions of difference. However, while Bourdieu identified three axes – the rare versus the common corresponding with total volume of economic, cultural and social capital; asceticism and self-cultivation versus hedonism and ostentation homologous with capital composition; plus the effect of trajectory – the British-based team revealed four. The first distinguished those who are engaged in all sorts of culture, both 'high' and popular forms, versus those who are disengaged – so omnivores of a kind versus the rest – and corresponds with their measure of class. Second, a taste for 'traditional' forms of culture versus more commercial forms corresponds with age, then an axis distinguishing 'inwardly oriented' practices versus 'outwardly oriented' practice corresponds with gender, and finally a fourth axis differentiates 'voracious' consumers of culture with inherited cultural capital (measured by father's education) from more moderate ones without.

Just how robust the CCSE team's model of the symbolic space, however, is open to question. After all, they too rely on various overly broad and arbitrarily aggregated genre categories – of TV, films, music, sports and so on – obscuring internal variation and modes of consumption. An overreliance on measures of frequency of attendance at or participation in certain institutions and activities also rather ineffectually taps into differences of *taste* – the difference between 'sometimes' and 'never' visiting a museum, for example, could simply be down to whether one has children in need of entertainment on a rainy day or not, no matter how dull the parent finds it, or the accessibility of museums – and therefore the phenomenology of class, i.e. the sense of one's place *vis-à-vis* others on perception of certain signs as well as symbolic violence. Do people really intuit their place relative to others they meet on the basis of whether they go to museums 'often' as opposed to 'sometimes', and denigrate those who go less often than them? At the same time, the researchers did not make much use, as Bourdieu did, of measures of cultural knowledge in constructing the symbolic space – how many and which composers, artists, writers etc. they know – even though they had the variables available. Nor did they mobilise measures capable of detecting the more hedonistic, opulent lifestyle identified by Bourdieu among the economically rich (e.g. boat ownership, holiday preferences, car value and so on), a move which may well have brought out the capital composition principle more strongly, but this time because the questions simply were not asked. Finally, as already discussed, there is the little problem of not actually having constructed a model of the social space against which any homology could be checked – relying on the NS-SEC meant that, while they could admit the first axis was more or less homologous with class, the other axes seemingly were not.

Things have obviously moved on slightly with the publication of the findings of the much-anticipated and widely trumpeted GBCS undertaken (with others) by one of the CCSE team (Savage *et al.*, 2013). Little support for the omnivore thesis is found, but a difference between 'established cultural capital' (high culture) and 'emergent cultural capital' (interest in sports, gigs, computer games and so on) is picked up instead. The logic is that a person can be high or low in either of these, and whether they are seems to correspond with age more than anything else. All very well, but the same mistakes that plagued Bennett *et al.* not only reappear but seem to have been amplified. They still rely on incredibly broad categories in their analysis, for example, and if anything these are *even less* differentiated than before – with categories of simply liking sports or gigs or not, without any further breakdown into type of sports or artists and performers liked. To give them credit, they do admit the possibility of internal variation (Savage *et al.*, 2013: 247n9), but they choose not to account for that in their final model.

We are left asking a rather obvious question: would the conclusion have been any different if things had been done differently? If the above limitations were circumvented by following different principles and making different methodological choices, more in tune with Bourdieu's logic and akin to Bourdieusian studies in other nations (e.g. Prieur *et al.*, 2008; Rosenlund, 2009), what would be the outcome? We will have to wait and see with the GBCS, since the full data is not yet (at the time of writing) available to others, but happily the CCSE data *is* available for re-analysis. In the following, then, I intend to use it to build a revised map of the space of lifestyles in twenty-first-century Britain and map the degree of homology with the social space. In order to balance out the limits of the CCSE survey, however, and supplement the picture of cultural difference and domination painted, data from elsewhere will also have to be brought in too.

The British space of lifestyles

First things first: to begin building a model of the symbolic space we must conduct a fresh MCA using carefully selected variables. Those tricky genre categories need to be left aside for reasons already stated, as do measures of degree of visitation of different cultural institutions or events (galleries, pubs, museums, etc.). Questions tapping knowledge of and interest in cultural producers and products also have to be largely avoided at this stage since too many 'positive v. negative' style variables (know/don't know) tend to distort the construction, though a single composite measure of number of artists known can be retained. Instead, variables comprised solely of positive categories (or 'modalities') constitute the bulk of the input data as they are better at tapping different tastes and their place in the system of tastes. This leaves only a select few variables in the CCSE dataset, however, namely tastes in sport (played, watched, and reason played), dress, newspaper, home decor and art, but these are enough for an initial construction which can then be bolstered with further analyses. Moreover, the chosen measures tend to have large numbers of categories spreading the respondents fairly thinly – a recipe for an unstable model – so an exercise in recoding had to be undertaken. Rather than arbitrarily lump modalities together, though, as Bennett *et al.* (2009) did (for sport in particular), a series of exploratory MCAs was conducted and modalities proximate in the resulting solutions, and judged to have some logical connection, were grouped together. This had the eventual effect in some cases of transforming variables from measures of taste into measures of broader dispositions underpinning tastes in a number of sports, decors and so on.[3] Some particularly noteworthy examples are the clustering together of sailing, skiing, tennis, water polo, horse-riding, cricket and golf as 'exclusive' sports to practise, on the basis that they all typically involve the use of more or less expensive equipment or club memberships, and yoga, jogging, cycling, dancing and gymnastics as 'self-cultivating' pastimes since they typically involve work on the body as an end in itself (or, in the case of dancing, a mode of expression), as well as some concept of mental or holistic 'wellbeing'. Moreover, when it came to stated reasons for practising sport – probably the best measure for getting at underlying dispositions – relaxation, escape, discipline and learning a skill were taken together on account of the fact that they all seem to revolve around a cerebral or 'mental' element, whether mental *release* or mental *stimulation* (cf. Atkinson, 2011), including, perhaps, the intention to 'learn a skill' as a projected end in itself rather than a taken-for-granted means to another end.

All in all, eight questions were included in the model, generating 45 active modalities.[4] Several indicators of social position, including the categories of the social space but also educational level, household income, age, ethnicity and gender, were included as supplementary variables; that is to say, they did not contribute to the construction of the symbolic space but were instead projected into it as a means of indicating homologies. The model distinguished three principal axes of the symbolic space which together explain 82 per cent of the total variation – a more than satisfactory amount. The first, primary axis accounts for 56 per cent of variation and is structured around a number of telling oppositions: knowledge of few artists versus knowledge of many artists; a taste for watching snooker or darts (both sports rooted in communal pub life) versus practising exclusive sports; a taste for a clean and tidy house (a sign of *functionality* but also *respectability*) versus a taste for a distinctive, imaginative or uncluttered home (i.e. *aesthetic* properties); a taste for sensationalist and human-interest/celebrity-focussed 'red top' newspapers (*The Sun*, *Star*, etc.) versus a taste for highbrow broadsheet newspapers (the *Independent*, *Guardian*, *Times* etc.); a tendency to refrain from practising sport at all versus an interest in practising sport for its 'mental element'; and a taste for no particular type of art versus a taste for Renaissance or Impressionist art – both forms of art, we might conjecture, demanding knowledge of particular styles in order to be appreciated (and even recognised in the survey) (Figure 3.1). Clearly this is an axis opposing elements of the dominated *modus vivendi* on the one hand and practices suggesting a degree of symbolic mastery, distance from necessity and economic interest on the other. Unsurprisingly, therefore, when proxies for position in social space are projected into the model it can be seen that this axis is largely homologous with total volume of capital, opposing the dominant and dominated classes and placing the intermediate class fractions in between (Figure 3.2).[5]

The second axis, which accounts for 18 per cent of the variance, opposes – in descending order from the top of axis 1 – exclusive sports and self-cultivating physical activities (as well as keep fit and swimming); tabloids (mostly right-leaning) and the liberal broadsheet newspapers; golf, cricket and horse-racing on the one hand and athletics and gymnastics on the other; pursuing sport for sociability (connections), so as a means to a (business) end, and pursuing physical activity for fitness, or as a self-oriented end in itself; and finally interest in landscape pictures and interest in performance and modern art. Knowledge of few versus all artists in the survey also makes a difference again. When indicators of capital and the categories of social space are projected into the model it becomes evident that this axis is homologous with capital composition, thus, we may suppose, opposing practices anchored in symbolic mastery (to different levels within the dominant and intermediate class fractions) and those grounded in economic capital, business interests and, of course, relative dearth of symbolic mastery. The picture is complicated, however, by the fact that this axis also corresponds with gender – perhaps

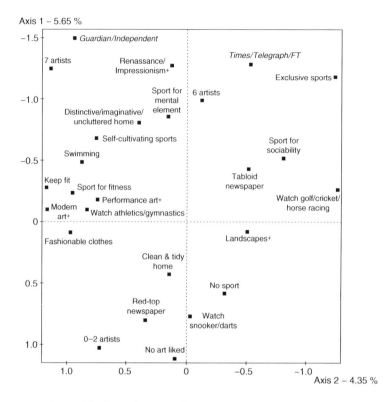

Axis 1 – 5.65 %

Figure 3.1 MCA plane of axes 1 and 2, active modalities with above-average contributions

not unexpected given the gendered nature of the social space – but also fairly closely with age, with younger respondents tending to fall on the left (symbolic mastery) side and older ones falling on the right (economic capital) (Figure 3.3). In other words, we have an interaction between capital composition and *trajectory* on this axis. This is hardly surprising since some of the class fractions richer in cultural capital are 'newer', in the sense that they are linked to jobs that have proliferated in recent years to soak up the growing pool of graduates in the UK and tend to be populated by younger people. It certainly demands a slightly more nuanced interpretation of some of the oppositions mentioned already, but it also explains why lack of knowledge of artistic producers is placed on the left side of the plane and why a desire to dress fashionably contributes to this axis within the dominated/intermediate class.

Axis 3 explains 7 per cent of the variance and seems to be a variation of the capital composition and trajectory axis, now only switching the direction of age to pull out the tastes of younger economically rich class fractions and older culturally rich ones (Figures 3.4, 3.5 and 3.6). Many of the key modalities are the same, but now we also see the younger economically rich favour modern art, fashionable clothes, keeping fit and pursuing sport for 'the buzz' and competition (reflecting the nomos of the economic field, perhaps) as well as its sociability, while the older culturally rich go for clothes that are comfortable.

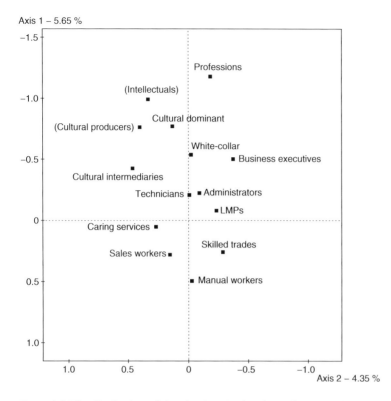

Figure 3.2 The distribution of class fractions in the plane of axes 1 and 2

The picture so far can be supplemented and refined through exploration of several practices and orientations not included in the active construction of the MCA model, including, to begin with, restaurant preferences, which can be projected as supplementary points (Figure 3.6). Fast-food restaurants, fish-and-chip shops and cafés – traditional, cheap or 'no frills' eateries – cluster in the section homologous with the dominated class, with traditional steakhouses – masculine, no airs and graces, but not so cheap – corresponding most closely with the older, masculine, economically rich fraction populated disproportionately by skilled workers while pizza houses correspond to the younger, cultural-capital-rich fraction. In direct contrast, French restaurants are associated with high volumes of capital, corresponding closely with the section of symbolic space homologous with the professions, though after them business executives are the class fraction most likely to name them as their favourite (16 per cent). Italian restaurants also seem more popular higher up in social space, but mostly amongst the white-collar workers (33 per cent) and secondarily the professionals (27 per cent), i.e. where the composition of capital is balanced – suggesting they require some degree of symbolic mastery or money as an entry ticket but not enough to mark out those with their capital stocks tipped one way or the other. In direct opposition to the tastes of the skilled trades, vegetarian restaurants are favoured most among fractions of the dominant and intermediate class richest in cultural capital.[6] Moreover, when *least* favourite restaurants,

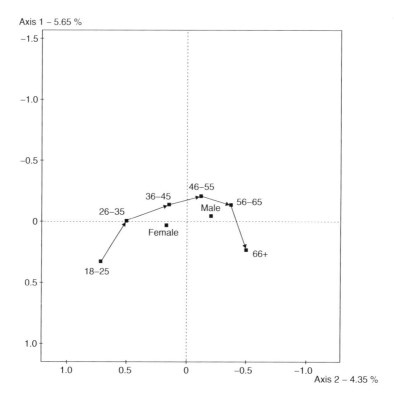

Figure 3.3 Age and gender in the plane of axes 1 and 2

as an indicator of *dis*taste and disgust, are examined we see a reversal of key elements of the pattern: the dominated seemingly dislike anything exotic ('foreign muck') while the dominant turn their noses up at fast-food restaurants, and the culturally rich, also the younger and more feminine segment of the population, once again oppose the male, older, economically rich in expressing their distaste for traditional steakhouses.

Next, we can turn our attention to some 'classic' markers of difference such as degree of familiarity with and participation in consecrated culture, i.e. the culture considered 'legitimate' and worthy since it acts as a sign of 'intelligence' (symbolic mastery) or material success (economic capital). First of all, as might be expected, there are apparent divergences in rates of playing a musical instrument (without even distinguishing what kind), partaking in the performing arts, engaging in painting or sculpture, practising photography, pursuing craftwork, writing stories or poetry and taking part in book clubs in one's leisure time (Table 3.1).[7] Some practices are, when broken down by gender, clearly more feminine – such as book clubs or crafts – and some are rather more masculine – such as photography – but in all cases the tendency to dabble in them generally follows the same pattern of increasing with cultural capital. This means their popularity does rise with capital volume, but more noticeably with possession of cultural capital relative to economic capital. Hence the cultural dominant, cultural intermediaries and to a lesser extent caring services tend to partake at a higher rate in most cases, alongside

Axis 1 – 5.65 %

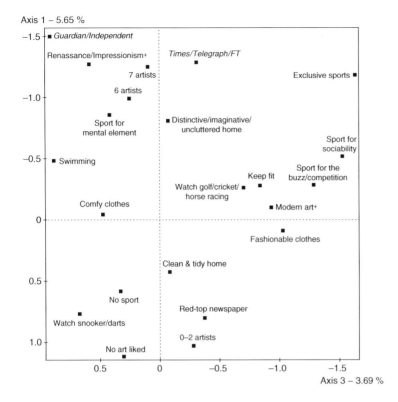

Figure 3.4 MCA plane of axes 1 and 3, active modalities with above-average contributions

professions, but not so much the business executives or LMPs, demonstrating that it is not simply money mediating preferences. Photography and filmmaking, interestingly, are equally as popular among the cultural intermediaries and the cultural dominant, suggesting that, though we do not know the differences in what is being captured and in what way, photography may be less of an obviously 'middlebrow' activity than it once was (cf. Bourdieu *et al.*, 1991). In line with its growth as a medium and the expanded universe of different technologies and techniques, elements of photography have perhaps been aestheticised and invested with greater cultural legitimacy than when it first appeared, the site of difference and derision now being less about engaging in photography *per se* rather than other arts but in the way in which photography is practised.

If proclivities for certain 'distinguished' practices are partitioned by class, then so too are likelihoods and frequencies – cut down to a key fault line to evade the problems mentioned earlier – of visits to certain sites of consecrated culture, i.e. museums, the theatre, classical concerts or operas, art galleries, historical sites and libraries, all of which demand a certain level of cultural capital and, in some cases, economic capital to be accessed and 'appreciated' (Table 3.2). There is a fairly apparent vertical differentiation, with visitation rates rising with capital volume, but there are also considerable differences within each class according to capital composition. In the dominant class the professions and the cultural dominant are the most likely to access consecrated culture,

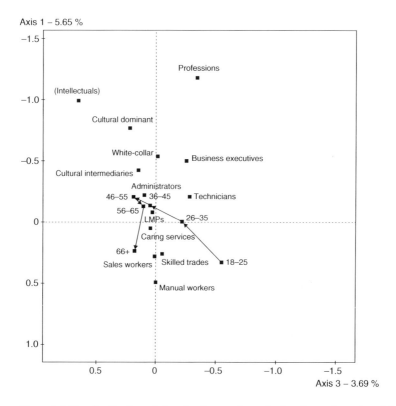

Figure 3.5 The distribution of class fractions and ages in the plane of axes 1 and 3

while the business executives are less likely, suggesting that while a balance of economic and cultural capital may maximise probability of attendance by increasing accessibility, in all senses, symbolic mastery, producing the desire and taste for the abstract and the contemplative, i.e. 'the love of art' (Bourdieu and Darbel, 1991), is the real key. The same oppositional structure is found within the intermediate class, with the cultural intermediaries most prone to frequent the institutions of legitimate culture (in some cases more so than the cultural dominant, though tellingly not in relation to the most 'traditional' sites, i.e. opera, art galleries, historical sites) – while the culturally poorest fraction, the LMPs, are much less likely, and within the dominated class, where the richest fraction in terms of cultural capital, the caring services, have the highest rates of attendance. Gender is a complicating factor in all cases, however, with museums, theatre, opera and libraries being more popular with dominant women than dominant men, especially among professionals – in some instances, perhaps, dovetailing with childcare or pedagogic work, which falls disproportionately to women, but it must also be remembered that women generally possess greater cultural capital than their male counterparts across social space. On the other hand, consecrated culture is often more popular among male cultural intermediaries than female ones, but then so too is the category of 'other concert', and while we can only guess at what might be included in that – covering many or all supposed 'genres' – it could well be that if there is any place for 'postmodern' or

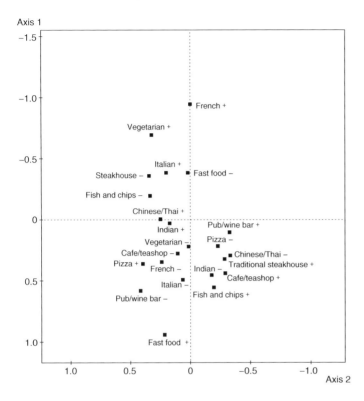

Figure 3.6 Restaurant tastes in the plane of axes 1 and 2

'omnivorous' consumption, or so-called 'emergent cultural capital', it is here, among the new petite bourgeoisie, the 'hipsters', as Bourdieu himself argued, perhaps evincing the 'dream of social flying' and attempt to evade being pinned down in social space which he postulated long ago for this particular class fraction.

Perhaps it is no surprise, given the foregoing, that responses to the statement that 'arts funded by the government aren't for ordinary people' are differentiated by possession of cultural capital (Figure 3.7). Replies will, of course, depend on the respondent's definition of 'ordinary people', but the question seems pitched in such a way as to encourage identification with the label, meaning the response is likely to reflect the sense of distance between the art funded by the government in museums, galleries and theatres, i.e. consecrated art, and the respondent's own aesthetic tastes and masteries. Rates of agreement thus generally increase with distance from the area of social space occupied by the professions and cultural dominant, *in all directions*, while rates of disagreement fall. Hence skilled workers, the furthest away both vertically and horizontally, record the highest level of agreement and the lowest disagreement of all, with the LMPs not far behind.

So far we have charted the correspondence between social space and practices generally associated with 'intelligence', 'cleverness' or 'brightness', i.e. symbolic mastery, but that is only half the story of consecrated culture. The other half, generally overlooked by most post-*Distinction* scholars yet perhaps of increased significance since the

Table 3.1 Cultural practices by class and gender (row%)

Class fraction	Playing a musical instrument		Engaging in performing arts		Painting, drawing, sculpting		Photography and filmmaking		Textiles and crafts		Writing stories, poetry, etc.		Member of a book club	
	Men	Women	Men	Women	Men	Women	Men	Women	Men	Women	Men	Women	Men	Women
Business executives	29.4	27.4	9.1	14.0	26.5	32.7	26.5	19.2	15.7	32.5	10.8	16.7	3.8	10.0
Professions	35.3	41.8	10.4	18.7	26.4	43.1	34.8	22.4	17.4	43.6	16.9	15.7	5.5	22.0
White-collar	28.5	19.8	10.3	12.1	27.2	35.4	29.7	17.1	16.9	39.3	13.0	14.6	3.9	8.4
Cultural dominant	42.4	40.7	24.7	30.2	41.7	46.7	48.9	29.2	24.0	51.2	28.7	26.7	8.0	17.7
LMPs	24.7	21.6	9.4	8.9	29.0	26.7	23.8	20.2	19.4	33.5	11.6	13.5	3.5	10.0
Technicians	26.6	12.6	8.0	5.7	25.8	31.0	27.7	11.6	18.9	34.5	12.5	8.2	4.5	6.9
Administrators	23.8	18.6	11.8	10.0	28.8	27.4	26.9	15.5	11.0	33.2	11.2	11.3	2.9	7.3
Cultural interm.	35.4	25.4	18.1	15.1	40.0	33.8	49.0	20.1	28.1	44.1	29.5	17.8	4.2	10.1
Skilled trades	23.7	22.7	7.8	5.4	27.7	33.8	22.3	21.9	23.1	48.7	8.7	14.9	4.3	11.6
Sales workers	21.3	15.0	8.1	11.2	24.0	25.2	21.6	17.1	13.3	31.2	10.8	10.5	4.1	6.7
Manual workers	16.4	16.3	8.3	9.9	26.4	28.5	19.8	13.9	18.5	34.0	9.4	9.3	5.4	5.5
Caring services	26.8	24.6	14.1	14.2	30.0	37.8	25.7	18.7	16.9	41.2	9.9	15.5	8.5	10.1

Source: BCS 2012

Table 3.2 Cultural venues and events by class and gender (row%)

Class Fraction	Museum (several times p/a)		Theatre (several times p/a)		Classical concert or opera (ever)		Other concert (several times p/a)		Gallery (several times p/a)		Historical site (ever)		Library (ever)	
	Men	Women	Men	Women	Men	Women	Men	Women	Men	Women	Men	Women	Men	Women
Business executives	25.0	22.9	18.5	29.8	32.2	40.9	18.9	22.8	16.5	17.9	29.8	23.0	57.9	63.3
Professions	33.3	41.3	19.4	25.9	40.8	60.2	20.9	20.6	26.4	35.8	34.2	43.6	67.6	75.2
White-collar	23.4	22.1	14.7	23.9	30.4	39.2	21.5	21.6	13.7	16.9	28.5	19.2	60.0	72.4
Cultural dominant	34.5	34.5	21.1	31.0	42.8	48.7	24.0	20.9	27.1	26.2	35.8	35.2	76.5	84.9
LMPs	15.9	17.5	12.4	23.6	27.0	31.5	15.5	15.4	14.6	14.2	20.5	17.7	48.4	57.1
Technicians	19.5	19.5	13.0	15.1	26.7	26.4	16.2	14.9	14.0	10.5	24.9	19.5	62.5	58.1
Administrators	19.9	15.6	13.5	18.3	24.0	23.7	17.0	14.9	18.6	11.6	24.6	15.6	58.5	67.6
Cultural interm.	34.4	18.8	23.4	17.6	39.6	42.2	28.4	20.3	26.0	13.9	21.9	20.5	68.7	80.4
Skilled trades	13.3	11.0	7.1	8.0	16.9	25.7	14.6	9.3	9.7	12.2	16.2	17.3	47.3	62.7
Sales workers	19.2	10.5	8.2	12.9	21.3	23.5	8.0	11.6	9.7	6.6	13.5	9.3	60.5	68.6
Manual workers	10.2	10.9	5.1	8.8	14.3	18.6	9.9	11.0	6.7	9.1	13.0	11.1	48.7	64.5
Caring services	21.7	16.1	10.1	16.2	22.5	28.1	24.3	12.4	12.9	11.2	28.2	17.8	62.0	73.1

Source: BCS 2012

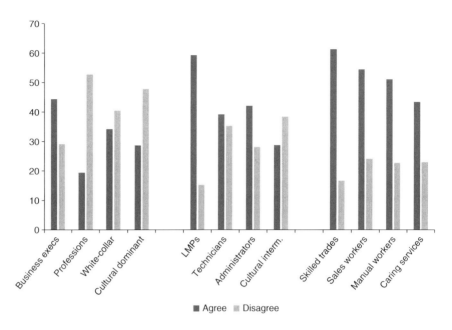

Figure 3.7 Arts funded by the government are not for ordinary people (%)

1980s, at least in Britain, with the growth of material wealth at the top of social space following neoliberal reforms, is the culture of the economically rich. Competing with the tastes of those richer in cultural capital – i.e. struggling within the field of power to impose their version of legitimate taste as the overall legitimate one, recognised by all, and perhaps successfully so these days – the key here is not symbolic mastery and exclusivity based on knowledge but luxury, ostentation and exclusivity by dint of money. The CCSE data is limited in this regard – one of the reasons, perhaps, why the business executives were less north-easterly in the MCA model than might have been expected. To examine empirical indicators of this we have to turn to government data yielding information on the average value of collectibles and valuables (i.e. antiques and artworks) – as symbols of distance from necessity, or distinctiveness – as well as rate of possession and average value of vehicles and personalised number/registration plates (Table 3.2). The patterns are fairly clear: the fractions of all classes richer in economic capital – business executives, LMPs and skilled trades, but also professionals, who possess most capital overall in a balanced composition – have, compared to their counterparts richer in cultural capital, a greater value of collectibles and valuables, which can be taken to indicate both volume and expense. Moreover, the economically rich are more likely to possess multiple cars and to possess private registration plates than their counterparts across the second axis of the social space, and the average values in most cases (indicating *exclusivity* or *distinctiveness*) are noticeably higher. Interestingly the average price of registration plate is highest among LMPs, perhaps indicating a level of striving for symbolic recognition which might be deemed 'crass' by those above. Doubtless other variables not currently available – such as boat ownership or holiday preferences – and greater data on the 'super-rich' – who have a

Table 3.3 Practices of the economically rich

Class fraction	Household collectibles and valuables (£)*	Own two or more cars (%)**		Mean value of car (£)*	Possession of private number plate (%)*	Mean value of private number plate (£)*
Business executives	23,600	59.3		12,700	11.2	1,700
Professions	16,800	46.1		10,200	9.0	1,400
White-collar	13,700	45.8		9,500	8.0	1,600
Cultural dominant	12,900	34.4	Intellectuals	7,500	7.0	1,000
			Teachers	7,100	5.3	1,500
LMPs	13,700	47.8		8,900	9.3	2,100
Technicians	8,400	47.8		–	–	–
Administrators	9,800	28.9		6,100	4.9	1,200
Cultural interm.	8,700	33.3		–	–	–
Skilled trades	12,700	44.9		6,600	5.9	900
Manual workers	6,000	25.2		5,500	2.8	1,300
Sales workers	9,600	17.9	}	5,200	3.4	1,000
Caring services	11,100	18.0				

* Source: WAS 2006–8. This data was very generously provided by the ONS at my request (full data is unavailable on grounds of confidentiality). As parts of the data were provided at different stages of the construction of the social space categories, some data is only available for more or less aggregated categories. Some data has been suppressed on account of insufficient numbers for robust comparison.

** Source: LCFS 2010

habit of escaping surveys – would further sharpen the opposition (cf. Beaverstock and Faulconbridge, 2014), and, indeed, it is notable that Bourdieu deployed a greater variety of data sources, such as magazine articles and adverts (of the kind still readily available today), to demonstrate the lavish, hedonistic lifestyle of the wealthy. Nevertheless the chiastic structure of the symbolic space and its homology with the social space is evident enough.

Finally, in order to evade common accusations flung at Bourdieu and those inspired by him that the dominated are only ever defined in terms of lack, we can pick out a few practices disproportionately engaged in by the dominated, or the low in consecrated cultural capital at any rate. This is not always easy since most surveys tend to focus on participation or lack thereof in legitimate culture, but four stick out from the CCSE survey and the BCS survey (Table 3.4). These are (i) bingo – a cheap, communal activity offering the possibility of economic reward, which increases in popularity lower down in social space; (ii) going to the pub once a week – again a relatively cheap, communal mode of relaxation, which is more popular among men than women and among male sales workers, skilled workers and LMPs in particular, though business executives and male professionals are not too far behind; (iii) gardening on a weekly basis (indicating it is a hobby rather than a necessity), which is most popular among skilled workers and technicians, no doubt as a mode of applying their technical capital and practical mastery to non-work ends, but also caring services; (iv) and engaging in DIY on a weekly basis, which is, again, a masculine practice and one more popular among skilled workers, technicians and other class fractions lower in cultural capital, perhaps for the same reason as gardening.

Table 3.4 Practices of the dominated (row%)

Class fraction	Pub (weekly)*		Gardening (weekly)*		DIY (weekly)*		Bingo**
	Men	*Women*	*Men*	*Women*	*Men*	*Women*	
Business executives	22.7	13.1	19.9	16.3	17.0	7.6	6.9
Professions	20.8	13.6	17.2	16.4	10.3	5.5	2.8
White-collar	19.3	17.0	17.0	21.1	10.2	6.7	8.7
Cultural dominant	14.8	8.2	20.0	19.8	11.7	6.8	6.1
LMPs	24.9	20.4	19.0	16.9	15.3	6.5	5.0
Technicians	18.1	6.9	22.1	18.4	25.6	9.2	11.8
Administrators	20.5	10.0	15.9	15.8	7.6	4.7	17.6
Cultural interm.	21.1	8.6	17.4	20.4	10.4	8.6	9.5
Skilled trades	25.2	10.8	26.3	32.0	29.0	16.0	9.0
Sales workers	33.8	8.8	15.8	19.4	9.2	7.3	19.2
Manual workers	19.3	12.5	20.2	21.0	20.9	6.4	21.0
Caring services	16.9	11.6	28.2	23.5	18.3	7.7	17.1

* Source: BCS 2012
** Source: CCSE 2003. Low total frequency precludes breakdown by gender.

Locating cultural products and producers

A second avenue for padding out the structure of the British symbolic space and its homology with the social space is through close examination of tastes for a selection of cultural products and producers. These can, no doubt, be subject to multiple readings and modes of consumption depending on class position, but they are still much more discerning than the giant genre categories often used by others and, for what it is worth, in line with Bourdieu's own methodological practice. Luckily the CCSE team asked their respondents about a range of artefacts and artists, including those from the fields of film, literature and music. In relation to the first, where the choices offered are film directors, a fairly clear opposition emerges. On the one hand, the most widely known directors – 'master of suspense' Alfred Hitchcock and Hollywood heavyweight Steven Spielberg – are more popular among the dominated and the economically richer intermediate class fractions, who are more likely to say that they would 'make a point of watching' one of their films if it were on: as regards Spielberg, for example, who is more popular all round than Hitchcock, 52 per cent of sales workers, 47 per cent of manual workers, 45 per cent of skilled workers and 47 per cent of LMPs, but also 48 per cent of the lowest category of the dominated class, the white-collar workers. The dominant class, and culturally richer fractions, by contrast, are much more likely to simply say they *might* watch one of their films: 60 per cent of professionals, 51 per cent of business executives and the cultural dominant and 46 per cent of the cultural intermediaries (as opposed to around only 35 per cent who would make a point of it in each case). As for Hitchcock, the starkest figures are only 23 per cent of professionals making a point of watching one of his pieces and 30 per cent of the cultural dominant – but 51 per cent and 46 per cent respectively saying they might watch it – versus 41 per cent of manual workers and 46 per cent of LMPs making a point of it. Spielberg and Hitchcock can thus be said to be more middlebrow/lowbrow overall.

On the other hand, when it comes to rather more obscure directors – Pedro Almodóvar, Ingmar Bergman, Jane Campion and Mani Ratnam – the chances of having even heard of them generally rises with cultural capital. Bergman is the most well-known on the whole, with around half the dominated having heard of him, but the figures are between two-thirds and three-quarters for other class fractions, and actually highest among business executives (81 per cent), white-collar workers (74 per cent) and LMPs (70 per cent), even though only 3 per cent, 11 per cent and 8 per cent respectively would actually make a point of watching one of his films (as opposed to 17 per cent of professionals), suggesting that a degree of cultural capital has brought them knowledge of but not taste for a more popular supposed highbrow director. The same patterns can be found in relation to Jane Campion, a touch less popular overall than Bergman: 27 per cent of business executives and 30 per cent of LMPs, along with 32 per cent of cultural intermediaries, have heard of her (the three highest), but the cultural intermediaries are most likely (10 per cent) to make a point of watching her films, while the others either might watch or probably wouldn't watch them.

If Bergman and Campion are thus somewhere between middlebrow and highbrow, then the class fractions richest in cultural capital find their road to recognition among the most obscure directors, with Pedro Almodóvar known by 28 per cent of professionals, 15 per cent of the cultural dominant and 16 per cent of the cultural intermediaries, as opposed to between 4 and 6 per cent in the dominated class and 8 or 9 per cent in the other fractions of the intermediate class and among business executives. The cultural dominant are, moreover, the most likely to make a point of watching his films (10 per cent), while the professionals are more likely to say they only *might* watch one (11 per cent). Mani Ratnam – a critically acclaimed Indian director of Tamil films – is the most obscure of all, with only the cultural dominant (among whom there are no Indians in the sample) hitting a double-figure percentage of having heard of him, while the rest of the social space (where there are Indians) hovers around 5 per cent. Some might put this down to a more cosmopolitan disposition, an interest in the exotic as the new site of difference, but it could equally be read as a novel application of the old disposition toward the *demanding*.[8] Of course, it might be said – and indeed it has been said (Kingston, 2000) – that the low numbers even within the cultural dominant of people having heard of these obscure producers hardly makes them characteristic of the tastes of the dominant class. But that misses the point: if there is a critically acclaimed yet obscure cultural producer out there, the cultural dominant are most likely to know about them, and while they might not have heard of Mani Ratnam they may have heard of Michael Haneke, or Pawel Pawlikowski, or someone else instead – but they are more likely to know someone who, because of the 'experimentalism' or 'difficulty' of (accessing) their work, are not generally known or favoured by the majority of moviegoers.

In relation to books, the CCSE team asked respondents to comment on specific titles rather than authors, allowing for a slightly more nuanced picture to emerge, but the underlying oppositions found in film preferences are reproduced here too.[9] Thus Maya Angelou's *I Know Why the Caged Bird Sings*, a critically acclaimed memoir often to be found on US school curricula, presupposing a knowledge of and interest in racism, civil rights and American history, i.e. a symbolic mastery and concern regarding social and political affairs, is unfamiliar to many in the dominated class and economic fractions of the intermediate and dominant class. Among men, only around 15 per cent of any fraction of the dominated class, as well as business executives, have heard of it, as opposed to 36 per cent of the cultural dominant and 42 per cent of professionals, though the fact that almost a fifth of the cultural dominant have actually read or are thinking about it compared with 13 per cent of professionals reveals a difference between knowledge and taste. Among women the book is more popular but still reveals differences by capital volume and, more so than among men, capital composition. So while still around 15 per cent of most of the dominated have heard of it, 20 per cent of the caring services workers have; while only 12 per cent of female LMPs have heard of it, 30 per cent of cultural intermediaries of the same sex have; and while 35 per cent of business executives have heard of it, 41 per cent of the cultural dominant have, with 25 per cent of the latter having actually read or thought about reading it (only just behind the professions on 27 per cent).

Similarly, Gustave Flaubert's *Madame Bovary*, a tale of feminine bourgeois existence now part of the canon of artistic, modernist literature and somewhat better-known across the sample, rises in familiarity and interest with volume of capital and especially cultural capital (Table 3.5). Jane Austen's *Pride and Prejudice*, an almost universally recognised yet still canonised 'classic' text, is, like *Madame Bovary*, more popular among women than men, with 53 per cent of women having read it as opposed to 22 per cent of men. Within this, however, there are clear class differences, with the book being read or considered for reading largely in line with cultural capital (though female LMPs also go in for it). J. K. Rowling's *Harry Potter and the Chamber of Secrets*, the most contemporary book on the list and one heralded as a paragon of children's literature, is known by around 90–95 per cent of all class fractions but not read and not likely to be read by the majority, no doubt because it is a children's book; but those who have read it or are thinking of doing so are mostly the professions (46 per cent of men, 55 per cent of women), the cultural dominant (31 per cent of men, 54 per cent of women) and caring

Table 3.5 Knowledge of and taste for two books (row%)

Class	Madame Bovary				Pride and Prejudice	
	Men		Women		Men	Women
	Read/ thinking of reading	Have heard of	Read/ thinking of reading	Have heard of	Read/ thinking of reading	Read/ thinking of reading
Business executives	9.1	60.0	12.5	43.7	38.2	70.6
Professions	26.1	65.2	36.4	63.6	54.2	91.7
White-collar	10.9	41.8	32.0	64.0	22.6	80.0
Cultural dominant	22.8	68.6	26.6	69.6	54.3	91.2
LMPs	5.6	41.7	8.7	26.1	36.1	83.3
Technicians	10.5	44.7	35.7	64.3	40.5	61.5
Administrators	20.0	52.5	13.0	52.1	38.5	69.3
Cultural interm.	18.2	72.7	11.1	57.1	60.0	74.6
Skilled trades	2.8	31.0	13.6	40.9	14.4	65.2
Sales workers	2.5	22.5	4.8	26.7	23.0	58.1
Manual workers	1.5	27.0	4.4	21.7	20.1	44.9
Caring services	0.0	45.0	13.0	37.4	38.1	59.9

Source: CCSE 2003

services (29 per cent of men, 50 per cent of women), perhaps partly because of a desire to read the books to or with their offspring.

Two other volumes, however, correspond with different sections of the social space. The first is John Grisham's *The Firm*, a best-selling American legal thriller, which is actually more popular among male professionals (71 per cent have read/are thinking of reading it), female professionals (50 per cent) female business executives (47 per cent), LMPs of both sexes (37 per cent) and sales workers of both sexes (30 per cent) than their cultural-capital-rich counterparts, since only 40 per cent of female cultural dominant, 10 per cent of male and 32 per cent of female cultural intermediaries and 19 per cent of male and 20 per cent of female caring services have read or are considering reading it. Clearly this is not only because the form of the piece is less demanding of cultural capital but because it bears upon, and perhaps requires for fuller appreciation some familiarity with (and interest in), the worlds of the professions and business, i.e. the machinations of the legal field and the economic field. The second divergent title is *The Solace of Sin*, a tale of forbidden passions and family secrets by Catherine Cookson, an author known for her focus on romance and working-class life. Barely read by men at all, among women this book is most popular with skilled workers (46 per cent have read it or are thinking of reading it), administrators (32 per cent), manual workers (27 per cent) and LMPs (26 per cent) and least popular with professionals (9 per cent), business executives (13 per cent) and the cultural dominant (15 per cent), marking out this dramatic account of the travails of amorous relationships – to which the dominated and intermediate feminine libido is disproportionately channelled – as a phenomenon of middlebrow/popular taste.

Finally we come to music preferences, where once again the question referred to specific compositions rather than the *oeuvres* of artists as a whole. Two preliminary remarks need to be made before plunging into the analysis here. First, music is a domain of cultural consumption known to be heavily influenced by age, as both the CCSE team and preliminary MCAs conducted here confirmed, but since the age profiles of the class fractions are inextricably constitutive of their character, as part of their seniority within their respective classes, that matters little. Second, music perhaps more than many other fields of cultural production has undergone significant transformation since Bourdieu's day, with the exponential growth of the popular music industry producing a diversified sub-field of non-classical production more or less homologous with the social space, opposing, on the one hand, those more interested in using themes, instruments and techniques of popular music in the service of (more) *restricted* production – focussed on artistic or creative impulse, experimentalism and sociopolitically conscious music, for example – which appeals more to those with greater symbolic mastery, and, on the other hand, those concerned (more) with *mass* appeal through standardised formulas and appeals to 'good times', dominated experience and physical release, with plenty muddling in between (cf. Bourdieu, 1993).

That said, familiar patterns emerge soon enough, with, in particular, an opposition between the various exemplars of classical music and the more 'popular' artists being fairly apparent, though within that there are interesting variations. The classical compositions, for example, are most widely known and enjoyed amongst the dominant class and least known and liked among the dominated, but to different degrees and among different class fractions according to their degree of popularisation. Vivaldi's *Four Seasons*, the most widely recognised and popularised among them – ubiquitous in film scores, advertisements, compilation albums and so on, and known by over 90 per cent of the dominant class and around 70 per cent of manual workers and sales workers – is most 'appreciated' in the dominant and intermediate classes but, noticeably, in the fractions with a more balanced capital composition primarily, the cultural fractions secondarily and the economic fractions least: 89 per cent of professionals, 86 per cent of the cultural dominant compared to 72 per cent of business executives in the dominant class; 71 per cent of technicians and administrators, 68 per cent of cultural intermediaries and only 49 per cent of LMPs in the intermediate class. Within the dominated class the distribution shifts to be more directly in line with capital composition, with the caring services most predisposed to a bit of Vivaldi (56 per cent) and the skilled workers least of all (39 per cent).

Parallel patterns are found in perceptions of Gustav Mahler's *Symphony No. 5*, although this piece is less familiar in general, with around 65 per cent of sales workers, manual workers and skilled workers never having heard of it and around 40 per cent of the intermediate class fractions reporting the same. This too is more popular among the professionals (49 per cent report liking it) than the cultural dominant (41 per cent) and the business executives (32 per cent) and among the technicians (28 per cent) and administrators (23 per cent) than the LMPs (20 per cent), although the cultural intermediaries are also relatively keen (29 per cent), while the dominant class are less likely to register a positive evaluation, including the caring services (18 per cent). The relationship shifts considerably, however, when it comes to Philip Glass' experimental opera *Einstein on the Beach*, barely known among the populace as a whole (14 per cent of the dominated, 18 per cent of the intermediate and 24 per cent of the dominant). The cultural dominant are the most likely to know of this long and unorthodox piece on the famed Austrian physicist (31 per cent) and by far the most likely to like it (10 per cent), suggesting a libido and habitus, or simply taste, disproportionately oriented toward the difficult, demanding and obscure, as an adaptation to conditions of life in which symbolic mastery is the primary route to recognition, in contrast to the professionals' taste for the most traditional, conventional or well-known classical pieces as markers of 'good taste'.

The chosen paradigms of popular music display an altogether different correspondence with positions in social space. The most pronounced is Britney Spears' *Oops!...I Did It Again* – a 'dance pop' song from 2000 aimed at teenage girls which references the tribulations of adolescent romance and finds its contemporary homologues in the fare released by Miley Cyrus or Rihanna. The song is far more popular with women than men, but particularly women in the dominated class and those less rich in cultural capital more generally – 50 per cent of female skilled workers report liking it, as do 50 per cent of female white-collar workers, 42 per cent of female LMPs and 36 per cent of female sales workers, in contrast to only 25 per cent of female cultural intermediaries and 31 per cent of the female cultural dominant. The song is liked least, however, by female business executives (just 13 per cent like it), who sit in the more masculine section of social space; interestingly, among men the section most likely to be keen on it are sales workers, i.e. men occupying positions in a particularly feminine zone of social space.

Wonderwall by the currently defunct indie-rock band Oasis, who had their heyday in the 1990s but spawned a thousand present-day homologues, is most popular among white-collar workers (66 per cent like it), sales workers (56 per cent), technicians (55 per cent), cultural intermediaries (52 per cent), business executives (51 per cent) and LMPs (48 per cent), but less popular among manual workers (37 per cent) and the professions and the cultural dominant (46 per cent), suggesting that a taste for the Manchester group may correspond most closely with more middling cultural capital, itself the product not only of present position but of age, or trajectory, within the social space. Very similar patterns are found for Eminem's *Stan*, a sombre hip hop song on the theme of fan obsession and alienation – and, it should be stated, a very particular example of the 'genre' different from (and perhaps somewhere between) the 'old skool', 'conscious' and experimental hip hop resonating more with highly educated 'backpack rap' fans on the one hand and the 'club bangers' celebrating monetary or romantic/sexual success on the other.[10] Once again the tune is most popular among sales workers (40 per cent like it), business executives (38 per cent) and white-collar workers (38 per cent) and least favoured among the cultural dominant (23 per cent) and professionals (26 per cent).

Body modification

So far I have covered similar ground to Bourdieu himself – orientations to decor, sport, art, film, music and so on – but I want now to turn to a couple of cultural practices which have increased in significance since the research on which *Distinction* was based was carried out. The first of these is 'body modification', i.e. piercings, tattoos and tanning oneself on a sunbed – a practice often seen as indicative of the creeping class-killing 'reflexivity' of our epoch (see Sweetman, 1999) yet, in reality, significantly differentiated by class, especially when broken down by gender (cf. Vandebroeck, 2016, on Belgium). Having one's ears pierced, for example, while a fairly widespread tendency among women of all classes, still varies notably by class fraction – 94 per cent of female business executives have their ears pierced (perhaps as a means of displaying expensive jewellery) compared to 79 per cent of female manual workers and 59 per cent of female skilled workers, for whom it might be less practical given the demands of work or less desirable in tune with their location within a more masculine zone of social space. Interestingly, a different set of patterns emerges when the piercing is somewhere else on the body (wherever that might be), with members of the dominated class as a whole more likely to have one than those in the other classes (16 per cent as opposed to 10 per cent of the intermediate and 8 per cent of the dominant class) and, cross-cutting this, cultural intermediaries (16 per cent), caring services (23 per cent) but also technicians (29 per cent) being far more likely than other fractions within their classes (e.g. 9 per cent of skilled workers, 8 per cent of LMPs and not a single female business executive in the survey) to have pierced their flesh.

Among men, the propensity to have one's ears pierced is rarer, and therefore a bolder statement, but also unevenly distributed, with those in the dominated class as a whole being more likely to puncture their earlobes than other classes (24 per cent as opposed to 14 per cent of the dominant and 11 per cent of the intermediate class). Within this, however, there are important differences by class fraction, with all those richer in cultural capital, and more toward the feminine pole of the social space, tending toward the practice at a much higher rate than those in the economically richer and masculine fractions: 22 per cent of the male cultural dominant as opposed to 7 per cent of business executives, 30 per cent of cultural intermediaries as opposed to 8 per cent of technicians and 38 per cent of caring and personal-service workers versus 20 per cent of skilled workers. As to piercings elsewhere on the body, while this is a very rare activity among men altogether (no more than 5 per cent in any class), this is extremely unevenly distributed by class fraction: 17 per cent of the cultural dominant, 10 per cent of cultural intermediaries and 24 per cent of caring and personal-service workers have such an adornment as opposed to barely more than a few per cent in any other class fraction. While piercing may still be associated overall with the dominated class, therefore, and thus potentially derided as 'vulgar' by those who would 'never do such things' to their bodies, there is perhaps some indication that the use of body piercing to express individuality, 'personal narrative', 'anti-fashion', rebellion and difference (i.e. *distinction*) often unearthed by qualitative researchers and psychologists (see Wohlrab *et al.*, 2007) is a sign not of a postmodern dissolution of hierarchies but of standardised resistance to the standardised and commercialised couture of the economically rich among those relatively wealthier in cultural capital.

Very much the same can be said for tattoos. Among men, 21 per cent of the dominated class possess one as opposed to 11 per cent of the intermediate and 7 per cent of the dominant class, but 14 per cent of the cultural dominant have one – far more than any other class fraction within the dominant. Among women, 15 per cent of the dominated are etched with ink, contrasted to 8 per cent of the intermediate class and 10 per cent of the dominant class. In this case the lower rate of tattooing in the intermediate class is perhaps due to the low level of inking amongst the most preponderant class fraction, the administrators, for whom 'presentability' and 'respectability' are woven into not simply their work but their mode of differentiation from those below; but it is also worth pointing out the cultural dominant again have a relatively high rate of having a tattoo (12 per cent), especially compared to other dominant class fractions (e.g. 6 per cent of business executives). Thus – and bearing in mind the possible effects of social mobility too – it may be that tattoos, historically a direct and immediate, and therefore efficient, symbol of belonging to a field in which some local power or recognition could be attained amongst the dominated class – an industry, a neighbourhood, a family, a gang – or as enhancement of bodily value, has in more recent years been appropriated by certain (cultural-capital-rich) sections of the non-dominated as a vehicle for expressing individuality, or distinction, with their artistic *form* overtaking their signifying *function* in importance (DeMello, 2000; Kosut, 2014). This has generated yet one more site of symbolic struggle and violence, as 'tasteful' tattoos are contrasted to 'distasteful' tattoos, but the differential rates of possession mean that having a tattoo *per se* can still act as an object of disgust for the dominant (see Lawler, 2005).

Finally, there are some telling differences in propensity to tan oneself on a sunbed. Among men, where rates of take up are generally lower as a whole, the class fraction most likely to have engaged in this activity is the business executives (20 per cent), in line with a focus on surface appearances, while the professions (8 per cent) and cultural dominant (14 per cent) are more likely to spurn them, on aesthetic rather than cost grounds one supposes, along with the intermediate and dominated classes (11 per cent in both cases). Among women the rates of using sunbeds, in line with dominant notions of femininity and beauty, are higher all round, but the patterning by class fractions is significant. Within the dominant class, 59 per cent of female business executives partake in it, compared to just 18 per cent of professionals and 28 per cent of the cultural dominant. The same distribution by capital composition can be found in the intermediate class, where 46 per cent of the LMPs absorb the UV rays compared to only 30 per cent of cultural intermediaries. In the dominated class, however, the pattern reverses, as those fractions putting greater emphasis on bodily appearance and maintenance are far more likely to subject themselves to ultraviolet (37 per cent of sales workers, 35 per cent of caring services) compared to the manual workers (20 per cent), for whom it is probably financially less viable, and more 'pretentious', and skilled workers (18 per cent), following the same orientation toward masculine practices already noted.

On television

Like body modification, television figures little in Bourdieu's original research, being so *nouveau* at the time, yet forms a central and seemingly innocuous part of the contemporary cultural landscape, even if nowadays in competition and integration with various so-called 'smart' technologies. Once the symbol of cultural massification and pacification for the condemners of the 'culture industry' like Adorno (2001), in more recent years it has, again like body modification, underpinned some arguments, at least implicitly, that old class practices might just be dwindling if for no other reason than because television delivers information on all sorts of lifestyles and views from all over the world into our daily lifeworlds constantly (e.g. Morley, 2000). From our point of view – extrapolating from Bourdieu's (1998) critical take on television – it might rather be said that it can be considered one of the most prominent media for the fields of cultural production (including the media field itself), providing extensive circuits of symbolic power through which the position-takings and categories of thought generated within the national and global field of power and beyond, glossed and framed in variegated ways, are transmitted to receiving habitus (or social surfaces) and interpreted accordingly. In any case, for our purposes there are four pertinent modes of differentiation *vis-à-vis* television-watching.

Number one: people in different classes watch television at vastly different rates. This is evident enough in the CCSE data, but more recent data comes from the 2012 sweep of the BCS. For example, the tendency to watch television for less than one hour per weekday increases with capital volume and greater relative possession of cultural capital, opposing professionals (32 per cent) and the cultural dominant (28 per cent) to the business executives (21 per cent) and the white-collar workers (17 per cent); the cultural intermediaries (19 per cent) to the technicians (14 per cent) and the caring services (16 per cent) to manual workers (11 per cent) and skilled workers (12 per cent). Watching 'the box' for more than five hours on a weekday, however, follows the reverse pattern, with few in the dominant class managing the feat but 8 per cent of skilled workers and sales workers and 11 per cent of manual workers doing so. Patterns of weekend viewing are similar, though telly-watching takes up more time on average for everyone then. Watching for less than an hour drops to 13 per cent among professionals and 9 per cent for the cultural dominant and intermediaries, but this is still a greater proportion than for business executives (7 per cent), LMPs (6 per cent), technicians (3 per cent), manual workers (6 per cent) and skilled workers (5 per cent). Watching for more than five hours, on the other hand, jumps up to a full quarter of manual workers, 18 per cent of sales workers and 15 per cent of skilled workers as opposed to just 4 per cent of professionals, 6 per cent of business executives and the cultural dominant and 9 per cent of the cultural intermediaries. The implication, of course, is that those not watching so much television are doing something else – going to art galleries, attending book clubs, writing poetry, maybe even writing poetry about book clubs in an art gallery. However, to see high rates of television-watching as indicative of 'cultural disengagement' among the dominated class, as it often is, would be not only misleading but itself infected with cultural prejudice – and if anyone thought that symbolic violence is not dispensed over television habits it is enough to remember that a common label for TV is 'the idiot box' – since it assumes that only dominant tastes and activities count as 'culture' and that television-watching does not involve engagement in itself (see Savage, 2012).

Number two: there is a distinct difference in the type of broadcaster favoured (Table 3.6). The tendency to prefer public-service broadcasting – including the publicly owned and somewhat 'experimental' Channel 4 – rises with cultural capital, while the

Table 3.6 Television channel watched most often (row%)

Class fraction	BBC1	BBC2	ITV	Channel 4	Other
Business executives	53.5	11.3	21.1	7.0	7.0
Professions	52.9	8.8	14.7	11.8	11.8
White-collar	63.8	10.0	13.8	10.0	2.6
Cultural dominant	61.7	6.1	9.6	14.8	7.8
LMPs	40.0	3.3	36.7	13.3	6.7
Technicians	51.0	5.9	27.5	5.9	9.9
Administrators	47.8	4.8	35.9	7.7	3.8
Cultural interm.	33.3	8.3	41.7	11.1	5.6
Skilled trades	41.3	7.2	35.3	7.8	8.4
Sales workers	27.4	2.1	58.2	6.2	6.2
Manual workers	28.8	4.7	44.8	6.3	15.3
Caring services	35.8	4.0	40.4	10.6	9.4

Source: CCSE 2003

preference for commercial television (e.g. ITV) declines, particularly among the dominant, suggesting a homology with the differing positions of organisations within the media field (cf. Bourdieu, 1998). The BBC, since it escapes the need to compete in the open market, maintains a greater degree of *autonomy* and can thus produce programmes for restricted markets, i.e. programmes measured against internal benchmarks of 'quality' set by cultural producers, and in line with its own paternalistic (and classed) founding ethos of 'educating' and 'informing' as well as 'entertaining' its audience. Indeed it is one of the key organs through which cultural producers can propagate their lifestyle as the legitimate one. Commercial organisations such as ITV, on the other hand, having to maximise revenues by maximising audiences, cluster at the *heteronymous* pole, yoked to the interests of the economic field more broadly, and favour programming designed for the mass market – i.e. more in step with the tastes of the most preponderant class, the dominated.

Number three: we can examine precisely what those tastes are a little since the CCSE team, trying to unpick the relationship between class habitus and televisual tastes and aware of the limits of genre categories (Bennett *et al.*, 2009: 144ff), though not enough to remove them from their MCA, included a question in their survey in which respondents were asked to pick their favourite programme from a long and relatively diverse list. These have been projected into the earlier MCA solution as supplementary points, revealing a number of pertinent oppositions (Figure 3.8). Within the broad rubric of drama and comedy, for example, *Six Feet Under*, *West Wing*, *Sex and the City* and *Absolutely Fabulous* appear to increase in favour the higher the class, with *Sex and the City* more popular amongst the younger, feminised, cultural-capital-rich side, whereas *Bad Girls*, *Big Brother*, *The Bill*, *EastEnders*, *Coronation Street* and *Two Pints of Lager and a Packet of Crisps* correspond with lower sections of social space. The opposition here is clearly between, on the one hand, programmes lauded for their exploration of and reflection on abstract themes (death in *Six Feet Under*, ethics in *West Wing*, sexuality and consumerism in *Sex and the City*),[11] centred on the fields and concerns of the dominant class (politics, media) and frequently described as ironic, satirical and 'intelligent' (on *Sex and the City* see Arthurs, 2003; on *Absolutely Fabulous* see Kirkham and Skeggs, 1998), versus, on the other, programmes (mostly soap operas) concerned with the immediate

Figure 3.8 The space of television programmes

emotional drama of ongoing, concrete familial and amorous relationships situated in the sites and resonating with the everyday experiences of the dominated (neighbourhoods, pubs, prisons, the police), though refracted in telling ways by the age/gender/capital composition axis. Within the general 'quiz' category, moreover, the clearest opposition is between *University Challenge*, which rises in favour with class position, and *Who Wants to be a Millionaire*, which descends, reflecting an opposition between the vaunting and valuing of pure symbolic mastery for no reward other than itself (and a modest trophy) and a show based more on trivia and luck (much like a pub quiz, and indeed *Who Wants to be a Millionaire* is a popular arcade game in pubs) as a means to the end of economic capital, and an escape or amelioration of conditions of existence, thus playing to the knowledges and desires of the dominated. Both are, however, united by being positioned slightly on the more masculine/older side of the symbolic space.

Number four: just as with any other stylistic possible we have to take into account the different *modes of consumption* of the same cultural good, or the reading of the same entity or sign through totally different lenses. Rates of watching *University Challenge* in the dominated class, for example, are not zero, and neither are rates of watching *Big Brother* zero among the most culturally resourced, but the different ways of appropriating them and using them, and the different judgements that can be dispensed against alternative readings, vary dramatically. One illustration, drawn from the observational research undergirding Part II, comes from Mr Newcombe and Ms Oliver, both notably rich in cultural capital (postgraduate qualifications in human/social sciences) but less so in economic capital, who, during a walk with their 15-year-old son and 10-year-old daughter to a coffee shop, begin to talk of their television tastes.[12] After registering a predilection for *Friends* and praising the programme *Frasier* for being 'a bit more thoughtful' (elsewhere they mention liking *West Wing* and *The Wire* because they are 'educational'), they arrive at *Big Brother*.

MR NEWCOMBE: Something else that we've all got interested in and is good learning for young people is *Big Brother*.
SON: I really like that.
MR NEWCOMBE: When we started watching it about three years ago, it was done quite well because not only did it have the hour of highlights each day but once a week. They'd have a discussion between psychologists about what situations had been artificially created and how different people had reacted. They [his children] were learning about scapegoating, about people presenting unfair images of each other.
SON: Power, power vacuums and yeah, power struggles.
MR NEWCOMBE: And at the time…
MS OLIVER: Social intelligence.

After a while of trying to remember the programme psychologist's name, the conversation continues:

MR NEWCOMBE: So obviously there's hours and hours of stultifying boredom, but the highlights programme often did draw attention to particular dynamics that were developing in the group. […]
MS OLIVER: Although again I think the view of our friends is 'What are you doing watching that?'
SON: Mmm.
MR NEWCOMBE: Yeah. Watching *Big Brother*!
Q: Why do you think they are saying that? Sorry, I've got to ask as a researcher!
MS OLIVER: Mmm, I think it's sort of, because it's reality TV, it's trash TV, it's kind of cheap and easy TV, it's not terribly…
SON: It's not like costume dramas.
MS OLIVER: …intellectually demanding.
MR NEWCOMBE: And if you just casually watch it, it looks like you're just being sort of, just prying on people's disintegrating, but what was interesting to us, the fact that there's quite an organised structure beneath it, that is controlled by some quite intelligent psychologists who are…
SON: Create tasks which bring out all the…
MR NEWCOMBE: So they say, 'Oh, did you see the stupid thing which George Galloway was pretending to be, a cat? Oh, my God.' But then if you listen to why they did that….so uhm…quite a lot of group dynamics. […]
MS OLIVER: I mean, I must say when I first started watching it, I thought 'Oh God, this is really, this is just contrived television' – they're kind of giving us these really extreme personalities, and kind of exposing them and, you know, 'Is this okay?' But over the years I've come to quite enjoy it and I think particularly … [Son] and I watched – well, we all watched – I particularly remember [son] and I watching

some Jade Goody, when she was bullying Shilpa Shetty, and there was some bullying going on at [son]'s school at the time, and it was just quite an interesting experience watching that and seeing how that was discussed.

Mr Newcombe adds:

> Yeah, the sort of lurid gloss on it, you get on it from the top tabloids, about who's having sex with who, we could do without that. But if you look beyond that, there's a lot of interesting learning – in the same way as watching *Friends*, you learn.

There is, then, a discredited reading of the show, the one apparently most prevalent (hence their slight defensiveness against friends), as 'lurid', 'trash', 'prying', 'cheap and easy', opposed to their own reading, focussed on 'learning' rather than entertainment, which goes 'beyond that', indicating a belief that it is a *deeper* reading, hidden to those lacking the mastery of certain codes (group dynamics, power vacuums, etc.).

Persistence through change (again)

So what are the consequences of all this, however limited the analysis might be, for understanding cultural domination today? First things first: with blanket genre categories removed from the analysis, the lingering spectre of omnivorousness has faded from view and in its place we find a familiar opposition between exclusive culture on the one hand – whether by dint of symbolic mastery or money – and indicators of necessity, corporeality and sociality on the other, with markers of middlebrow taste clustering in between. This does not mean that *no one* rich in cultural capital *ever* regularly consumes what would be deemed 'popular' cultural products, as some lazy caricatures of Bourdieu's position might suggest, and not only because of the effect of social mobility demonstrated by Van Eijk (1999) and Friedman (2012). Yet the salient source of sociocultural difference in twenty-first-century Britain would appear to remain the restricted versus the common; and even where popular cultural products are consumed by the cultural fraction of the dominant class, the underlying disposition, and the source of misrecognition, continues to revolve around the same-old cultural arbitrary of differential symbolic mastery (Bourdieu, 1984: 40, 329; Atkinson, 2011). Familiarity and ease with musical history, styles and 'classics', or preference for more 'thoughtful', 'intelligent', 'radical' or 'meditative' versions of this or that, differentiating the *mode* of consumption, the *types* of popular items consumed, etc., is crucial, not some new disposition toward 'openness' and 'tolerance' postulated by defenders of the omnivore thesis (cf. Holt, 1997; Prieur and Savage, 2015).[13] I sometimes wonder whether the omnivore thesis represents a scholastic projection of the cultural sociologist's head, with a certain perception of their own tastes, onto the body of the music-listener, film-watcher etc., much as Sartre imposed the philosopher's head on the waiter's body according to Bourdieu.

A second, important point is that the capital composition principle, so often muddied in pro-omnivore research and downplayed in the CCSE study, persists. True, everything would appear to suggest that it entwines fairly closely with two factors. The first is age, or youth culture and traditional culture, avant-garde and rear-guard, but that only confirms Bourdieu's stress on trajectory (or seniority within a class) as an important structuring principle. The second is gender, even if the prominence of this has not been as obvious as it was in the original CCSE model, where the division between feminine 'inwardly oriented' tastes and masculine 'outwardly oriented' tastes was a distinct axis, on account of an avoidance of genre categories, which are evidently good discriminators in this regard but poor measures of differences associated with distance from necessity and symbolic mastery. The left and right poles are, respectively, feminine and masculine, meaning the lifestyle associated with symbolic mastery is also likely to be seen as more effeminate or 'soft' and that associated with money as 'manly', no matter who displays them.

In any case there is no reason to think that the underlying nature of symbolic difference and domination in contemporary Britain is vastly different from 1970s France, or contemporary Norway, Denmark or other Western capitalist societies with developed education systems. That is not to say it is universal – in pre- or even early capitalist social orders and socialist societies other forms of recognition and capital, giving rise to different symbolic markers, have held sway – even if it is interesting to note the historical ubiquity of the mastery of symbolic systems, whether religious or secular, as a principle of misrecognition and domination opposed not only to the dominated against which that mastery is defined but to other sources of misrecognition and domination within a social order – martial skill (physical capital) or aristocratic manners (symbolic capital) in feudalism, bureaucratic position and favour (political capital) in socialist societies, and possession of money and wealth (economic capital) today. Nor is it to say the situation is exactly the same as 1970s France, as if the contemporary British working class enjoy playing the accordion and driving Renault 4s, only that the underlying dispositions and their relational differentiation seem remarkably consistent. New artists, fashions, styles and products may have emerged to play the signifying function once performed by older ones thanks to the ongoing struggles and strategies within the fields of cultural production, and so too may have new stylistic possibles – body modification, television preferences and so on – each of which, as we have seen, may act roughly as a differentiator *per se* but also as a universe of internal differentiation through which long-standing masteries and dispositions (including dreams of social flying) are expressed.

Notes

1 I have found only very occasional uses by Bourdieu (1984) himself of genre categories, notably for books and in reference to 'classical music', but they are absent from his constructions of the lifestyle spaces for the different classes. Genre categories need not be banished altogether from analysis, but they do need to be very carefully constructed and handled.

2 This is not to say regression analysis and so on do not have their place, only that they are unsuited to constructing models of fields and checking homologies.

3 Strictly speaking, this means that the analysis is tapping into elements of both the space of lifestyles and the space of dispositions mediating between it and the social space. I am under no illusions that the clustering is without limits, particularly insofar as it necessarily has to suppress what differences there may actually be, and that may have emerged with a larger sample size, between the constituent practices or tastes.

4 A 'specific' MCA was conducted, which just means that certain modalities are excluded from the model, in this case all the 'don't knows', refusals to answer and modalities with fewer than 5 per cent of respondents. For details of eigenvalues and contributions, see Appendix II.

5 The homology is not absolute, in that some class fractions appear in slightly different positions compared to their place in the social space, but that is as much down to the variables available as anything else. Specific technical procedures can only ever offer approximations, of greater and lesser degrees, of the epistemic spaces in question. Correspondence with some other indicators of capital, for comparison, is documented in Appendix II.

6 Although vegetarian restaurants correspond closest to the cultural intermediaries, it is actually the cultural dominant who register the highest rate of considering them their favourite type of eatery.

7 The data here derives not from the CCSE study but from the 2012 BCS, which benefits from a much larger sample size and has the added effect of neutralising age as a factor, since all participants are aged 42. See Appendix II.

8 '[T]o go to a foreign film is to be *challenged* and *provoked*. We've got to find new ways of encouraging people to make that *mental leap*': Jason Wood, artistic director at Manchester's Home art centre, interviewed by the BBC in 2015 (www.bbc.co.uk/news/entertainment-arts-31585429) (emphasis added).

9 For a complementary analysis of literary tastes using the 2012 BCS, see Atkinson (2016).

10 Hip hop, while sometimes lauded as a paradigmatic 'postmodern' musical style given its heavy reliance on sampling and blending existing songs (see e.g. Potter, 1995), was in fact a form of music clearly born of proximity to necessity in the US, albeit one inflected with ethno-racial significance. Those charged with providing musical entertainment, from Kool Herc to Afrika Bambaataa, at block parties in the Bronx in the 1970s, the latter serving as a collective release from the pressures of penury, did not have the equipment, instruments or valued skills necessary to compose music afresh so instead took what they had available – record players and records (usually funk) – and made something new out of them (including scratching records to produce new rhythmic sounds), while commands to dancers or stories told in rhythm to the music spawned rapping. Incidentally, this places the genesis of hip hop outside of, or at least at the very edges of, the field of musical production *per se*, but soon enough it was co-opted, commercialised and expanded into a diverse sub-field of musical production with its own internal hierarchies and homologies.

11 *Empire* magazine described *Six Feet Under* as 'a wonderful meditation on life, love and grief' (www.empireonline.com/50greatesttv/default.asp?tv=27), while *West Wing* was famously championed as a 'pedagogical tool' for political science students (Beavers, 2002). Both shows were generously decorated with the specific 'symbolic baubles' of the field, particularly Emmy awards. A more recent equivalent might be *Breaking Bad*.

12 See Appendix III for details of Ordinary Lives participants.

13 Where I differ from Prieur and Savage (2015), however, is that I would describe all this not as a new *form* of cultural capital but as simply a new *expression* within the symbolic space of the *old* form of cultural capital, symbolic mastery. The shadow of Savage's conflation of the social and symbolic spaces perhaps looms in their language.

References

Adorno, T. W. (2001) *The Culture Industry: Selected Essays on Mass Culture*. London: Routledge.

Arthurs, J. (2003) 'Sex and the City and Consumer Culture' *Feminist Media Studies*, 3(1): 83–98.

Atkinson, W. (2011) 'The Context and Genesis of Musical Tastes: Omnivorousness Debunked, Bourdieu Buttressed' *Poetics*, 39(3): 169–186.

Atkinson, W. (2016) 'The Structure of Literary Taste: Class, Gender and Reading in the UK' *Cultural Sociology*, 10(2): 247–66.

Beavers, S. (2002) '*The West Wing* as a Pedagogic Tool' *PS Online*, June, pp. 213–16.

Beaverstock, J. and Faulconbridge, J. (2014) 'Wealth Segmentation and the Mobilities of the Super-Rich' in T. Birtchnall and J. Caletrio (eds.) *Elite Mobilities*. London: Routledge, pp. 40–61.

Bennett, T. Savage, M., Silva, E., Gayo-Cal, M. and Wright, D. (2009) *Culture, Class, Distinction*. London: Routledge.

Bourdieu, P. (1984) *Distinction*. London: Routledge.

Bourdieu, P. (1998) *On Television*. Cambridge: Polity Press.

Bourdieu, P. and Darbel, A. (1991) *The Love of Art*. Cambridge: Polity Press.

Bourdieu, P., Boltanski, L., Castel, R., Chamboredon, J.-C., and Scnhapper, D. (1991) *Photography: A Middle-Brow Art*. Cambridge: Polity Press.

Chan, T. W. and Goldthorpe, J. H. (2007) 'Social Stratification and Cultural Consumption: Music in England' *European Sociological Review*, 23(1): 1–19.

Coulangeon, P. and Duval, J. (2015) 'Introduction' in P. Coulangeon and J. Duval (eds.) *The Routledge Companion to Bourdieu's Distinction*. London: Routledge, pp. 1–12.

DeMello, M. (2000) *Bodies of Inscription*. Durham: Duke University Press.

Dennis, N., Henriques, F. and Slaughter, C. (1969) *Coal is Our Life*, 2nd edition. London: Tavistock.

Friedman, S. (2012) 'Cultural Omnivores or Culturally Homeless?' *Poetics*, 40(5): 467–89.

Gilroy, P. (2000) *There Ain't No Black in the Union Jack*. London: Routledge.

Hall, S. and Jefferson, T. (eds.) (1999) *Resistance Through Rituals*. London: Routledge.

Hebdige, D. (1979) *Subculture: The Meaning of Style*. London: Methuen.

Holt, D. B. (1997) 'Distinction in America? Recovering Bourdieu's Theory of Tastes from its Critics' *Poetics*, 25: 93–120.

Jarness, V. (2013) *Class, Status, Closure: The Petropolis and Cultural Life*. Bergen: University of Bergen.

Kirkham, P. and Skeggs, B. (1998) 'Absolutely Fabulous: Absolutely Feminist?' in C. Geraghty and D. Lusted (eds.) *The Television Studies Book*. London: Arnold, pp. 287–98.

Kingston, P. (2000) *The Classless Society*. Stanford: Stanford University Press.

Kosut, M. (2014) 'The Artification of Tattoo' *Cultural Sociology*, 8(2): 142–58.

Lawler, S. (2005) 'Disgusted Subjects' *Sociological Review*, 53 (3): 429–46.

Morley, D. (2000) *Home Territories*. London: Routledge.

Peterson, R. A. (1992) 'Understanding Audience Segmentation: From Elite and Mass to Omnivore and Univore' *Poetics*, 21: 243–58.

Peterson, R. A. (1997) 'The Rise and Fall of Snobbery as a Status Marker' *Poetics*, 25: 75–92.

Potter, R. A. (1995) *Spectacular Vernacular: Hip Hop and the Politics of Postmodernism*. New York: SUNY Press.

Prieur, A. and Savage, M. (2013) 'Emerging Forms of Cultural Capital' *European Societies*, 15(2): 246–67.

Prieur, A. and Savage, M. (2015) 'On 'Knowingness', Cosmopolitanism and Busyness as Emerging Forms of Cultural Capital' in P. Coulangeon and J. Duval (eds.) *The Routledge Companion to Bourdieu's Distinction*. London: Routledge, pp. 307–18.

Prieur, A., Rosenlund, L. and Skjott-Larsen, J. (2008) 'Cultural Capital Today: A Case Study from Denmark' *Poetics*, 36(1): 45–71.

Rosenlund, L. (2009) *Exploring the City with Bourdieu*. Saarbrucken: VDM Verlag Dr Müller.

Savage, M. (2012) 'Broken Communities?' in W. Atkinson, S. Roberts and M. Savage (eds.) *Class Inequality in Austerity Britain*. Basingstoke: Palgrave Macmillan, pp. 145-62.

Savage, M. *et al.* (2013) 'A New Model of Social Class?' *Sociology*, 47(2): 219–50.

Skeggs, B. (2005) 'The Re-branding of Class' in F. Devine, M. Savage, J. Scott and R. Crompton (eds.) *Rethinking Class*. London: Palgrave, pp. 46–68.

Sweetman, P. (1999) 'Anchoring the (Postmodern) Self? Body Modification, Fashion and Identity' *Body and Society*, 5(2–3): 51–76.

Vandebroeck, D. (2016) *Distinctions in the Flesh*. London: Routledge.

Van Eijk, C. (1999) 'Socialisation, Education and Lifestyle' *Poetics*, 26(5–6): 309–28.

Willmott, P. and Young, M. (1960) *Family and Class in a London Suburb*. London: Routledge and Kegan Paul.

Wuggenig, U. (2007) 'Pitfalls in Testing Bourdieu's Homology Assumptions Using Mainstream Social Science Methodology' *Poetics*, 35(4): 306–16.

4   The space of political position-takings

What we think of as 'politics', so often cordoned off as a discrete sociological specialism, is no less 'cultural' than predilections for particular sports, music, books or films; it may be more about ethics than aesthetics, but it is no less embedded in the variegated orientations to the world – how it is and how it should be – adapted to variegated conditions of existence, and no less entwined with the incessant search for justification and recognition at the heart of the human condition. It is, therefore, for good reason that the final substantive chapter of *Distinction* was devoted to this old topic, sketching the different approaches of the classes and class fractions to matters political or ethical and rooting them in oppositions born of volume and composition of capital, and it is, therefore, why the final chapter of our own journey through the spaces of practice homologous with the social space in twenty-first-century Britain will train its sights on this topic, replicating selected aspects of Bourdieu's own method in order to assess the applicability of his postulated theses, and our model of social space in the process, but also heeding subsequent developments in the protracted debates over the relationship between class and politics.

Bourdieu's (1984) point of entry into the murky waters of political sociology is, in fact, somewhat unconventional: he begins not with the correspondence between class position and political positions or opinions, as might be expected, but with the differential tendency attached to class position to feel one even *has* a political position or is *entitled* to an opinion – the degree to which one is, in other words, a 'political animal' at all. An opinion poll, or a government survey of political views, is a very peculiar instrument which, far from being clear of class prejudices, is itself the product of classed dispositions insofar as it embodies and articulates the dominant way of thinking and describing the world. The questions posed, the way in which they are framed and the vocabulary used to express them emanate not from the neutral gaze of some hypothetical objective observer, but from the concerns, perceptual schemes and struggles of players in the political field, materialised and transcribed in so many bits of paper or, these days, computers, and are foisted upon respondents who are, to greater and lesser degrees, socially distant from them. Three elements in particular are in play here. First, symbolic mastery, and with that mastery of the categories of political discourse, plays its part: a question such as 'are homosexual relations always wrong?', for example, presupposes an abstract, codified principle, generalising from practical experience in a quasi-theoretical manner alien to many. Second, and more important, is symbolic capital, that is, the degree to which one sees oneself as a *legitimate authority* on the question at hand since one is endowed with a mode of knowledge deemed worthy, generating a differential sense of confidence or even entitlement to speak on politics. Third, one must also take into account the relevance of the question or problem to everyday practice and everyday *interests*, namely, how to accumulate or maintain the properties securing worth in our society.

On the one hand, therefore, there are those richer in capital, who decipher and respond strongly to the pollster's questions because, being distant from necessity, they are the kind of question they might have asked of, or discussed with, others before; because, feeling themselves 'knowledgeable' or 'a bit of an expert' on how to run society or the economy, they believe their opinions matter; and because the ins-and-outs of the education system, the tax system or international relations are directly relevant to their mode of recognition and its reproduction as played out through the economic field or the field of educational institutions. On the other hand, the dominated, being asked abstract questions that bear little on the everyday experience of meeting the demands of necessity – there is a disjunction between the conceptual practices of the field of power and the problematics of the everyday world, to twist Dorothy Smith's famous formulas – and believing themselves less entitled to speak ('what do I know?') and less likely to be listened to, are more likely to refrain from answering, to tick the 'don't know' option or to take a neutral stance. This is not to say they do not have views, only that when they are faced with so-framed 'political issues' they feel an instant discomfort and disconnect.

The division between entitlement and disconnect is complicated, however, by what Bourdieu refers to as the different 'modes of production' of opinion. For the most part people's view of right and wrong, good and bad, desirable and undesirable on any matter is a question of class ethos: ethical dispositions and interests attuned to the practicalities and relevances of everyday experience – 'lower taxes would be good for business', 'immigrants are stealing manual jobs', 'higher wages would be good' and so on. In some instances people may codify their class ethos by formulating it as an explicit political 'line' followed more or less assiduously, but more important is the production and circulation of ideologies and set stances associated with particular agents in the political field – parties, trade unions, lobbyists and pressure groups. Certain questions and responses may be interpreted as being in tune with the 'line' of one or the other parties and followed or avoided on that basis – the affinity or lack of affinity being based on the degree to which the party line appeals to, perhaps even codifies, the class ethos or individual line. Inevitably this broaches the importance of the dynamics of the political field, and the shifting, solidifying or weakening homology between class ethos and party ideology on the basis of the relatively autonomous struggles for power therein.

Returning to the question of disconnection, Bourdieu goes on to argue that where there is no official party 'line' on an issue and people are thrown back on their class ethos to formulate a view, not only do the 'don't knows' proliferate among the dominated but all sorts of apparently contradictory stances can emerge. For instance, while the dominated may be progressive on questions concerning material standing and industrial relations, which Bourdieu sees as explicitly 'political' issues because they have long been formulated and struggled over by political parties, when it comes to 'moral' questions outside the usual discourse of politics – such as family values, sexuality and so on – their responses mark them out as apparently reactionary or authoritarian because practical experience (such as direct competition for work with immigrants) and class sense opposes them to 'long-haired liberals' (Bourdieu, 1984: 432ff).

As a final piece of the puzzle, Bourdieu maps out a space of political position-takings.[1] This seems to be based on two operations (1984: 439, 452–3): first, following the work of others, a simple algorithm in which the proportion of left-wing votes is subtracted from the proportion of right-wing votes within each class fraction; and second, a number of exploratory correspondence analyses, the details of which are never revealed. In both cases the overall pattern is the same. A first, vertical axis opposes those leaning left and those leaning right and corresponds more or less with volume of capital, pitting industrialists and professionals against manual workers but also artists and primary teachers. A second, horizontal axis then distinguishes those with particularly 'classifying' choices, i.e. extreme views, whether right- or left-wing, and those holding more moderate, mixed or unclear views, which Bourdieu sees as roughly corresponding with capital composition – those richest in economic capital have stronger views, those richer in cultural capital tend to be more centrist or apathetic. To contemporary users of CA and MCA this might suggest Bourdieu had a kind of Guttman effect on his hands – an 'extreme versus moderate' axis – produced by interaction between the two axes. In any case it marks an important specification of the point on the differential sense of entitlement: clearly it is the economically rich who feel most entitled to have a view, perhaps because they are most likely to feel their views matter and will be taken seriously by the state since they wield so much power over it.

From politics and morals to materialism and liberalism

In mainstream political sociology what Bourdieu called 'political' issues – wealth redistribution, industrial relations, property ownership – are generally referred to as 'materialist' questions, and what he dubbed 'moral' concerns – sexuality, immigration, ecology, etc. – are usually described either as 'post-materialist' topics, as for Inglehart (1977, 1990), or, more frequently, as subjects tapping into a long-evident opposition in Western societies between liberal and authoritarian worldviews (Lipset, 1960). Interestingly, for users of unidimensional conceptualisations of class, including the EGP scheme, this partition has proved somewhat thorny. In a nutshell, while materialist issues may well correspond fairly closely with their chosen measures of class, post-materialist/ liberal-authoritarian questions stubbornly refuse to (Evans, 1999), and although Goldthorpe tries to ascribe it to the effects of 'situs', i.e. public- versus private-sector work, or status, education is the real key, casting a fracture between those who are more highly educated, and more liberal, and those with lower educational attainment, who are more authoritarian, *within all classes*, but most notably the service class at the top, where professionals in the social and cultural services stand opposed to managers and business leaders (Houtman, 2003; Flemmen, 2014). This has led some to question whether class is really all that important in shaping attitudes nowadays, since these non-class, non-materialist issues have steadily permeated political debate and shape party choices at the ballot box (Sarlvik and Crewe, 1983; Giddens, 1991; Pakulski and Waters, 1996).

Bourdieu did not construct his space of political position-takings on the basis of both materialist and liberal/authoritarian attitudes, but his multidimensional model of class nevertheless reframes the whole debate. If the tendency to lean and to vote left or right on material issues differs by 'class' as measured by existing schemes, then this is perhaps a phenomenon of what those schemes crudely approximate – total volume of capital – while if the liberalism-authoritarian opposition corresponds essentially with high and low education, then this is likely a product of *capital composition*, the second axis of social space. In other words, rather than the explanatory power of class being thrown into question, we should expect a rough homology between the social space and the space of political position-takings a little different from the one presented by Bourdieu, with the vertical axis opposing left- and right-wing attitudes on economic questions while the horizontal axis opposes liberal and authoritarian attitudes.

As it happens, however, studies inspired by Bourdieu and using MCA to map the homology, particularly Harrits *et al.*'s (2010) analysis of the Danish space of political position-takings, have found it comes out slightly differently in their statistical models: the two spaces are homologous, but tipped over, with volume of capital and the left–right polarity running from one corner to its opposite and the capital composition axis and liberal-authoritarian opposition stretching across the corners perpendicular to the first schism. As an additional twist they found that these were not even the two lead axes in the MCA: the liberal/authoritarian or post-materialist, and thus capital composition, axis, came out first and the materialist/volume axis third – the second axis opposed those who took a stance and those who registered a more neutral position. Harrits *et al.* (2010) dismissed this axis as sociologically trivial, but could it not be revealing something of the differential confidence and sense of competence to speak? Of the sense of entitlement? We will never know, unfortunately, because the team omitted any analysis of the axis from their write-up. An addendum of sorts did, however, surface a few years later in a paper by Harrits (2013), wherein a 'space of political participation' (attending meetings, discussing politics etc.) and a 'space of political resources' (degree of knowledge of and interest in politics) were mapped out using MCA and determined to have loose – and no more than that – homologies with social space, with the economically rich the most engaged and resourced. Yet this is an unsatisfactory move, needlessly fracturing a single epistemic space – the space of political position-takings – into multiple MCA models and thus obscuring the relation between non-stances and stances of different persuasions and, ultimately, the fact that not taking a position *is* a position-taking, much as if someone interested in anatomising a musical composition analysed the tone and tempo separately without considering how they together constitute the whole.

The space of political position-takings

The first task before us, then, is obvious: we must construct the British space of political position-takings, i.e. draw out the maximal similarities and differences in stances on as broad a range of political-moral issues as is feasible, and, armed with our trusty measure of position in social space, determine the nature and extent of the homology and, from that, the dispositions mediating it. The space of political position-takings is not, of course, the product solely of class but of an intricate mesh of interrelated factors – religion, gender and nationality play their part too, as do all manner of lifeworld particularities – but a pattern broadly similar to that found by Harrits and her team in Denmark can still be hypothesised. To get us on our way, we can draw on data from the British Social Attitudes (BSA) survey of 2010, chosen because it was undertaken in an election year marking an important turning point in the UK political field. 'New' Labour, the centrist reimagining of the party set up a century ago to represent workers, once so popular but then irreparably undermined by the fallout from the deeply divisive invasion of Iraq and the cataclysmic economic crisis of the late 2000s, finally came crashing down. In its place stood a two-headed beast: a coalition government headed by David Cameron's right-wing Conservative Party but incorporating Nick Clegg's small band of Liberal Democrats – a party, itself born of an unsteady amalgamation of the old Liberal Party and a defecting right-leaning fraction of the Labour Party in the 1980s, with a broadly centrist view on economic matters but an effusive liberalism on all else.

The BSA survey, being designed to pick the populace's brains on a whole raft of pertinent issues, as determined by academic and political minds, contains an abundance of material for analysis. As an initial entry point we can zone in on three discrete clusters of questions – or more accurately, statements with which respondents are asked to rate their (dis)agreement on a five-point Likert scale – specifically used by the survey designers to represent the core axes of differentiation. The first two of these, rooted in decades of scholarship on political cleavages, target materialist issues (redistribution, exploitation etc.), aiming to pull out those leaning left and those leaning right, and liberal/authoritarian views on crime, nationalism, censorship and so on. In recent editions of the BSA survey these have been joined by a third set of statements ostensibly measuring attitudes to welfare – whether it is too generous, whether people abuse it, and so on. Undoubtedly its presence is underpinned by debates over 'benefits scroungers', 'cultures of dependency' and 'generations of joblessness' whipped up by the New Right in the 1980s and 1990s and persisting into the twenty-first century. While the statements seem, at first sight, to overlap with the materialist questions, they do so only in a particular way, opposing those championing self-responsibility, self-help, independence and individualism to those in favour of centralised state support for all.

The administrators of the BSA survey have used each of these clusters to form three scales running from one to nine, with one signifying extreme left-wing views, extreme libertarianism and extreme pro-welfare attitudes respectively and nine representing extreme right-wing views, extreme authoritarianism and extreme anti-welfare individualism. Some might be tempted to plot the average scores on these scales for each class fraction in a three-dimensional space, but scales suffer too many problems to be taken especially seriously – there is never much dispersion, for example, since the end points are calculated to be so extreme, and there is no way of pulling out precisely which issues constituting the scales are the most classifying (Savage, 2000). Is it attitudes to the death penalty, for instance, that pulls one into the authoritarian camp, or something else, and do different issues underpin the apparently shared authoritarianism of different fractions, themselves perhaps revealing telling class differences? To rely on the scales would also be to automatically assume the distinctiveness of the three measures, taking over, in an act of epistemological laxity, the existing definition of political reality without question, when, in reality, the principal sources of difference and similarity may cut across them.

To avoid these pitfalls we can turn instead to an MCA of selected indicators from all three clusters of statements. Not all of them could be used, however, for the simple reason that views on them are distributed in such a way as to seriously distort any solution they might be a part of, and considerations of balance between the three clusters had to be borne in mind for an agreeable outcome. The statements retained were:[2]

- The government should redistribute income (redist)
- Working people do not get a fair share of the nation's wealth (wealth)
- There is one law for the rich and one law for the poor (richlaw)
- A boss will get the better of employees if s/he gets the chance (boss)
- Sometimes the death penalty is the only appropriate sentence (death)
- One should always obey the law, even if a particular law is wrong (wronglaw)
- Censorship of films and magazines is necessary to uphold morals (censor)
- The government should spend more money on welfare benefits for the poor (morewelf)
- Most unemployed people could find a job if they really wanted one (unempjob)
- Many people who get social security don't really deserve any help (sochelp)
- Most people on the dole are fiddling in one way or another (dole fiddle)

To these was added a question asking for party identification – not membership or voting intention, but simply with which party the respondent most identifies – as an indication of alignment with certain 'lines'. The resultant model distinguished three axes which, together, accounted for 90 per cent of variance.[3]

The first axis, accounting for 36 per cent of the variance, opposes those who lean left and those who lean right on materialist issues, including some of the welfare-related questions. Those who are in favour of redistribution, who believe that workers do not get their fair share, who agree that there is one law for the rich and one for the poor, who think bosses will try to get the better of their employees, who affirm that more money should be spent on welfare, who think the unemployed could not just get a job if they wanted to, who cast doubt on the assertion that most people claiming benefits do not deserve them or who are 'on the fiddle' and who align with the Labour Party, no doubt on grounds of historical association, thus stand opposed to those against redistribution, against the idea that workers get a rough deal, against the suggestion that employers want to get one over on their employees, against the notion that the rich and poor are subject to different laws, against the possibility of the government spending more on welfare and in step with the bastion of right-wing thought, the Conservative Party.

The second axis accounts for 30 per cent of the variance and would seem to pit those with strong views, particularly on material and welfare issues, and who vote

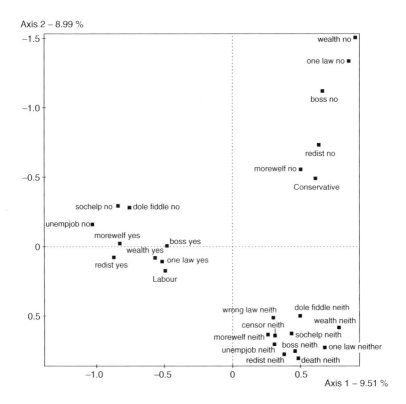

Figure 4.1 MCA plane of axes 1 and 2, active modalities with above-average contributions

Conservative, against those who plump for the 'neither' option (which, after recoding, includes 'don't know' and refusal to answer) on all issues. Here, perhaps, we have the opposition between those with a sense of competence and entitlement and those feeling unconfident, uninspired or disenfranchised. Axis 3, finally, explains 23 per cent of the variance and, though it implicates some material issues once again, is more strongly shaped by views on liberal/authoritarian and welfare issues, opposing those possessing more liberal attitudes on censorship and the death penalty, as well as more pro-welfare views, to those with more authoritarian and individualistic outlooks.

The plane of axes 1 and 2, reminiscent of several diagrams displayed by Bourdieu (1984: 423, 427), takes the form of a rough triangle, its three tips counterposing those with irresolute or indifferent views on all issues, those with unswerving right-wing materialist views and those with left-wing, but evidently not as consistent, stances (Figure 4.1). When indicators of social position are projected into this space a few things become clear (Figure 4.2). First, on axis 1, business executives and professionals, the richest class fractions economically, are closely associated with a conservative view on capitalist relations, followed by technicians, LMPs, administrators and white-collar workers – in other words, the Eastern and centrist sections of the higher classes in social space – while manual workers and the cultural dominant – the furthest class fractions West and South – correspond with the left wing. This is hardly surprising. The

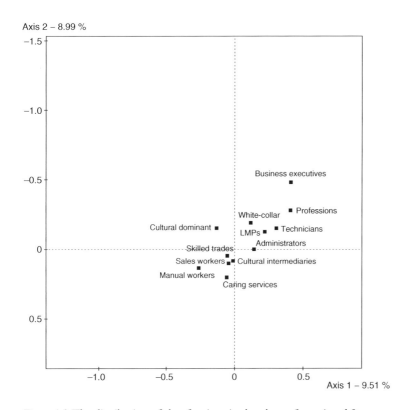

Figure 4.2 The distribution of class fractions in the plane of axes 1 and 2

economically richer fractions of the social space, most implicated in capitalist industrial relations and dependent on profit for maximisation of their preponderant source of mis-recognition, are likely to favour measures calculated to preserve or amplify their capital stocks, and to view themselves as justified and reasonable in their own daily striving to that end, while the dominated perceive their position relative to the economically rich as rather more unjust and political intervention as their only realistic chance of signifi-cantly improving their standing. The cultural dominant's leftism, on the other hand, is likely to take on a somewhat more abstract character: being outside of direct capitalist relations and dependent to a greater extent on the state than the market for the repro-duction of their mode of recognition, their orientation doubtless rests more on their opposition to the profit-driven economic libido and a form of symbolic mastery of social and human relations predisposed toward denaturalisation and questioning of the current socioeconomic order.

Second, the business executives and professions have the most consistent views, while the various fractions of the dominated class, plus the cultural intermediaries, fall closer to the disconnected and non-partisan pole. This, we might suppose, is the difference between those who see themselves as the most competent and entitled on economic issues, the captains of capitalism, and those who feel less sure or engaged. Third, although men are more likely to have strong views and women weaker ones, reflecting to some degree the effects of patriarchal relations on a differential sense of the right to speak, the dispersion is not very strong, nor is it in relation to age – though the younger are slightly more disengaged than the older (see Appendix II for coordinates). Ethnicity and religion, however, are slightly more implicated: black Britons tend to be a little more left-wing and disengaged, and Asian and Jewish Britons the most right-wing and consistent, but this seems to reflect the class distribution of these different categories. Then again, even the dispersion of the class fractions is not vast, affirming the relative autonomy and multi-determination of the space of position-takings (cf. Harrits, 2013).

The plane of axes 1 and 3, meanwhile, reveals precisely the kind of distribution hypothesised earlier (Figure 4.3). There are, first of all, four quadrants to the space: a North-East marked by firm right-wing views on capitalist relations, a South-East most strongly distinguished by anti-welfare, individualist and authoritarian attitudes, a South-West characterised by resolutely left-wing views on materialist issues and a North-West possessing clear liberal and pro-welfare tendencies. Projection of two 'post-materialist' variables excluded from the final model, attitudes toward homosexuality and the envi-ronment, as illustrative points confirms this interpretation, with the most liberal on sexuality and the most conscious of environmental issues gathering in the North-West, while the most anti-homosexual and least concerned about the environment cluster is in the South-East.[4] Likewise we can see a correspondence with the Liberal Democrats and the Green Party in the North-West, even though identification with the first party does not contribute significantly to the axis and alignment with the Green Party was set as a supplementary modality due to low numbers.

With indicators of social position cast into the space, we can see the same skewed homology between the space of political position-takings and the social space discov-ered by Harrits *et al*.: as already seen, the business executives and professionals are most right-wing, opposed to the dominated, particularly the manual workers, who are the most left-leaning on material issues; but now we also see the cultural dominant and, to a lesser extent, the cultural intermediaries occupy the most liberal and pro-welfare posi-tions, contrasting with the more anti-welfare and authoritarian elements of the domi-nated and the petite bourgeoisie: technicians, LMPs, and skilled workers (Figure 4.4).

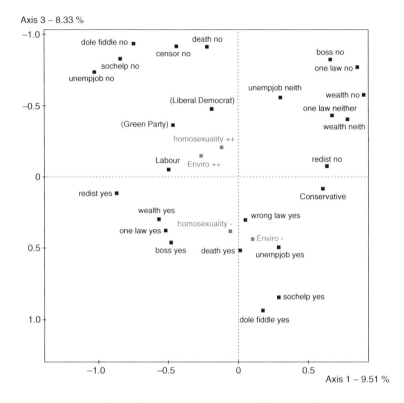

Axis 3 – 8.33 %

Figure 4.3 MCA plane of axes 1 and 3, active modalities with above-average contributions and two supplementary variables

This latter opposition is nourished by many of the same ingredients feeding into the first division – symbolic mastery versus the economic libido – but it also seems to tap into the petit-bourgeois ethos of independence, thrift, self-responsibility, aspiration to be like those above, attachment to the established order as the path to success and hence fear of instability, and it might be conjectured that welfare becomes a more pressing issue, a more salient point of distinction, the 'final difference' ('I am not like them'), for those socially closer to its statistically typical claimants. Once again, age and gender are only minimally dispersed across the axes.

Cynicism, powerlessness, disenfranchisement

It is revealing that liberal and authoritarian attitudes are subordinate in structuring the space of political position-takings to the tendency to actually take a position or not. The rather ambiguous category of 'neither' defining this principle of opposition, however, is not especially helpful for unpicking the different relations to the political field which may play into it – it cannot, for example, pick up the difference between the aloof refusal to be 'pigeonholed' among some sections of the cultural dominant, as discovered

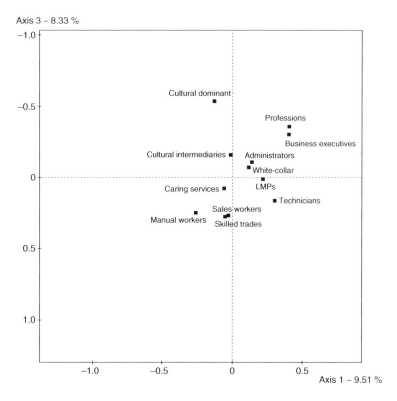

Figure 4.4 The distribution of class fractions in the plane of axes 1 and 3

by Bourdieu (1988), and the abject political alienation of others. Alternative indicators can help in this regard. In particular, and in line with Bourdieu's original analysis, it can easily be shown that the dominated are by far the most cynical, disenfranchised and self-consciously powerless when it comes to politics – a cluster of dispositions rooted in a mismatch between the language and position-takings characterising the political field on the one hand and the masteries and ethos of the dominated on the other.

Picking up on the disjunction between the modes of knowledge and language operative within the political field – in other words, the specific manifestations of symbolic mastery and schemes of perception implicated – and those of the dominated class, for example, it is interesting to note the distribution of responses to the statement that 'sometimes politics and government seem so complicated that a person like me cannot really understand'. Members of the dominated class are by far the most likely to agree – 70 per cent of sales workers, manual workers and caring services, 59 per cent of skilled workers – and the dominant least likely – a quarter of business executives, 22 per cent of professionals and 30 per cent of the cultural dominant – while the intermediate class fractions hover around 40 to 50 per cent. White-collar workers, interestingly – the lowest and youngest fraction of the dominant class – register a fairly high level of agreement, at 64 per cent, but when this is broken down by strength of agreement it can be seen that only 7 per cent strongly agree that politics is too complicated for 'people like me' compared to a full 18 per cent of manual workers and 15 per cent of caring services. Yet differences in symbolic mastery or 'competence' – which could, in the wrong hands, be twisted to support the symbolically violent and potentially anti-democratic assertion that people are 'too stupid' to understand politics or 'know what's good for them' – are only a small part of the picture and, if taken in isolation, could mask the major springs of disengagement and their origins in the machinations of the political field.

First, the dominated are most likely to register a certain amount of *cynicism* regarding politics, as observable in responses to any indicator of distrust or suspicion of politicians and their motives. They are, for example, the most likely to claim that politicians 'almost never' put the needs of the country above their party needs, with 48 per cent of manual workers and 36 per cent of the rest of the dominated ticking that box as opposed to just 21 per cent of the cultural dominant, 25 per cent of white-collar workers and 26 per cent of the professionals. They are, moreover, the most likely to state that they 'almost never' trust politicians of any party to tell the truth when they are in a 'tight corner' (defending a policy U-turn, for instance), even though rates of agreement with that option are generally high across the board, with 69 per cent of sales workers, 66 per cent of manual workers, 61 per cent of skilled workers and 59 per cent of caring services in contrast to 42 per cent of the cultural dominant, 46 per cent of business executives and 48 per cent of professionals. Among the intermediate class fractions, interestingly, the cultural intermediaries (who were toward the disengaged pole in the space of political position-takings) are the most cynical in this respect (59 per cent) and technicians the least (44 per cent). Similarly, caring services and manual workers are the most likely to strongly agree with the statement that politicians 'lose touch' once they become Members of Parliament (30 per cent), along with LMPs (29 per cent), administrators (23 per cent) and skilled workers (21 per cent), whereas professionals (7 per cent), white-collar workers (9 per cent), the cultural dominant (15 per cent) and business executives (18 per cent) are rather less distrustful – perhaps as much because politicians are less likely to actually 'lose touch' with them as because of any less suspicion of self-interest. Finally, and perhaps providing the bluntest evidence of cynicism, a third of manual workers strongly agree that politicians 'are only interested in people's votes, not their opinions', followed by a quarter of caring services and LMPs, compared with 7 per cent of the cultural dominant, 19 per cent of business executives and, most starkly, just 4 per cent of professionals.

This last statistic perhaps owes something to the fact that there is a differential likelihood of having one's opinion taken seriously, and a sense of that difference, shading into a perception of oneself as *powerless* and a feeling of *disenfranchisement*. The former is also attested by the fact that manual workers are the most likely to strongly agree with the statement that 'people like me have no say in what the government does' (27 per cent), followed by skilled workers (22 per cent), caring services (21 per cent) and sales workers (19 per cent), but also white-collar workers (25 per cent) and LMPs (22 per cent), as opposed to 12 per cent of the cultural dominant, 9 per cent of business executives and just 4 per cent of professionals. This dovetails, of course, with a more general tendency to view oneself as powerless in tune with conditions of existence and symbolic capital (Figure 4.5). Disenfranchisement, on the other hand – in the sense of having no stake in political struggles because no one offers a clear line encapsulating class ethos – is gaugeable from views on the specificity and efficacy of political parties, particularly whether there is any noteworthy difference between the policy programmes they offer and whether it matters who is in power. On the first question, when asked whether there is any appreciable divergence between the Conservatives and the Labour

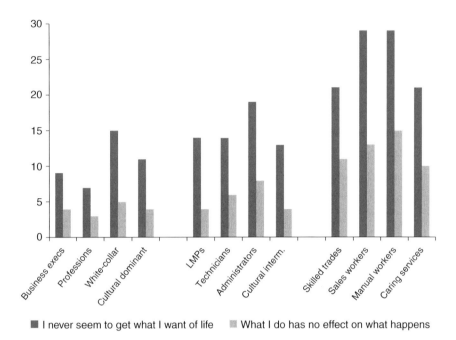

Figure 4.5 The sense of powerlessness by class fraction (%)

Party – the supposed representatives of warring class interests – the sections of the social space most likely to declare there is not much difference at all are the skilled workers (47 per cent), manual workers (42 per cent) and then sales and caring workers (35 per cent), standing in stark opposition to professionals (15 per cent), though other fractions of the dominant are less discerning. On the second question, when faced with the statement 'it doesn't really matter which party is in power, in the end things go on much the same' – i.e. there is no conspicuous amelioration of conditions of existence either way, a damning indictment of the efficacy of the Labour Party – those most likely to agree strongly are caring services (26 per cent), manual workers and skilled workers (23 per cent) and then LMPs (19 per cent), contrasting with 12 per cent of business executives, 9 per cent of the cultural dominant and just 4 per cent of professionals.

The effects of transformations in the political field

The cynicism, powerlessness and disenfranchisement of the dominated class and, to a lesser extent, fractions of the intermediate class may well correspond with relatively long-standing perceptions of not being listened to or taken seriously by politicians in capitalist society, but there is no doubt they have become more widespread in recent years. For example, using the equivalent BSA survey for previous years, we can see that the tendency to strongly agree that politicians will put their party's interest over the nation's has jumped up 13 percentage points among manual workers since 1991 and 17 percentage points among caring services, as well as 12 per cent among LMPs and

16 per cent among cultural intermediaries, the two extreme poles of the intermediate class, whereas the dominant class have either increased their likelihood of agreeing strongly marginally (4 percentage points for business executives and the cultural dominant) or have even become less likely, as with white-collar workers (a drop of 1 per cent) and professionals (a drop of 7 per cent). Or again, the chances of strongly agreeing that it does not matter which party is in power because life will go on more or less the same regardless, while generally increasing across the board and indicating a broad trend of dissatisfaction with the state of politics, has risen at different rates for different class fractions over the same time period. Caring services are up from 10 per cent to 26 per cent, skilled workers from 12 per cent to 23 per cent, manual workers from 16 per cent to 23 per cent and administrators from 6 per cent to 15 per cent, while among the dominant class the rise has been rather more modest – 4 per cent for the professions and cultural dominant, 5 per cent for the business executives.

The reason for this increase in cynicism and disenfranchisement is not hard to finger: the struggles and transformations of the UK political field over the last thirty years have amplified the disparity between the supply of political 'lines', visions of the social world and programmes for change on the one hand and the ethos of the dominated class on the other, robbing those lower in social space of a clear and influential representative, of a 'voice', and leaving them with a feeling of being abandoned by politicians looking to bolster their own standing instead. The trajectories of two sets of agents effective within the field of politics are key here. The first is the decline and mutation of trade unions, established and granted legal recognition in the nineteenth century as representatives of workers, and even 'the working class', codifying the dominated class ethos on materialist issues into a vision of the world and how to transform it in a way they could identify with. Even if political delegation – conferring to trade unionists the authority to speak on one's behalf – requires a certain degree of sacrificing the capacity to speak directly for oneself, and even if a trade union, with its various staff and internal hierarchy, forms its own internal field of forces and competes with other unions in its own subspace of struggle to represent workers, all of which shape the production of political visions and strategies which can then be imposed unilaterally upon members, unionists constituted the first effective agents of the newly emerged dominated class of capitalism within the British political field – or at least the male members thereof. Their various strategies in the political field, premised on a sense of what was possible, were responsible for delivering multiple improvements to working conditions and pay levels over the years, and though the balance of forces shifted back and forth through the twentieth century, with periods of rupture and reinvention, they were, by the 1970s, at the height of their influence, fundamental to the downfall of both Ted Heath and James Callaghan. But then came the conservative revolution in the political field and the Thatcherite counter-strategy: a cluster of general and specific measures were taken wholly or in part designed to diminish the relative standing of trade unions. Most of these were made possible by an inherent power imbalance built into the field – the unions depended on the state and legislation for their place at the table, and so they were at the mercy of any government determined to take them on (Howell, 2005). Closed shops were banned, wage councils were weakened and then abolished, regulations bearing on strikes and ballots were tightened, employment laws were loosened, and so on. More systematically, the government embarked on a campaign of *derecognition* of trade unions, i.e. of stemming their symbolic power, not only by excluding them from the kinds of state-level negotiations of policy they had theretofore become partners in but through a smear campaign, branding them 'the enemy within', and sought to *individualise* worker grievances and struggles by encouraging the movement of negotiations over pay and conditions from the industrial scale, involving collective bargaining between unions and industry representatives, to the firm or even workplace level (Fraser, 1999).[5] Finally, and most fundamentally, the Conservative government, reacting to global economic change, seized the opportunity to demolish the industries that had, historically, been most unionised and most active – mining being the most emblematic – to make way for the growing, but casualised and poorly unionised, service sector. Trade unionists fought back, of course, but with greater symbolic capital in the hands of the opposition there was little they could do but eventually concede defeat.

The effects of these strategies have been dramatic. Union density (the percentage of the working population affiliated with a union), for instance, halved from 50 to 26 between 1980 and 2010 (OECD), and the number of strikes has plummeted since 1979 (Figure 4.6). Yet these general omens of decline mask important shifts in the nature of trade unions too. Since the reordering of the economic field charted in Chapter 2 effectively drained them of their staple membership, and thus further sapped their quotient of symbolic capital within the political field, unions undertook a three-pronged recovery (or, we might say, compensation) strategy. The first tactic was amalgamation, seeking to rescue the principle of strength in numbers, and thus were born some of the giant super-unions like UNITE and UNISON that currently dominate the field of trade unions. The second prong was to try to battle the inherent weakness of their position – their dependence on state support – by trying to push a pro-EU agenda, and campaign for adoption of the EU's 'Social Chapter' setting out labour law regulations, which would effectively lock the state into recognising certain union powers and safeguard their symbolic capital. The third prong, critically, was a widening of the pool of

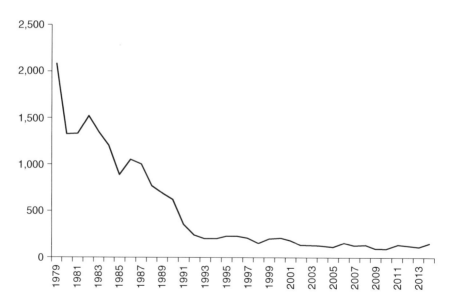

Figure 4.6 The decline of work stoppages since 1979.

Source: ONS, data available at www.ons.gov.uk/employmentandlabourmarket/peopleinwork/workplacedisputesandworkingconditions/datasets/labourdisputeslabourdisputesannualestimates

Table 4.1 Class composition of trade union membership (%)

Class fraction	1991	2010
Business executives	3.4	2.9
Professions	2.3	3.2
White–collar	1.4	2.5
Cultural dominant	12.4	22.5
LMPs	2.7	3.9
Technicians	4.3	10.3
Administrators	12.9	4.2
Cultural intermediaries	5.9	8.1
Skilled trades	15.1	8.4
Sales workers	2.5	4.1
Manual workers	31.7	18.2
Caring services	5.5	11.7
Total*	100.1	100.0

Source: BSA 1991 and 2010

* Column totals may add up to more than 100 due to rounding.

members beyond the traditional zones of social space, and a major move in this regard was a Trades Union Congress policy document entitled *Organising for the 1990s*, which advocated a concerted effort to attract public-sector workers, women, and what they referred to as 'white-collar workers' and 'professional workers' as the only viable strata- gem for maintaining recognition and legitimacy within the political field. Hence the gender disparity of union membership has reversed between 1991 and 2010 according to the respective BSA surveys, from 56 to 44 per cent in favour of men to the same balance in favour of women. More interestingly, the class composition of trade union members has altered significantly in the same time period (Table 4.1). There has been a predictable loss of manual workers and skilled workers, and a slight increase among caring services and higher-skilled technical workers; but rather than professionals and white-collar workers (as defined here) joining the fray, by far the biggest gain in trade union membership – and, indeed, the largest segment of trade union members nowa- days – are the liberal, pro-welfare, left-leaning cultural dominant. Not only that, but while 'professions' undertake, according to a 2011 survey (WER), the majority of strike action (42 per cent, with administrators in second place on 23 per cent), this is only so using the undifferentiated definition of professions available in the dataset which includes the cultural dominant, and has to be balanced against the fact that UNISON – the union of public-sector workers, particularly teachers and sociomedical services (as well as doctors) – and UCU – the union of higher education teachers and researchers – have been particularly active in the last few years, spearheading large strikes in 2011, the survey year, and 2013 respectively. Moreover, the BSA surveys for 1991 and 2005 reveal that the cultural dominant and cultural intermediaries have become the most likely to say they would protest or demonstrate in the face of injustice, at 29 per cent (a rise of 11 per cent) and 26 per cent (a rise of 14 per cent) respectively, compared with 11 per cent of manual workers (a drop of 4 per cent), confirming the relative politicisation of those rich in cultural capital – despite the already-seen relative cynicism of the cultural intermediaries, which may be a sign of their disaffection with 'mainstream' politics and a preference for so-called 'sub-politics' – to match the depoliticisation of the dominated.

To recruit from a wider social base, and then to articulate its new members' class ethos, the issues trade unions campaign on and the lexicon they deploy have undergone considerable change. Gone is the language of class and class conflict; gone is the founding notion that unions represent 'the working class'; gone is any serious aspiration for radical social reform. In their place are indistinct talk of 'working people', concern with fuzzy and abstract issues of 'social exclusion', broader campaigns against poverty and inequality and orientation around liberal tropes of gender and racial parity (Bradley, 2008; Bradley and Hebson, 1999). Whatever the real gains in this for women and minorities, and without lapsing into the error of thinking that unions ever had the 'true' or most useful notion of class and class conflict, the state of the symbolic struggle has thus shifted: 'class' as a scheme of perception has been stripped of the political tint it acquired through the nineteenth and twentieth centuries and the dominated have been deprived of a clear, concrete and potent line to articulate their experience of the world and the changes to material conditions of existence necessary to improve it (cf. Atkinson, 2010a, 2010b). No wonder feelings of powerlessness and disenfranchisement are more prevalent than ever.

The second trajectory within the British political field bearing on the dominated class' experience is that of the Labour Party. Like the trade unions, with which it has had a long if rocky alliance, this particular body – a microcosm of clashing interests in itself, of course – was established to act as a parliamentary voice for 'the working class' of early twentieth-century Britain. Tellingly, it had roots in the reformist Fabian intelligentsia, part of the cultural dominant of the day, but over the next hundred years it recruited plenty of politicians to its ranks from lower reaches of social space, usually via the trusty conduit of trade union representation. As is well known, however, the party underwent revolutionary alteration in the course of the 1980s and 1990s. Rather than seek to strike against the Conservatives' dominance by doggedly challenging the neoliberal political orthodoxy they propounded, they opted to align with it instead, at first slowly under Neil Kinnock and John Smith, and then wholeheartedly under Tony Blair. Hence the dropping of any constitutional commitment to socialism or nationalisation (the famous Clause Four), Blair's talk of 'no more workers against bosses' and the attempt to broaden the electoral base by courting business interests and enticing those rich in cultural capital with a liberal agenda on, for example, gay rights. Underpinning this was a shift in the driving principle of political practice: the point of the Labour Party, and struggles over political/symbolic capital, no longer seemed to be to represent the dominated class at all costs, who were deemed to be shrinking anyway and therefore no sure ticket to office, but to do whatever it takes to win power.

One visible manifestation of this transformation of the Labour Party's programme, and the objective social distance and subjective disconnect it fostered between itself and the dominated class, is a shift in the class composition of its MPs. In 1979, when Labour lost the general election to the Conservatives off the back of their mishandling of the Winter of Discontent (a wave of strikes against pay caps), but before the sweeping success of Thatcherism in the wake of the Falklands War had prompted the rethink of party orientation (which actually took a leftwards turn amongst this intake of MPs before a fresh batch shuffled rightwards after 1983), there was a reasonable spattering of MPs drawn from lower down the social space (Table 4.2).[6] True enough, in tune with the reformist class ethos which actually founded the Labour Party, the majority of its MPs were drawn from the cultural dominant – usually teachers and lecturers – and the professions – nearly always lawyers – but technicians (almost exclusively engineers of various specialities), skilled workers and manual workers (especially miners and metal workers), generally

Table 4.2 Class background of UK Members of Parliament by party, 1979 and 2010 (%)

Class Fraction	Conservatives		Labour		Liberal Democrats★	
	1979	2010	1979	2010	1979	2010
Business executives	43.6	47.1	5.4	11.5	9.1	32.7
Professions	27.2	32.0	17.9	21.0	27.3	27.3
White-collar workers	3.9	2.3	6.2	2.8	0.0	9.1
Cultural dominant	12.2	6.2	32.3	39.3	27.3	21.8
LMPs	5.4	5.2	2.3	0.8	9.1	1.8
Technicians	2.1	0.7	10.5	4.0	9.1	1.8
Administrators	2.1	2.3	4.7	5.6	9.1	3.6
Cultural intermediaries	3.0	3.9	4.3	7.5	0.0	1.8
Skilled trades	0.6	0.3	5.1	3.2	9.1	0.0
Sales workers	0.0	0.0	1.2	0.4	0.0	0.0
Manual workers	0.0	0.0	10.1	3.6	0.0	0.0
Caring services	0.0	0.0	0.0	0.4	0.0	0.0
Total	*100.0*	*100.0*	*100.0*	*100.0*	*100.0*	*100.0*

★ 1979 figures refer to the Liberal Party, of which there was only a handful of MPs.

recruited through the unions, together made up almost a quarter of the party's elected members. By 2010, however, the homology with the social space had altered not only in terms of volume of capital but composition too. On the one hand, the number of Labour MPs drawn from the cultural dominant has increased – though now they tend to be drawn from public-service executives, i.e. heads of various social-service or public-sector organisations – but so too has the proportion who used to be business executives, i.e. directors, managers and chief executives in manufacturing, construction and especially finance, along with brokers of various kinds, doubtless attracted by the new pro-business agenda of the supposed 'workers' party'. On the other hand, the number of Labour politicians who were once manual workers, skilled workers or engineers has dwindled to a combined total of 11 per cent, and those who remain tend to be the older, long-serving MPs, such as ex-miner Dennis Skinner, who may well find themselves replaced before too long. Within the intermediate class, moreover, cultural intermediaries – nearly always journalists – have also increased at the expense of the dominated class. Accordingly, the distribution of cultural capital possession within the party has shifted too, with far more MPs holding degrees and postgraduate degrees and the number with education below degree level – whether apprenticeships, (G)CSEs, A levels or no qualifications at all – dropping off dramatically (Table 4.3). There are still evident differences from the Conservative Party, which has only the barest showing of MPs from the dominated class or engineering backgrounds and which was, in 2010 as in 1979, constituted primarily by business executives of one sort or another, and secondarily by lawyers (and fewer cultural dominant than in the past). It may thus be said that, in this respect, the Labour Party is still at least *more* 'representative' of the dominated than their long-time political adversary, but the direction of travel is nevertheless toward the dominant class, providing the conditions of possibility for the impression amongst the dominated that Labour MPs, and indeed all MPs, are increasingly 'not like me', whether on account of money or education, and therefore harder to believe when they say they are battling in their interests.

Table 4.3 Highest educational qualification of UK Members of Parliament by party, 1979 and 2010 (%)

Education	Conservatives		Labour		Liberal Democrats	
	1979	*2010*	*1979*	*2010*	*1979*	*2010*
Postgraduate	8.3	22.1	12.6	28.7	9.1	26.8
Degree	60.9	62.2	42.0	53.5	36.4	58.9
Below degree	30.8	15.7	45.4	17.8	54.5	14.3
Total	*100.0*	*100.0*	*100.0*	*100.0*	*100.0*	*100.0*

A second indicator of the disconnect between the Labour Party and the dominated is a drop over time in the number of the latter who claim to identify with it and, by implication, its line on any particular issue. Between 1991, when the Conservatives were still in full swing, and 2010, when the sun had finally set on New Labour, identification with the party had dropped among skilled workers by 15 per cent, sales workers by 11 per cent, manual workers by 9 per cent and technicians by 4 per cent (Table 4.4). Conversely, alignment with Labour, and their new centrist line, has risen among all fractions of the dominant class, the LMPs and, most dramatically, the cultural intermediaries, all of whom display a marked reduction in identification with the Conservatives to match. Support for the Conservatives among the dominated is relatively static, so they are hardly recruiting the disaffected dominated class. Nor are the Liberal Democrats, who continue to appeal mainly to the dominant and intermediate classes, especially the fractions richer in cultural (or technical) capital. In fact the main shift is toward identifying with no party at all, and while this applies to all sections of the social space the dominated class are the most likely to state that no party speaks to or for them, with around a fifth of skilled workers, manual workers and caring services saying as much, up 13, 12 and 11 per cent respectively, closely followed by the LMPs. Some have also switched allegiance to other parties – e.g. the eco-socialist Green Party or the far-right nationalistic UK Independence Party (UKIP), depending on the general position-takings of the class fraction – but far more no longer feel any party gives them a line, a vocabulary or a vision they can draw on to confidently articulate their ethos.

In summary, then, the two sets of agents who once spoke and acted in the name of 'the working class', who codified the class habitus of the dominated into a specific, recognisable discourse and who contended within the political field to improve their lot no longer do so to quite the same degree. Both may well still claim to champion the cause of 'working people', but that label purposefully stretches over quite broad expanses of social space, including business leaders, in order to broaden support as far as possible and, at the end of the day, both trade unions and the Labour Party look less and less like the dominated class and more and more like the cultural dominant, whose leftism, and therefore the driving impetus of the two bodies once fighting for 'the working class', is more strongly oriented by liberal and non-materialist issues than materialist ones. Everything examined in the foregoing would seem to indicate that this shifting homology has something to do with the dominated feeling *increasingly* voiceless, abandoned, illegitimate, unrecognised – desperately looking for someone who can offer clear and strident words to encapsulate and explain the everyday experience of privation and deeply dissatisfied with those who no longer do. Is it therefore any surprise, when the

Table 4.4 Party identification, 1991 and 2010 (row%)

Class fraction	Conservative			Labour			Liberal Democrat			None		
	1991	2010	Difference	1991	2010	Difference	1991	2010	Difference	1991	2010	Difference
Business executives	61.8	48.0	-13.8	13.2	19.0	5.8	13.9	16.5	2.6	3.5	8.0	4.5
Professions	60.6	42.4	-18.2	15.5	20.7	5.2	15.5	15.2	-0.3	2.8	10.9	8.1
White–collar	50.0	40.0	-10.0	21.4	26.9	5.5	14.3	13.8	-0.5	5.4	8.3	2.9
Cultural dominant	38.8	25.1	-13.7	25.4	30.0	4.6	18.2	20.6	2.4	4.8	11.1	6.3
LMP	51.6	36.7	-14.9	18.5	27.2	8.7	13.4	8.2	-5.2	7.6	17.1	9.5
Technicians	46.2	37.2	-9.0	25.3	21.3	-4.0	9.9	18.1	8.2	3.3	11.7	8.4
Administrators	49.1	37.8	-11.3	23.0	25.1	2.1	12.3	14.1	1.8	5.9	12.9	7.0
Cultural interm.	49.5	25.0	-24.5	19.8	35.9	16.1	17.6	14.1	-3.5	4.4	10.9	6.5
Skilled trades	27.9	28.8	0.9	45.3	29.9	-15.4	10.4	7.8	-2.6	7.3	19.8	12.5
Sales workers	29.1	28.8	-0.3	44.9	33.9	-11.0	8.2	9.3	1.1	10.1	14.8	4.7
Manual workers	22.8	17.8	-5.0	47.9	39.2	-8.7	10.6	8.6	-2.0	9.4	21.2	11.8
Caring services	32.6	20.7	-11.9	33.1	34.0	0.9	17.1	12.3	-4.8	9.1	19.8	10.7

Source: BSA 1991 and 2010

dominated have witnessed a yawning gap between themselves and the players in the political field and when all means of articulating their interests have dissolved in a sea of calculated centrism, that the second most significant dimension in the space of political position-takings revolves around the propensity to be engaged, to feel involved, to play the game, to hold a view, to trust the line-providers, to even take a position and stake a firm place for oneself in the extant universe of political discourse?

Postscript: the 2015 general election

The 2010 general election was, in the end, a transition point. Labour may have been defeated, but by such a narrow margin that the two parties of the opposing fractions of the dominant class, the Conservatives and the Liberal Democrats, had to enter into government together. Five years on, the turn toward the Conservatives had deepened – much to many commentators' surprise, that party managed to secure a slender majority in the 2015 general election, while the Labour Party suffered its worst defeat for almost thirty years. Three key factors underpinned this dramatic result, and it is worth using what we have learned in the foregoing – in lieu of available good-quality data – to reflect a little on their potential relationship to class. The first is the rise of the Scottish National Party (SNP), which usurped Labour's representation in Scotland to the point of almost total annihilation. Now, the Scottish electorate have often been claimed to be disproportionately left-leaning on materialist issues, as evidenced by the paucity of Conservative MPs returned there in years of Scottish politics and the dominance of Labour even in the era of Tony Blair. The 2010 BSA data certainly confirms this, with the Scottish tending to be further toward the left and pro-welfare poles of their respective scales than the English. The industrial heritage of the nation, which has resulted in an over-representation of the dominated class, their ethos, their institutions (including trade unions) and their experiences (including the ravages of deindustrialisation), often bleeding into the ethos of other locally situated class fractions on account of a spontaneous, substantialist conflation of preponderant class experiences and ethos with national experience and 'character' (especially *vis-à-vis* England), is likely to be key here (see Chapter 6). Perhaps, then, the Scottish National Party, being an overtly socialist party – it pitched itself as the true 'anti-austerity' option – which proved itself capable of governing via the Scottish Parliament, and its nationalist demands being muted by the failed referendum on Scottish independence in the previous year, offered a line that chimed with, and codified, the ethos of the dominated class, and others, more closely than that offered by Labour (even if pitching themselves as more left-wing than in previous years). It was thus only a question of finally abandoning a party they felt had abandoned them years before anyway.

The second factor was the demolition of the Liberal Democrats, who were reduced to having just eight Members of Parliament and lost their long-standing place as the third party of the UK. Their electoral base being the fractions of the social space richest in cultural capital, opposed to the social conservatism of the economically rich and more left-leaning in general, the coalition with the Conservative Party did them immense damage. Their practice and their policy, it seemed, pulled away from the ethos of its voters, generating a sense of betrayal; but since those voters are far more likely to be politically engaged and confident than the section of the electorate abandoned by Labour, rather than refuse to vote they opted instead to switch to Labour, the SNP in Scotland and the Greens – the last of these doing better than ever before across the nation, even if only securing one MP. Third, there was the rise of UKIP. A party seemingly of the old petite bourgeoisie insofar as it explicitly championed the interests of small business – opposing corporate oligopolies as much as government bureaucracy under the banner of Euroscepticism – they had worked to broaden their line to appeal to the ethos of other classes too. On the one hand they 'interpellated' sections of the dominated class not just on the basis of nationalism, which construes migrants as a threat to the established order, but by espousing the notion that migrants from the European Union were to blame for low pay, unemployment and scarce social housing (rather than the neoliberal revolutions in the political and economic fields). In so doing they managed to usurp both the British National Party, which had imploded for a variety of reasons, by occupying the authoritarian/traditionalist zone of political position-taking *and* the Labour Party by offering apparent solutions to material struggles. On the other hand they attracted members of the economic fraction of the dominant class by present-ing their opposition to the European Union in terms of gaining freedom from business regulation, which would allow them more efficiently to accumulate their source of power and authority at the expense of others. Hence UKIP's breakthrough came not so much in securing MPs – they managed only one in the end – but by gaining a large share of the vote and coming second place in constituencies where Labour and the Conservatives had traditionally dominated.

The rise of both the SNP and UKIP, as well as the Greens, demonstrates a prolifera-tion of potential political lines, some of which have not yet been proven untrustworthy by experience of government, to which people could yoke their own ethos, generating a greater sense of representation, and therefore higher voter turnout, than in previous elections. But how long will it be until disenchantment among the dominated sets in once again? In Scotland that will depend on the performance of the SNP at Westminster, but in England and Wales, where there is no unified or credible party more left-wing on material issues than Labour, everything would seem to indicate that alienation will deepen. After their loss, and especially following the party members' election of left-wing rebel Jeremy Corbyn to the leadership, no shortage of key figures in the Labour Party asserted their need to become more pro-business, more pro-entrepreneurialism and, ultimately, more like New Labour so that they may win over those who tend to vote rather than win back those who, because of Labour's past strategies in the political field, no longer see any reason to vote.

Notes

1 To be accurate, Bourdieu calls it the 'political space', but that label seems too close to, and may thus potentially be confused with, the notion of political field, or the field of struggles between certain agents (politicians, party members, trade unions etc.) to represent and transform the world, which he developed later (see esp. Bourdieu, 1991) – at this point he was using 'field of ideological production' to describe the latter, but he dropped that probably in order to signal a clearer break from Marxism. 'Political position-takings' seems more apt.
2 In order to counter the effect of low numbers in some categories, all questions were recoded into a three-category variable of 'agree', 'neither' and 'disagree'. All modalities containing less than 5 per cent of the sample were treated as supplementary.
3 For eigenvalues, modality contributions and the spaces of individuals, see Appendix II.
4 Homosexuality ++ refers to the response 'Homosexuality is never wrong', while Homosexuality – denotes the statement 'Homosexuality is always wrong'. Enviro ++ indicates the respondent is 'very concerned' about the environment, and Enviro – indicates they are 'not concerned at all' about it. These two variables were excluded from active construction of the space because, being filled in by only half of the sample (the survey administrators administer different versions of the survey to

different sections of the sample to get a wider coverage of issues efficiently), the MCA tended to pick them out on this artificial basis.

5 It is, as I have argued before, only in this limited sense that theories of 'individualisation' have any purchase, i.e. as an indicator of the shift in symbolic struggles and ways of carving up the world in perception, working against the category of 'class', not in any sense as a diagnosis of structural trans-formations (Atkinson, 2010a).

6 In order to allocate elected politicians to class fractions, last known occupation before entering poli-tics was converted into a SOC unit (as a 'best guess') and then, from that, into the class scheme used here. Since the criterion was last job before entering politics rather than parliament, work as local councillors or as researchers, agents, aides and assistants to politicians, parties, think-tanks or trade unions was discounted. Military service during the Second World War was also ignored. One quirk of focussing on last job held is that it overlooks social mobility – the hypothetical MP who started off as a miner, for example, but then worked their way up to management before entering politics. In a select few instances – the real 'career politicians' – there were actually no jobs between leaving education and political employment of one form or another, and so in these cases those jobs had to suffice and a suitable code was found for them. The principal sources of information were *The Times Guide to the House of Commons* for 1979 and 2010, supplemented in many instances with other publicly available sources, including MPs' own constituency websites, newspaper obituaries, Debrett's *People of Today* website and, in some exceptional circumstances, Hansard as navigated through the TheyWorkForYou.com website run by the UK Citizens Online Democracy charity.

References

Atkinson, W. (2010a) *Class, Individualization and Late Modernity: In Search of the Reflexive Worker*. Basingstoke: Palgrave Macmillan.

Atkinson, W. (2010b) 'Not Either-Or but Both-And?' *Sociological Research Online*, 15(4): www.socresonline.org.uk/15/4/7.html.

Bourdieu, P. (1984) *Distinction*. London: Routledge.

Bourdieu, P. (1988) *Homo Academicus*. Cambridge: Polity Press.

Bourdieu, P. (1991) *Language and Symbolic Power*. Cambridge: Polity Press.

Bradley, H. (2008) 'No More Heroes?' *Work, Employment and Society*, 22(2): 337–49.

Bradley, H. and Hebson, G. (1999) 'Breaking the Silence: The Need to Re-articulate Class' *International Journal of Sociology and Social Policy*, 19: 178–203.

Evans, G. (ed.) (1999) *The End of Class Politics?* Oxford: Oxford University Press.

Flemmen, M. (2014) 'The Politics of the Service Class' *European Societies*, 16(4): 543–69.

Fraser, W. (1999) *A History of British Trade Unionism 1700–1998*. Basingstoke: Macmillan.

Giddens, A. (1991) *Modernity and Self Identity*. Cambridge: Polity Press.

Harrits, G. (2013) 'Class, Culture and Politics' *The Sociological Review*, 61(1): 172–202.

Harrits, G., Prieur, A., Rosenlund, L. and Skjott-Larsen, J. (2010) 'Class and Politics in Denmark' *Scandinavian Political Studies*, 33(1): 1–27.

Houtman, D. (2003) *Class and Politics in Contemporary Social Science*. New York: Aldnine de Gruyter.

Howell, C. (2005) *Trade Unions and the State*. Princeton: Princeton University Press.

Inglehart, R. (1977) *The Silent Revolution*. Princeton: Princeton University Press.

Inglehart, R. (1990) *Culture Shift in Advanced Industrial Society*. Princeton: Princeton University Press.

Lipset, S. M. (1960) *Political Man*. New York: Doubleday.

Pakulski, J. and Waters, M. (1996) *The Death of Class*. London: Sage.

Sarlvik, B. and Crewe, I. (1983) *Decade of Dealignment*. Cambridge: Cambridge University Press.

Part II

Lifeworld analysis: class, place, family

5 National space, urban space

The focus hitherto has been on field analysis, that is, the mapping-out of the abstract space of relations constituting the twenty-first-century misrecognition order in the UK and its various homologous spaces of position-takings. Now, however, we begin to shift gear, transitioning toward lifeworld analysis, i.e. the exploration of how class determinations combine with forces emanating from other fields in structuring everyday experience and, with that, social surfaces. We start, in this chapter and the next three, by examining the entwinement of class, and the circuits of symbolic power sprawling forth from global, national and local fields of power with which it is enmeshed, with the quotidian experience of, and practice within, physical space and place. To be a little more precise, three overlapping themes will move centre stage. The first is the two-way relationship between class and lifeworld topology, i.e. how conditions of existence and class experience are given concrete form yet also specified, complicated and even modified by spatial location and the material and social relations inhering therein. These are the 'site effects' broached, but underexplored, by Bourdieu (1999), encompassing the patterning of recurrent pathways through time-space, the sensory texture of one's territory and the properties of the objects and others one typically tends to encounter, perceive and interact with in the usual daily round, all of which furnish conditions of existence and the solicitations of the social world with their individual hue and specify the nature of the classed habitus. The second theme, bumping into the burgeoning literature nowadays on 'mobilities', some of which claims to question or necessitate a rethink of class analysis (e.g. Urry, 2007), is *reach*, also known as *motility*, with its double face: the differential potentiality for movement through time-space generated by capital possession and its phenomenological correlate in the form of perceptions of the possible (see further Atkinson, 2016). Finally, attention will turn to the symbolic struggles taking place within localised physical spaces, connecting with and nuancing the existing mass of contemporary research on gentrification and urban marginality but also spotlighting otherwise overlooked clashes between fractions of the dominant class on the basis of capital composition within what would, in the language of spontaneous sociology, be described as a homogenously 'middle-class' area.

Rather than proceed thematically, however, the analysis will unfold according to *scale* and let the three themes interweave like the channels of a braided river. We thus begin with the national level, indicating the rough homologies of social space and physical space and the differentiation of reach,[1] before then dropping down to the plane of the contemporary Western city. Our case study at this scale will be the English conurbation of Bristol, which, with its core population of roughly 450,000 and an encompassing 'larger urban zone' of almost 900,000, is the UK's eighth largest city.[2] Although not quite a Sassen-style 'global city' on the scale of New York, London or Tokyo, the general mechanisms that have oriented and continue to permeate this city's classed composition, including those born of increasingly globalised circuits of symbolic power, are common to urban areas not only across Britain but beyond it too; yet the particularities of Bristol – its specific industries, its specific geography and districts, its local powers – are significant for unpacking the constitution of the thousands of unique individual life-worlds anchored in its environs. After this we will descend, in the next chapter, to the level of specific neighbourhoods, where data from local government and the Ordinary Lives project combine to paint portraits of spatial experience and localised symbolic struggles in three contrasting areas of Bristol. The final drop, to the level of domestic space, is reserved for Chapters 7 and 8, and serves as a bridge, or meeting place, between the focus on class and space and the focus on the relationship between class and the familial field which will detain our attention more fully in the final substantive chapter.

National geographic space

The major homology at the national level between social space and physical space, however modest, rough and refracted at lower levels it may be, is that between volume of capital and latitude, with height in social space inversely related to northerliness in Britain (cf. Cunningham and Savage, 2015). Thus, on the one hand, the Southern regions – including the South-West, of which Bristol is the premier conurbation – are weighted ever so slightly toward the dominant class compared to other parts of the country (LFS 2015). Over a third of the South-East's population, for instance, hail from the dominant class, and almost a third of the residents of the South-West fit the same bill, compared with just 24 per cent in the North-East and Wales and 25 per cent in Tyne and Wear. Or, to look at it from a different angle, the South-East is home to 26 per cent of all business executives in the country and 23 per cent of all white-collar workers, but only 16 per cent of manual workers. The limit case is, however, Inner London, the heart of the capital city and the heartland of capital (cf. Bourdieu, 1999: 125). In London as a whole one will find 19 per cent of all business executives, 21 per cent of all professionals, 17 per cent of all the cultural dominant and 20 per cent of white-collar workers, compared with just 12 per cent of all manual workers and sales workers, 11 per cent of caring services and 11 per cent of skilled tradespeople; but in the core of the city about half the resident population, no doubt drawn by the City, Whitehall and the multiple universities there, is made up of business executives, professionals, the cultural dominant and white-collar workers, concentrating countless key players in the field of power within a few square miles. One is, therefore, disproportionately likely to come into contact with – to see, to typify, to interact with – such people and all the symbols of their social position (tailored suits, briefcases, polished shoes, or somewhat scruffier intellectuals) here, whether in the street or on the tube. Then again, the sheer number and diversity of tourists and students from exotic climes in London, particularly its inner core, swallows such experiences within a general sense of 'everyday cosmopolitanism' unlike anywhere else in the country and which might just give those who live or work there (including in the universities…) a very particular, and perhaps skewed, view of the world. Be that as it may, the class composition of the South of Britain is at least in part a knock-on effect of the concentration of capital in London, since (i) executives in large financial and legal firms, pursuing so many strategies carved out in the context of the economic field (and the internal struggles of its participant organisations), opt to site their offices where property prices and rents are cheaper yet transport to London straightforward and inexpensive; (ii) executives in manufacturing firms opt to locate their research and executive functions at a distance from the sites of production to fragment the field formed by its employees and quell worker disquiet (cf. Massey, 1995); and (iii) as we shall see, those working in Central London elect to reside outside of the city, where property is cheaper, and commute in.

The obverse of the disproportionate siting of the dominant class in the South is the over-representation of the dominated in the North (and in Wales), itself a legacy of the industries that have been and still are, though to a lesser extent, situated there as monuments to the innumerable strategies and struggles within the economic field, past and present, factoring in proximity to sites of extraction, or of import and export, labour supplies, and so on (a species of the 'profit of localisation' described by Bourdieu, 1999: 126). Over or almost half the whole population of the North-East and North-West, Merseyside, Yorkshire, Wales and the Midlands, for example, are situated in the dominated class, and around 20 per cent are manual workers alone, while Inner and Outer London and the South-East are characterised by lower numbers of individuals from the dominated class as a whole: 30 per cent, 41 per cent and 40 per cent respectively. There is, therefore, a greater chance of being amongst the dominated in the course of one's routine journeys in the North, of crossing paths with them, with all the effects for one's sense of belonging, of being more or less 'at home', amidst 'people like me', but which also differentiates the daily experience, self-perception and anxieties of the business executive or intellectual in Kent and the business executive or intellectual in Newcastle. Indeed, the disparity contributes to the fuzzy conflation in many people's minds of the North/South divide with oppositions structuring the social and symbolic spaces – poor/affluent, vulgar/posh, hard/soft, masculine/feminine, etc. (Taylor, 2012).[3] We have already seen, in the last chapter, the effect this can have on the political culture of a locale, but, when coupled with regional pay and sectorial discrepancies, it also means the chances of describing oneself as 'working-class' rises in the North whatever position of social space one occupies (with the exceptions of the cultural dominant and sales workers) and, the mirror image of that, the chances of identifying oneself as 'middle-class' increase with residence in the South no matter what class fraction one belongs to (again excepting the cultural dominant) (Table 5.1).

Yet the uneven distribution of class fractions over geographical space, as indicated by current region of residence, only tells half the story of the knotty nexus between class and space at the national level. It may well indicate the patterning of a key hub in individual lifeworlds, but it tells us less of the routine pathways traversed to, from and around those hubs, or the propensity to reposition hubs and refashion the lifeworld, and, with these, the differential spatial *reach* or *motility* that comes with capital – or put another way, the 'mobilities' or 'flows' of people across the face of the planet and their differentiation by class (seen as a specific individual strategy to *appropriate* space by Bourdieu, 1999: 128). To tap into this – albeit very crudely, in lieu of better (purpose-built) data – we can examine a few statistics from the LFS. The first of these is rates of relocating residence, as measured by the proportion of people who lived within a different region (including outside the country) one year ago (Figure 5.1).[4] A basic indicator, for sure, limited by its reliance on officially defined 'regions' and, thus, its inability to distinguish distances travelled (it may have been just a short hop across an arbitrarily drawn border), as well as its lack of insight into reasons for relocation, but still one which reveals a few telling patterns. Rates of residential transfer in a single year for all class fractions are small – no more than a few per cent in any case – even if it must be remembered that that still represents many tens of thousands of people once

Table 5.1 Rates of identification with class labels by class and region (row%)

Class fraction	Middle-class identity*		Working-class identity	
	North**	South	North	South
Business executives	55	73	45	21
Professions	57	70	43	30
White-collar	50	69	46	22
Cultural dominant	69	69	25	25
LMPs	44	61	56	36
Technicians	39	38	62	58
Administrators	35	46	60	43
Cultural intermediaries	41	65	59	31
Skilled trades	12	28	89	65
Sales workers	28	27	67	68
Manual workers	13	20	81	75
Caring services	20	38	77	57

Source: BSA 2005

* Combining answers to the questions 'Do you see yourself as belonging to a particular social class' and 'If you had to choose middle or working class…'
** 'North' = North-East, North-West, Yorkshire and Humberside. South = South-West, South-East, East and London.

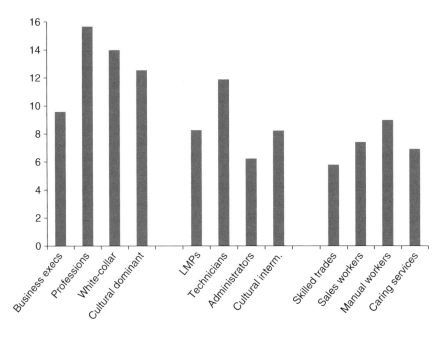

Figure 5.1 Five-year spatial fluidity (%).
Source: LFS 2011, 2012, 2013, 2014, 2015

weighted for population estimates. To get a clearer view, then, we can aggregate data for the past five years using the LFS from 2011 to 2015, though since this does not distinguish one-time movers from individuals moving more than once in successive years (or even within a single year) the resulting statistic is best viewed as a measure of the general five-year spatial fluidity of class fractions. In any case we see that the most likely to have resited their lifeworld hubs are the professionals, white-collar workers, the cultural dominant and technicians – in other words, <u>those with valued and portable skills, namely symbolic or technical mastery, as well as enough economic capital to facilitate moving abode.</u> The rest of the intermediate class and the dominated are rather less likely to have relocated, as are business executives, but in the latter case there appears to be a very particular explanation, unearthed when we switch attention to differential chances of residing and working within different regions of the country as an indicator of recursive path lengths (Figure 5.2).

Similar riders as for the chances of relocating within a year have to be issued: the precise distance of paths is not known, nor are the frequency or the phenomenology of the path – but it still provides a rough-and-ready measure of relatively *routine*, as opposed to occasional, spatial reach and mobility. In any case, once the stark disparity between male and female mobility across all class fractions has been registered (indicating, one would imagine, differences in constraints, expectations and investments in childcare and home-making anchored in the familial field) it emerges that male business executives are the most likely to live and work in different regions. This suggests a few potential explanations for their lower likelihood of relocation. They may, for example, be more able, and given more

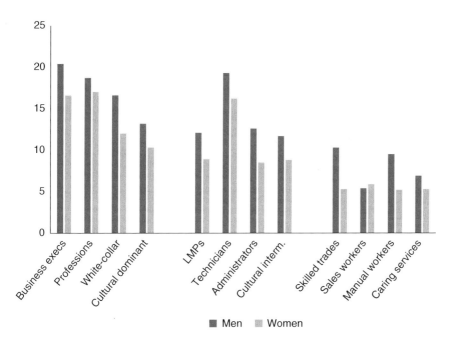

Figure 5.2 Region of usual workplace is different from region of usual residence (%)

Source: LFS 2015

autonomy, to work remotely, but they may also be happier to commute longer distances. Most of these commutes are, to be fair, clustered in certain tracts of the UK, between northern regions or between southern regions and London, for example, but business executives residing in London, the South-East and the Midlands seem particularly likely to have long commuting paths – up to the North of England, Wales and even beyond the UK – indicating possession of enough economic capital (as well as desired-enough housing and possibly family considerations too) to make them feasible and appealing. After business executives it is the technicians, professionals and white-collar workers who seem particularly mobile (with meta-regional circuits taking the same rough form as for business executives, but to an attenuated degree), whereas the dominated, the remainder of the intermediate class and the cultural dominant, both male and female, seem either rather less able to work remotely or somewhat less tolerant of long pathways between domains of the lifeworld. In many cases this may be due to limits of economic capital, and the objective and subjective impossibility or implausibility of significant travel it furnishes, but among the cultural dominant the genetic principle may well include other elements too, since they are hardly impoverished economically. Perhaps keeping workplaces and domiciles in closer spatial proximity is a tactic for managing the clashing demands of fields (intellectual, organisational, familial) in tune with a desire for greater 'work-life balance', or parity of libidinal investment, and a disposition toward some degree of gender egalitarianism in the family. Perhaps – as we will broach later – gentrification of inner-city areas closer to their places of work rather than long commutes is a strategy that fits better with their balance of capital and their habitus. Or perhaps ethical or political views in tune with their position – their concern for the environment glimpsed in Chapter 4 and elsewhere (Atkinson and Deeming, 2015) – play into their decision to spurn the cars and airplanes usually facilitating lengthy home-work paths.

This brings us, finally, to the task of filling in at least some of the blanks on the *form* of pathways, and, joining with the analysis in Chapter 3 of multiple car ownership, to indicate some of the mobility-specific *symbols* associated with different class fractions we can examine differential propensities for utilising particular modes of transport, whether for work or pleasure, this time drawn from the 2010 BSA survey (Table 5.2). For instance, the dominant class, but especially the business executives, are by far the most frequent flyers. They could be attending meetings and conferences at a distance, or jetting off on holiday, or both, or it could even be part of the routine commute for some, but it indicates a relationship between air miles and volume of economic capital, including via claimable 'expenses' and business accounts, underpinning the common association, pervasive in the media and popular cultural production, of the 'jet-set lifestyle' with (monetary or business) 'success' (cf. Mau and Mewes, 2009). Yet the more modest air travel among the cultural dominant is also likely to dovetail with their ethical concern and environmentalism, as an opposition, born of the struggle for recognition on the basis of what they have, i.e. symbolic mastery, to the 'ignorant' excesses of the economically rich. Indeed, according to the same survey the cultural dominant are the most likely to strongly agree that the current level of air travel has a serious effect on the environment (29 per cent) and the business executives the least likely (11 per cent). Moreover, the dominant are least likely to say they never take the train to their destinations, and business executives least of all. This is, after all, a relatively direct and swift, yet often expensive, method of traversing tracts of space beyond the home town or city, allowing the commuter or meeting/conference-attender to work – i.e. feel the pressure of and forge more or less mundane strategies in the field(s) to which their employment is oriented – on the move. And, of course, like air travel it has 'class' differences explicitly built into it,

Table 5.2 Uses of modes of transport by class fraction (row%)

Class fraction	Number of plane journeys within the last 12 months				Never use the local bus	Never use the train
	None	One	Two to Four	Five plus		
Business executives	24.5	20.5	29.0	26.0	60.0	20.5
Professions	33.7	18.5	35.9	12.1	44.6	22.8
White-collar	34.5	25.5	29.6	10.5	42.8	29.7
Cultural dominant	38.6	19.1	29.7	12.8	45.1	23.7
LMPs	48.7	19.0	28.5	3.6	55.1	43.7
Technicians	51.1	14.9	23.5	9.6	42.6	33.0
Administrators	49.5	21.4	25.1	3.8	40.1	42.0
Cultural interm.	49.2	20.3	26.6	4.0	40.6	36.7
Skilled trades	60.8	21.2	15.9	2.1	54.7	53.8
Sales workers	63.6	18.2	16.0	2.1	32.6	44.1
Manual workers	68.5	14.9	15.4	1.1	37.9	56.5
Caring services	58.3	17.9	21.0	2.7	40.4	45.7

Source: BSA 2010

separating out those who can afford exclusive carriages from the rest of the locomoting population so as to maximise space and comfort and minimise contact with others.

Rather different patterns are to be found, however, when it comes to taking the bus, a prosaic mode of transport where there are no in-built spatial class barriers, where proximity to constantly changing others is more pronounced, the routes of which are usually both more circuitous and more localised, and which is, ultimately, relatively inexpensive. In this case the likelihood of never taking the bus appears to be related less to *volume* of capital than *composition* of capital, with those richest in economic capital in all classes – business executives, LMPs and skilled tradespeople – the least likely to be seen on a bus. Among the rest of the dominated we might conjecture that catching the bus instead of driving is likely to be rooted in economic necessity, but among the cultural dominant, once again, ecological concerns are likely to play their part – they are, for example, highly likely to state that they are using public transport in place of a car more than they were two or three years ago 'for the sake of the environment' (23 per cent), compared with just 11 per cent of manual workers and 13 per cent of sales workers. This doubtless provides them with a defensive weapon, or a counter-strike, against the symbolic violence peddled against bus use on account of its close association with the dominated class, as captured in the declaration famously popularised by an aristocrat, though frequently misattributed to Margaret Thatcher, that anyone riding the bus over the age of 30 should count themselves a failure.

Class in the city

The homology between social space and geographical space plays out not just over regions and zones of the country but within cities too, where different class fractions are dispersed and clustered to different degrees in terms of their residences, their workplaces, their paths and thus their statistically probable and improbable encounters and where, as a result, different tracts of space within the city with their own formal and informal appellations (certain streets, estates, tower blocks or 'neighbourhoods') are associated in manifold ways with the symbols and behaviours of different classes and judged according to their social distance from the position of the person perceiving them. The classed geography and urban environment of any city, Bristol included, must be situated in historical context, of course, specifically the transformations upending metropolises across the Western world in the last few decades, for these mutations not only bear down in varying fashion upon the diverse sections of social space, impressing upon the sense of space and place (both physical and social), but are themselves the product of a melange of class strategies undertaken in and ricocheting through a variety of relatively autonomous fields – the bureaucratic field, the political field, the field of local powers (e.g. the city council, town planners and local agencies), the field of architectural production, the economic field and so on (cf. Bourdieu, 2005; Fogle, 2011; Bacqué *et al.*, 2015).[5] To be precise, the cityscape of Bristol, and thus the individual worlds and spatial trajectories of those who dwell and move within it, has been irreversibly wrought over the last thirty-odd years by the twin processes of *deindustrialisation* – which, as we have already seen, was not just bound up with transformations in the structure of the social space but propelled by the interests associated with certain dominant class fractions – and, following in its wake, apparent '*regeneration*' – which, in many ways, is oriented toward the tastes of certain dominant class fractions.

Most emblematic, perhaps, is the recasting of the core of the city, the old docks and 'floating harbour' which, through a series of locks, manages to maintain a constant water level unaffected by the substantial tidal surge carried along the River Avon. Originally designed and constructed in order to facilitate the passage of brittle merchant ships – thus objectifying in space the interests of economic capital – the harbour, this industrious nucleus of Bristol, came to be lined with warehouses large and small, loading bays, cranes, train lines along which cargo was hauled and numerous boatyards – central hubs of the everyday worlds of so many (male) labourers, where the air was thick with the sounds and smells of industry, where bodies wove amongst and attuned to machines, goods and other people, where the objective likelihood and subjective expectation of toil, danger and misery hung heavily but also where workplace banter and solidarities, making virtues of necessity, alleviated the strains (cf. Willis, 1979). To the south and the east, a short distance away, were the workers' homes, rows of terraces punctuated by numerous pubs and shops, where women's worlds were more continuously anchored; to the north and the east, especially in Clifton, a district standing atop a hill overlooking the mercantile traffic on the river and the hubbub of the centre, were the large residences of the merchants and their families.

Today, however, the centre of Bristol bears the stamp of different class interests. The harbour, no longer able to accommodate increasingly large cargo ships, ceased industrial operations in the mid-1970s, the warehouses were abandoned, the railway went quiet and the space was largely cleared of industrial labour. Remaining dock operations were relocated – sequestered, one might say – from the city centre to Avonmouth, far to the north-west where the river flows into the Bristol Channel, while workshops and distribution centres were pushed into St Philip's Marsh, east of the centre; tobacco manufacturing, which had been a staple, disappeared overseas in search of cheaper labour, leaving only offices behind. In order to combat escalating inequality and poverty as a result, and in line with the changes in the economy encouraged by the national government in the 1980s, mediated through council plans for redevelopment and 'regeneration' (largely framed by the discourse of 'encouraging investment' and 'economic growth'), the city developed a specialisation in hi-tech production as well as financial services and higher education (Boddy *et al.*, 1986). While the former was, again, isolated from the city centre in the northern area of Filton, however, the latter has come to have a profound impact on the shape of the city centre in two ways. First, by etching spaces of production and accumulation of both cultural capital and economic capital into the landscape: the University of Bristol, spurred by its own strategies within the field of higher-educational institutions, has purchased a series of old merchant houses in Clifton to transform into various departments and continues to erect imposing scientific laboratories which, being sited at the crest of a steep hill, are visible to all in the centre; Lloyds Bank, in the context of the ascendancy of financial services in the economic field, redeveloped an old patch of land previously dominated by a large warehouse and built an ostentatious columned edifice and accompanying amphitheatre; and the Temple Quay area near the main train station was transformed from a dense mass of distilleries, soap and bottle factories and mills into the legal and financial district, where large (at least for the city) plate-glass buildings belonging to bank headquarters (RBS), corporate and financial-service companies (KPMG, Deloitte), law firms and suchlike nestle alongside one another around enclosed squares and walkways. Second, the 'regeneration' of the city centre essentially took the form of redeveloping the old sites of labour into sites of consumption for the dominant class: an old iron and tea warehouse was converted into the Arnolfini art gallery; several aged industrial sheds have been converted into the Watershed arthouse cinema and media centre, a large warehouse has been transformed into a museum (with remaining period cranes and train lines recast as side 'heritage' attractions); an old tobacco factory was refitted to become a theatre playing Shakespearean and avant-garde plays; a science museum was planted on abandoned soil; and vastly expensive apartments were constructed along the waterfront. True, general-purpose public spaces, squares and fountains acting as 'temporary constellations of trajectories', as Massey (2005: 153) puts it, wherein social differences are negotiated and habitus tweaked, have been constructed, and a mix of bars, clubs and eateries dot the waterfront (though these each draw their clientele from different sections of the social space to different degrees). Yet the major landmarks are art galleries, museums, theatres and the arthouse cinema, and while the capital-rich Labour councillors involved in the planning process may well have been motivated by patronising desires to improve 'access' to the forms of culture they value in building them, in fraught alliance with local business interests in attracting investment and increasing tourism (see Bassett, 1993), these sites are, as we already know from Chapter 3, disproportionately visited by the dominant, particularly the cultural dominant.[6] One final development worthy of mention is the expansion of the Broadmead and Cabot Circus shopping areas, in tune with the general economic shift to services, as these have concentrated the time-space paths of sales workers and lower managers and channelled those of consumers (who visit different shops there at different rates depending on their class tastes).

The significance of all this is that the class-refracted network of routinised paths through the city, the hubs or 'domains' concentrating people in fixed points in space at certain times and, with that, the prepredicative pairing of certain geographical coordinates with certain types of people, activity and symbols of greater or lesser remove from the perceiver have been transfigured. On the one hand, in Temple Quay, where once the dominated worked and dwelled, populating the streets like J. S. Lowry's 'matchstick men', now business executives, professionals and white-collar workers, in their formal work attire, checking the time on their pricey watches, talking or browsing on their smartphones, swarm, and, other than for those passing through, or those who maintain the buildings and streets and work in nearby cafés and eateries, is now a virtual no-go area for the dominated, ensuring a cloistered existence for the former and perhaps generating a sense of discrepancy and non-belonging among the latter (the same cannot be said for the area around the Lloyds building, which, due to its central location and specific design, has been appropriated by skateboarders as a key site for honing and displaying their skills).[7] On the other hand, distinct hubs of the city centre now lure the culturally rich, at least at certain times, turning buildings and locations once peopled by the dominated and paired in perception with physical toil into spaces of exclusion – not by dint of money, since most attractions are free, but by dint of symbolic mastery and a sense that such places are 'not my thing' or 'not for the likes of me' – paired in perception, one would suppose, with the potential for symbolic violence. Meanwhile the dominant overlay even the old industrial buildings that remain, stripped of their old (profane) functions and set to the background of Bristol's transformed spaces, with a new significance, as objects of contemplation, on the basis of the abstract historical themes and 'lessons' they embody, and even aesthetic 'charm'. One large old warehouse occupying a prominent position in the skyline, for example, a participant in the Ordinary Lives project (Mr Quinn) describes as a 'fascinating' and 'interesting' 'symbol of Bristol', defending it against (and thus trying to overturn) his teenage son's 'naive' view that it is simply ugly, while the old swing bridge that used to carry industrial traffic across the river, now functioning as a footbridge, is described as having 'its own charm' because it 'harks back to the industrial heritage'.

Entwined with the peppering of the city centre with dominant-class bastions and the removal of industry to the urban periphery is growing *residential* segregation. As part of inner-city slum clearance programmes in the early and mid-twentieth century, and in the clamour to reside close to their places of work and consumption and to shorten their journeys, those rich in cultural and economic resource have pushed the dominated class increasingly to the edges of the city, lengthening their paths to the centre, with all its amenities and shops, making them more arduous and expensive and thus lessening their frequency – in short, removing the 'regenerated' harbourside from their every-day lifeworlds. Instead they are either confined to their own locales or contained in the purpose-built 'out-of-town' shopping centres and entertainment complexes (main-stream cinemas, bowling alleys, arcades and low-cost eateries), the so-called 'cathedrals of consumption' (Ritzer, 2010) drawing malicious stigmatisation as 'trashy' or – as the contemporary vocabulary of denigration has it – 'chavvy' by others (Box 5.1).

Box 5.1 Place and symbolic violence

iLiveHere.co.uk is a website, otherwise known as 'chavtown' (playing on the still-pervasive label of 'chav' for describing the dominated), designed as an outlet for people – particularly young people – to vent their hatred, under the cloak of anonymity, toward those at the bottom of the social space, particularly where they live, where they go and what they consume. Regarding Cribbs Causeway, the major out-of-town shopping complex to the north of Bristol, one user decries it as a site of 'the average retard "chav"', otherwise known as 'our favourite sub-species', venturing forth from 'the seething estates' nearby and enticed by its various fast-food outlets (McDonald's, KFC, Pizza Hut, etc.) and 'jewellers specialising in the large hoop [earring]'. *Another user describing Bristol in general pays particular attention to Cribbs Causeway, sneering at the supposed 'smell of BO [body odour] (tracksuits, eurgh), cheap perfume and the leather of Nike trainers [that] hits you' once you enter the shopping mall, musing over the lone Starbucks amidst the fast-food outlets as 'no chav would be seen dead' in there and denigrating one encountered woman in particular for having a 'typical short chavette haircut' and 'the tacky gold earrings, the trainers' and for referring to conversational others as 'love'.* **

*www.ilivehere.co.uk/cribbs-causeway-regional-shopping-centre.html
(last accessed 01/06/2016)
**www.ilivehere.co.uk/bristol.html (last accessed 01/06/2016)

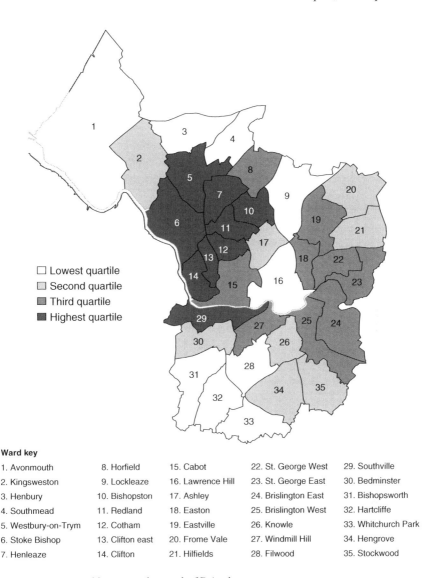

Ward key

1. Avonmouth	8. Horfield	15. Cabot	22. St. George West	29. Southville
2. Kingsweston	9. Lockleaze	16. Lawrence Hill	23. St. George East	30. Bedminster
3. Henbury	10. Bishopston	17. Ashley	24. Brislington East	31. Bishopsworth
4. Southmead	11. Redland	18. Easton	25. Brislington West	32. Hartcliffe
5. Westbury-on-Trym	12. Cotham	19. Eastville	26. Knowle	33. Whitchurch Park
6. Stoke Bishop	13. Clifton east	20. Frome Vale	27. Windmill Hill	34. Hengrove
7. Henleaze	14. Clifton	21. Hilfields	28. Filwood	35. Stockwood

Figure 5.3 Net weekly income by ward of Bristol

This apparent reversal of the famous Burgess model, where a dilapidated inner core is contrasted to the leafy outer suburbs, is revealed by mapping Census data on the distribution of net weekly income and possession of higher education (Figures 5.3 and 5.4).[8] Notwithstanding the absolute centre itself, Cabot, with its high proportion of student housing and flats pulling the distribution of economic and cultural capital downwards, the affluent and culturally dominant northwestern zone enveloping the areas surrounding the University of Bristol (Cotham, Redland) and the old merchants' quarter (Clifton, Clifton East, Southville) is opposed to the outer rim of depressed

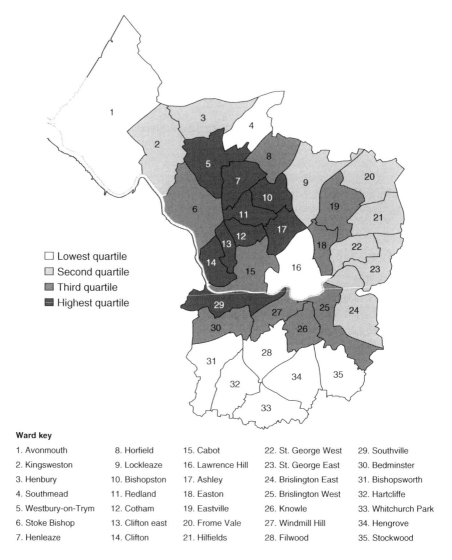

□ Lowest quartile
▨ Second quartile
▩ Third quartile
▦ Highest quartile

Ward key

1. Avonmouth	8. Horfield	15. Cabot	22. St. George West	29. Southville
2. Kingsweston	9. Lockleaze	16. Lawrence Hill	23. St. George East	30. Bedminster
3. Henbury	10. Bishopston	17. Ashley	24. Brislington East	31. Bishopsworth
4. Southmead	11. Redland	18. Easton	25. Brislington West	32. Hartcliffe
5. Westbury-on-Trym	12. Cotham	19. Eastville	26. Knowle	33. Whitchurch Park
6. Stoke Bishop	13. Clifton east	20. Frome Vale	27. Windmill Hill	34. Hengrove
7. Henleaze	14. Clifton	21. Hilfields	28. Filwood	35. Stockwood

Figure 5.4 Rate of possession of higher education by ward of Bristol

capital-poor council estates (Southmead, Hartcliffe, Avonmouth, etc.), especially to the far northwest and south. The exception is Lawrence Hill, with the single lowest average income in 2001, which perhaps serves as the city's last ungentrified inner-city zone of urban marginality, though it is interesting to see figures from 2011 indicate possession of HE here is not as low as in other areas. This is, in fact, up a touch, from 20 per cent in 2001 to 25 per cent in 2011, perhaps indicating a nascent gentrification around the edges by those with a little in the way of cultural capital and attracted by its proximity to the centre but with few economic resources. More middling levels of capital distribution – which may well indicate the greater presence of the intermediate class, or simply a more heterogeneous mix of classes – often characterise areas nestling between the affluent core and the more depressed areas, or else sit out to the east, with the latter marked by its higher economic capital relative to its cultural capital distribution. Indeed, the disparity between patterns of income and patterns of education suggest other homologies by capital composition. Most strikingly, there is an opposition between Stoke Bishop to the West of the central hub and Ashley to the east. Everything would seem to suggest that the former, being the single richest area of the city (average income of £620 per week) and consisting largely of ample detached and semi-detached housing plus a few quiet tree-lined streets of veritable mansions, but not being so high in cultural capital distribution, disproportionately houses the economic elite of Bristol. Ashley, in contrast, packs individuals rich in cultural capital into its lines of narrow terraces but lies within the third income quartile, reflecting its folk reputation in the city as 'the artists' quarter', that is, a place popular with younger contenders in fields of cultural production and mediation in one way or another, including, given its proximity to the University of Bristol, the intellectual field. Unsurprisingly, therefore, organic food shops, vegetarian cafés and radical bookshops abound, anti-capitalist graffiti adorns public walls (some of Banksy's first works are to be found in this area) and far-left or anarchist groups meet in dusty backrooms – all of which, alongside what we know from Chapter 4 on the politicisation of the cultural dominant and cultural intermediaries, helps throw fresh light on the violent street protests over the opening of a Tesco that erupted in this area in 2011.

Then again, even within each of these expanses of space stamped with 'official' names, which are only ever more or less in accord with everyday perceptual and linguistic categorisations of territory built up through practical experience, class fractions can be more or less concentrated, sometimes with fringes or enclaves of social difference, sometimes in relative parity with other classes and class fractions. Even in otherwise exclusively expensive areas there are variations in housing tenure, prices and biographical circumstances leading people from lower down the social space to reside there, and even in areas otherwise overwhelmingly populated by the dominated there are still professionals or business executives to be found. A whole gamut of forces structuring the everyday lifeworld and tugging on the libido, beyond the sense of 'fit' with not only the aesthetics and amenities nearby but the people who live there, draws individuals to the place they inhabit: local school performance (factoring in the sense of the state of the field of education), proximity to the work-place (though this matters to different degrees in different sections of the social space, as we will see), attachment to family (as the site of recognition in the form of love), childcare facilities, ethnic solidarity, etc. (see e.g. Bridge, 2003, 2006; Ward *et al.*, 2010; Benson, 2014; Bacqué *et al.*, 2015). On top of that, of course, people of different social locations 'pass through' each area to different degrees depending on the geography of their pertinent lifeworld hubs and the transportation networks of the city, refracting the probabilities of bumping into someone from remote reaches of social space. Nevertheless, the rate of representation of different classes feeds into the sense of an area's 'mix', the perceptual classification of people who typically live there, the intuition of one's place relative to them (and one's area relative to proximate or renowned others), the anticipation of certain behaviours and the everyday symbolic struggles between those living in close proximity – all of which are amongst the most salient ways in which the class differences mapped in a national social space are actually experienced, comprehended and sedimented in everyday existence. To properly demonstrate some of this, however, we need to move our focal scale down a notch, from the contemporary Western city to its constitutive neighbourhoods.

Notes

1 Some may balk at what they would cast as a 'methodologically nationalist' orientation here. Yet everything would seem to indicate that the circuits of symbolic power constituting distinct social orders and working in dialectical interplay with social spaces continue, amidst the global mesh, to operate along grooves forged by national fields, not least the bureaucratic field (see e.g. Ray, 2007). Until evidence suggests otherwise, the sharp distinction between methodological nationalism and methodological cosmopolitanism and outright rejection of the former is thus – like so many strategies revolving around false dualisms – a hindrance to good social science. The two perspectives should instead, like field analysis and lifeworld analysis, be seen as complementary (Atkinson, 2007).

2 City population figures come from the ONS Compendium of UK Statistics: www.neighbourhood. statistics.gov.uk/HTMLDocs/dvc134_a/index.html. 'Larger urban zone' population estimates come from Eurostat: http://epp.eurostat.ec.europa.eu/portal/page/portal/statistics/search_database.

3 A simple correspondence analysis was run on a table crossing class fractions by usual region of residence and revealed two oppositions: the primary one, closely homologous with capital volume, opposed London and the South-East to the rest of the country, while the second (much weaker) one opposed the deindustrialised and 'regenerated' Northern regions (homologous with sales, caring and manual work but also the cultural dominant) to Southern and Midlands regions (homologous with LMPs, technicians and skilled workers but also business executives). The weight of London in determining the axes (and the South-East when London was removed), however, was too great to deliver a robust and balanced enough model to report in detail.

4 Central, Inner and Outer London are treated as a single region here and in Figure 5.2.

5 This should, hopefully, dispel any perception that Bourdieu-inspired analyses of class and space are limited to the 'consumption' side of the equation, i.e. the differential perception and appropriation of space in line with class habitus, while Marxists hold the monopoly on analyses of the production of space (e.g. Lees *et al.*, 2008). Much of Henri Lefebvre's (1991) turgid thought on space, for example, can be recast and nuanced with relational phenomenology via examination of struggles and strategies in the various fields concerned with the management and alteration of physical space (government, architecture, etc.), the circuits of symbolic power through which they are realised and the mismatch between the schemes of perception of the producers of these field effects and the schemes of perception of those whose worlds the effects enter as forged by the contrasting conditions of existence to which each is adapted.

6 There has, in fact, been a study on the Arnolfini's visitors by June Bianchi (1999), who explicitly confirmed that it falls in line with Bourdieu and Darbel's (1991) thesis that art galleries are largely the preserve of those rich in cultural capital.

7 Now as then, however, Temple Quay is a somewhat masculine space given the gender ratio within the typical class fractions frequenting it, though perhaps less so than in the past in light of the feminisation of the clerical workforce upon which the financiers and solicitors rely. It is also a largely white area for the same reason, but this time, perhaps, more so than in the past since immigrant labourers are likely to have worked here in the past.

8 'Higher education' includes undergraduate and postgraduate degrees and top-level professional/ vocational qualifications, with data coming from the 2011 Census. Average net weekly income (before housing) has been modelled and equivalised by the ONS, i.e. modified to control for size and composition of households, and, unfortunately, comes from the 2001 Census, meaning changes since then cannot be grasped. Quartiles are calculated with reference to the rank order of city wards, not national figures. The data used is available through the ONS Compendium of UK Statistics: www. neighbourhood.statistics.gov.uk/dissemination/.

References

Atkinson, W. (2007) 'Beyond False Oppositions: A Reply to Beck' *The British Journal of Sociology*, 58(4): 707–15.

Atkinson, W. (2016) *Beyond Bourdieu*. Cambridge: Polity Press.

Atkinson, W. and Deeming, C. (2015) 'Class and Cuisine in Contemporary Britain' *The Sociological Review*, 63(4): 876–96.

Bacqué, M.-H. *et al.* (2015) *The Middle Classes in the City*. Basingstoke: Palgrave Macmillan.

Bassett, K. (1993) 'Urban Cultural Strategies and Urban Regeneration' *Environment and Planning A*, 25(12): 1773–88.

Benson, M. (2014) 'Trajectories of Middle-Class Belonging' *Urban Studies*, 51(14): 3097–3112.

Bianchi, J. (1999) 'Changing the Frame: Access and Exclusion on Gallery Education' Paper presented at the British Education Research Association Annual Conference, University of Sussex at Brighton, 2–5 September 1999. Available at: www.leeds.ac.uk/educol/documents/00001239.htm.

Boddy, M., Lovering, J. and Bassett, K. (1986) *Sunbelt City?* Oxford: Clarendon Press.

Bourdieu, P. (1999) 'Site Effects' in P. Bourdieu *et al.*, *The Weight of the World*. Cambridge: Polity Press, pp. 123–9.

Bourdieu, P. (2005) *The Social Structures of the Economy*. Cambridge: Polity Press.

Bourdieu, P. and Darbel, A. (1991) *The Love of Art*. Cambridge: Polity Press.

Bridge, G. (2003) 'Time-space Trajectories in Provincial Gentrification' *Urban Studies*, 40(12): 2545–56.

Bridge, G. (2006) 'It's Not Just a Question of Taste: Gentrification, the Neighbourhood and Cultural Capital' *Environment and Planning A*, 38(10): 1965–78.

Cunningham, N. and Savage, M. (2015) 'The Secret Garden? Elite Metropolitan Geographies in the Contemporary UK' *The Sociological Review*, 63(2): 321–48.

Fogle, N. (2011) *The Spatial Logic of Social Struggle*. Lanham, Maryland: Lexington Books.

Lees, L., Slater, T. and Wyly, E. (2008) *Gentrification*. London: Routledge.

Lefebvre, H. (1991) *The Production of Space*. Oxford: Blackwell.

Massey, D. (1995) *Spatial Divisions of Labour*, 2nd edition, Basingstoke: Macmillan.

Massey, D. (2005) *For Space*. London: Sage.

Mau, S. and Mewes, J. (2009) 'Class Divides Within Transnationalism' in T. Ohnmacht, H. Maksim and M. Bergman (eds.) *Mobilities and Inequality*. Farnham: Ashgate, pp. 165–85.

Ray, L. (2007) *Globalization and Everyday Life*. London: Routledge.

Ritzer, G. (2010) *Enchanting a Disenchanted World*. London: Sage.

Taylor, Y. (2012) *Fitting Into Place?* Basingstoke: Palgrave Macmillan.

Urry, J. (2007) *Mobilities*. Cambridge: Polity Press.

Ward, K., Fagan, C., McDowell, L., Perrons, D. and Ray, K. (2010) 'Class Transformation and Work-life Balance in Urban Britain' *Urban Studies*, 47(11): 2259–78.

Willis, P. (1979) 'Shop Floor Culture, Masculinity and the Wage Form' in J. Clarke, C. Critcher and R. Johnson (eds.) *Working-Class Culture*. London: Hutchinson, pp. 185–98.

6   Local space

For most people the area in which they live – their village, town or city neighbourhood – is fundamental to their everyday experience of the world. The streets they regularly walk or drive down, the buildings and faces they routinely see, the conversations and interactions they habitually have are all so many means through which the possibilities and impossibilities mapped by the social space are delivered, felt, sedimented and negotiated and through which capital is maintained, accumulated or even lost. 'Relative distance from necessity' may be a handy formula for boiling down the rich fullness of quotidian experience to a single element efficient for explaining large amounts of variation but, when viewed from the perspective of the individual living their life more or less within the confines of a concrete patch of time-space, it becomes evident not only that the formula can be manifest in experience and practice in vastly different ways but that place, the product of so many struggles, can have its own effect in return. Topography and infrastructure have their impact on motility, or one's objective and sensed reach – facilitating or hindering certain activities aimed at capital conservation or accumulation – and the social composition of the area specifies one's sense of place in society.

Riding a swelling tide of research demonstrating the significance of place for understanding class (e.g. Rogaly and Taylor, 2009; McKenzie, 2012; Bacqué *et al.*, 2015), this chapter explores all of this by zooming in on three contrasting residential areas of Bristol and unpacking a little bit of what makes them what they are and what it is like to live there. The first, Lockleaze, scores highly on just about every index of deprivation, while the second, Redland, is generally a locale of the affluent and educated; Southville and Bedminster, two conjoined neighbourhoods making up the third zone in focus, are deep in the throes of gentrification. Beneath the general profiles reflecting the *typical* resident, however, lie multiple tints of internal difference, some fairly drastic, others being so many 'final differences', as Bourdieu put it, that is, differences flowing from relatively modest objective distances in the national social space but, because they relate to people seen on a daily basis, amongst the most significant for people's sense of who they are.

Lockleaze: a forgotten estate[1]

Lockleaze, wedged between the M32 and Ashley to the east and Horfield to the west, is one of those housing estates, like the Greenleigh of Young and Wilmott's (1962) classic anthropology of kinship and family life in London, built after the Second World War to accommodate people shipped out of city-centre living spaces as part of the government's slum clearance agenda. Like Greenleigh, therefore, it bears the imprint of the dominant modernist ideas of the architectural and town-planning fields of the day, filtered through the strategies and struggles within the local council and space of building firms: instead of tightly packed rows of cramped terraces along higgledy-piggledy streets reflecting decades and centuries of ad hoc construction, sprinkled with small pubs, shops and markets, one encounters wide avenues, meticulously planned roadways, distinctive grey concrete roads over which tyres bump and rumble audibly, open patches of tufty grass in the middle of crescents and closes, files of semi-detached houses, many in stark rufous brick, all converging on the core of the neighbourhood, Gainsborough Square, a green space bordered on two sides by shops and overlooked by the omnipresent Purdown telecommunications tower visible from almost anywhere on the estate.

The resultant transformation of the lifeworlds of new inhabitants is likely to have been the same too. No longer, for example, is everything and everyone of significance within walking distance – time-space hubs are now dispersed over larger expanses of space, necessitating longer routine pathways. A full 73 per cent of residents in Lockleaze thus either drive or catch the bus to work, above the city average of 64 per cent, while only 13 per cent walk, in contrast to around a fifth of the city as a whole, and only 17 per cent say they are satisfied with job opportunities in the local area. Even routine shopping excursions unfold over greater expanses, as vendors encompassing the Square are deemed too dear compared to the large supermarkets within driving distance: 'I don't use the local shop up there, I must be honest,' says Mrs Nash, for example, 'because it's too expensive. It's cheaper to go to Tesco's or Asda.' No longer, moreover, are the dominated class's streets bustling with activity and kith and kin bumping into one another on their way from one place to another – in Lockleaze the pavements are often eerily empty, the grass spaces are infrequently exploited and overgrown and the few commercial enterprises present struggle as people retreat into their homes for entertainment or opt to drive or take public transport to anywhere of importance (a pub prominent on Gainsborough Square has been boarded up for years). Hence only 17 per cent of residents say they have visited a park or green space in the last week, despite the fact that Purdown, a large expanse of open land, lies to the immediate east, compared with over a third of the city as a whole. Mrs Nash, for instance, admitted that despite having lived in Lockleaze all her life she did not even know there were woods next to the estate, revealing how her experience and use of place is structured by the relevances, in Alfred Schutz's (1970) sense, furnished by her particular place in the social world and its solicitations. Home-based leisure pursuits, on the other hand, such as gardening, pets, DIY and playing computer games, are among the most over-represented practices in the area according to the Acorn analysis commissioned by Bristol City Council.[2] No longer, therefore, are people encountered nearly always known in their particularity through a history of face-to-face interactions – the foundation of elementary forms of domination and distinction, as one might still find in certain locales – but, rather, perceived as anonymous exemplars of certain categories on the basis of a reading of certain symbols.

In more recent years the story of Lockleaze has been one of unemployment, lack of investment and council inattention. Some homes have fallen into various states of disrepair, the local environment has been left to deteriorate and rates of illegal activity have been amongst the highest in the city. Almost three-quarters of residents complain that litter is a problem in the neighbourhood, half think vandalism a daily blight, 30 per cent believe anti-social behaviour in their vicinity is a real issue and 22 per cent claim their daily life is disturbed by the fear of crime – figures which will come into their full starkness once contrasted with the respective numbers for Redland. House prices have tumbled as a result, attracting poorer migrant families looking for decent-sized homes, particularly from Poland (following its EU entry) and Somalia, with 11 per cent of the local population now being Muslim. Taken together with specific statistics on health and physical wellbeing – rates of adult and childhood obesity are well above average, as are rates of smoking and ill-health – a picture of the mix of people a typical resident comes across in daily travels around the neighbourhood, and the kinds of symbols against which one places and judges oneself (as more or less like them, as superior or inferior, and so on), begins to emerge.

Yet Lockleaze, for all its deprivation and social troubles, is not like some other areas of Bristol, whether St Paul's, Hartcliffe or Lawrence Weston, which have garnered city-wide stigmatisation as hotspots of danger and degradation. While it may be true that, as Mrs Green put it, 'Some people don't have many good things to say about Lockleaze', it is more of a 'forgotten' area, overlooked and left to slowly decay by local powers.[3] Nor is the Lockleaze district all of a piece: on certain streets where former council residents have bought and renovated their homes house prices have been elevated, and parts of the estate closer to the main road which passes it, and/or sealed off from the core of Lockleaze by allotments, fields and woods, are more costly and suffer fewer of the ailments afflicting the interior. There are, therefore, real objective social differences patterned over the local geography, jarring clashes of *modi vivendi* in daily experience and resultant efforts at social distancing.[4] Smaller differences manifest in the struggle between fractions of the dominated class, with those possessing (or having possessed) a modest amount of widely consecrated capital stocks and valuing 'respectability' and 'getting on' being opposed to those who, lacking legitimated resources, turn to violence and crime as a means of recognition or drink and drugs as a mode of escaping their vilified position at the bottom of society.[5] Stories thus abound among the former of confrontations with youth on the estate, of no-go areas, of distaste or fear of local drug-users and of contentment with their little sanctuaries within the estate (cf. Reay and Lucey, 2000). The Golden Bottle pub, for example, is viewed as off-limits according to Mrs Nash because 'drug-dealing goes on in there, it's a place I wouldn't take the kids'. When asked what kinds of people do frequent it, Mr Nash adds: 'the ones who's on it all day, like the drunkards, the drunks. Because obviously you could go in at seven o'clock and have 'em sittin' there drunk. It's not a very nice environment'. They contrast this with their particular street, which is, in Mrs Nash's words, 'quite quiet' and experiences 'no aggro'. Others denigrate 'druggies' having 'rows' in the flats nearby (Mr Cavendish), or note that 'some streets and some bits of Lockleaze is probably worse than where I live. I'm lucky that I've got a little dead-end quiet street, not a lot goes on around here' (Mrs Green). Mr Duncan, a former naval chef and lorry-driver, and his wife, a cleaner, provide a vivid example:

MR DUNCAN: We don't like living here.
MRS DUNCAN: I used to love it when I was little. I hate it now.
Q: Why?
MRS DUNCAN: It's just the people round here.
MR DUNCAN: People.
MRS DUNCAN: It is awful. Groups of kids that are so intimidating.
MR DUNCAN: Anti-social behaviour round here.
MRS DUNCAN: Really bad.
Q: Has that changed since…?
MR DUNCAN: Oh my goodness, yeah.
MRS DUNCAN: Oh God, yeah.
MR DUNCAN: Society has…

MRS DUNCAN: I mean, we went up to Co-op going back, what, five, six months ago, and there were two boys in there that we know of, and they've been in and out of prison and for no reason they just started on us. They said to him [Mr Duncan], 'What you looking at?', when he wun't even looking at 'em. And when we came out the shop he were outside waiting for us and he was having a go at us and he threatened to bundle me in the boot of a car and all sorts, just for no reason. That's what it's like round here.

Q: So what did you do?

MRS DUNCAN: Well, to be honest, we made a bit of a joke of it in the end and they couldn't handle it and they walked away. But it got to the stage, every time I went up there I was thinking, 'I hope I don't bump into them again.'

MR DUNCAN: I'm one of these people that because of my past in the forces, I won't back down from anybody, unfortunately.

MRS DUNCAN: I worry about the kids as well, 'cos he [Mr Duncan] will stand up to 'em, and I think 'Oh no, our kids gotta walk past these.'

Here we have testimony of the tussle of different forms of value splitting the dominated class in the locale and framing their everyday interactive relations: the physical capital of 'hardness' esteemed by the youth in question is, in the researcher's interaction with the Duncans, portrayed as undesirable on a wider scale, something of which they want no part, even if, in the specific convergence of paths, it demands recognition *in situ*. Mrs Duncan went on to recount the story of a female neighbour who had recently been released from jail after serving a sentence for fraud and seemed to be in receipt of ample money from unidentified sources, 'doing up her house, buying Blackberries for [her] kids, things we could never afford'. When asked what they thought of that, Mr Duncan replied: 'It's made me sick, sick, very angry.' This was a tale of undeserved and ill-gotten fortune contrasted to their own unrewarded hard labour and honesty. Mrs Duncan also added that this apparently disreputable woman had shown her a particular piercing she had received in prison and described it as a 'jailbird thing', i.e. a signification of position within the prison microcosm, to which Mrs Duncan, indicating her fixation on altogether different, 'legitimate' forms of recognition and desire to be seen as 'not like that', appended 'I just thought, I wouldn't be proud of a jailbird thing.'

The yawning gap and intensifying struggles between the fractions of the dominated class in Lockleaze have, in fact, yielded distinct perceptions of the local space, refash-ioned motilities and generated long-term mobility strategies among some of those ori-ented toward legitimated capitals. There are, without a doubt, many firmly rooted in the area, content with their quiet little patch and harbouring no intention or desire to permanently relocate further afield. It is, as yet at least, irrelevant to their classed projects in the misrecognition order, whether through work, family or some other means – indeed it could well be that these founts of recognition act as anchors, since spatial and/ or interactive remove might diminish their standing and their 'returns' in the sets of relations they value. For others, however, Lockleaze and certain people within it have become nothing short of *repellent*, in the sense not only of being objects of disgust but of actually inducing a desire to get away. The degree to which this yearning can be realised, however, varies. On the one hand there are those who, being in possession of enough capital to make it possible, are able to formulate and successfully pursue exit strategies. Ms Jeffers, for example, who had grown up in Lockleaze but moved to the other side of Bristol when she left home, states that she was always 'determined' to 'get away', that she 'was always going to move away from Lockleaze', and elaborates:

It was quite a rough council estate. Nothing wrong with that because that makes you the person that you are, but I knew that I didn't want to stay there. But Dad still lives in the house we were brought up in, and when you go back there, you know, just sometimes you think 'Oh, I'm so glad I got out of that,' really. Don't know why. I don't think I'm a snob, I didn't think I was, but just glad to be away from it. You see the massive gangs of kids on corners dealing drugs and smoking drugs and…I know you get it everywhere, but it just seemed too much in your face when you lived there – there was always lots of theft going on, lots of drugs, people had nowhere to go, there was no youth clubs there, there was nothing for them to do, so it just…You know, as soon as your car was parked up, the window was smashed and whatever was inside was stolen – that was just the time it was, there was nothing there, and I didn't want to be brought up in that and I didn't want any children of mine to be brought up in that.

On the other hand, there are those who want to get away but cannot – capital stocks are not ample *enough* for it to be realised, even if of a level conducive to pursuit of widely (mis)recognised capitals rather than their rejection. Mr Duncan and his wife have, for instance, *fantasised* about moving away 'many times' – a phenomenological state anchored in desire yet divorced from the field of possibles – but know that it 'just isn't gonna happen'. In other words, though it does enter consciousness, it is already pre-predicatively, and frustratingly, seen under the aspect of being impossible given the level of resources possessed. When asked about the prospect of moving abroad, moreover, he admits he has contacts in other countries from his time in the navy, but states he simply 'couldn't do it', indeed that there is 'no chance whatsoever'. 'It's just the cost,' he continues. 'I mean, you look at airfares – what's that for us?' – 'No chance,' adds his wife. The subjective field of possibles has, therefore, aligned with the objective possibilities delivered by possession of limited economic capital.

Larger social distances, meanwhile, generate an even starker sense of (mis)placement, spawn all kinds of efforts at disaffiliation and time-space segregation and spur inter- rather than intra-class symbolic violence. Take, for instance, the Buchanan family. Mr Buchanan being a well-paid electrical engineer, and his wife being a medical receptionist, everything would appear to indicate they are both sited somewhere within the intermediate zone of social space. They live on the edge of Lockleaze, near the main bypassing road, and describe their patch of the neighbourhood as a 'nice', 'clean', 'quiet', 'family' area accommodating – in their words – the 'lower-middle class' or 'upper-working class', but this is clearly constructed in opposition to all-too-proximate, denigrated spaces with a different profile. When mentioning that there are a lot of children in their immediate vicinity, they continue:

MR BUCHANAN: They're not ASBO [Anti-Social Behaviour Order] kids.[6]
MRS BUCHANAN: That's down the road.
MR BUCHANAN: That's down the road, yeah.
MRS BUCHANAN: Or up the road.
MR BUCHANAN: Up the road. No, there's no… It's a nice area.
Q: So, up the road, where do you mean?
MR BUCHANAN: Lockleaze.
MRS BUCHANAN: Lockleaze.
Q: Okay.

MRS BUCHANAN: That's ASBO area.

Q: And what's that like?

MRS BUCHANAN: Underclass.

MR BUCHANAN: Yeah.

MRS BUCHANAN: Yeah, so, at the top, it's different.

From the first sentence here they are keen to emphasise their difference from nearby others, to draw a perceptual boundary around themselves buffering them from the taint of Lockleaze, the core of which is but a few minutes away yet set at an important symbolic distance ('up the road', 'at the top'). At another juncture, when taking the researcher around their territory, they compare their area to nearby Eastville, which they perceive as somewhere they would fit in, adding:

MRS BUCHANAN: There's more of a difference between where we live and Lockleaze, which is only at the top of our avenue. That's quite rough, isn't it?

MR BUCHANAN: Yeah.

MRS BUCHANAN: You notice a difference there, and that's just a few hundred yards up the road. You don't notice any difference here from where we live.

MR BUCHANAN: No.

Q: So you don't…Lockleaze is quite near to you, isn't it?

MRS BUCHANAN: Yeah.

MR BUCHANAN: As you go up [the] road where the postcodes change, we're basically in Horfield and then [it] changes into Lockleaze.

Once again, despite their location and inclusion under the label 'Lockleaze' in official and other people's spatial classifications, the Buchanans deploy physical and behavioural markers of difference ('quite rough'), and even attempt to manipulate administrative categories (i.e. the postcode – which is actually the same for them and the core of Lockleaze), to extricate themselves from that designation in the eyes of others and attach themselves to the farther afield, but less stigmatised, area of Horfield.

In the Michaels family, however, a more blunt and disparaging assessment is offered, perhaps because Mr and Mrs Michaels, both being degree-educated social-service workers, are further away both vertically and horizontally in the social space (and thus symbolic space) from the typically encountered inhabitant of their locale, and also perhaps because the discussion is led by their teenage daughter who, since she goes to school in and all her friends are from Cotham and Redland, feels the disjunctive difference all the more keenly. They live even further from the core of Lockleaze than the Buchanans, on the periphery, where the streets blend subtly into St Werburghs and Ashley, yet, when asked about their relationship to the local area, the following ensued:

DAUGHTER: I just feel like we're not the same, not in like a snobby or like better way, but just not the same as the people who live here at all. Like them next door [on one side], and them next door [on the other side] – them, I hate. [To her parents, who are worried the neighbours might overhear her] They can't hear! And then them [across the road], they've lived there like…oh, and they've lived in their house all their life and they're brother and sister, and just like we're not like that at all, we just live here because we have to […][7] it's just that's not like us at all. And like across the road, people like that, we're just not the same as them at all.

Unlike others in a similar position in social space cosseted by an *Umwelt* inhabited by 'people like them', by virtue of her family dwelling's site she is surrounded in her daily life by people deemed to be socially distinct and is thus, one might infer, constantly ill at ease. Indeed, she tries to spend as much leisure time as she can away from the area, routinely trundling along extensive paths through time and space on her scooter (a necessity for just this purpose) to do things and see people others need only a short jaunt to accomplish or visit. Not only that, but, despite her opening claim not to be 'snobby', her sentiment, born of a desperate dissatisfaction, becomes laced with symbolic violence: 'they're just horrible, horrible, horrible people'. Searching for ways to further articulate the difference, she explains: 'They're all like really like born-and-bred like Bristolian.' Her father challenges her on this, more on a point of logic than anything else, by interjecting that she and her school-friends were born and bred in Bristol:

DAUGHTER: Yeah, but they're not in the same way.
MR MICHAELS: But you are.
DAUGHTER: Not in the same way.
MR MICHAELS: You were born in Bristol.
DAUGHTER: I can't describe it. I don't know. I don't know how to say it without sounding really, like, snobby.

Such is the logic of practical sense: she knows she is not 'the same' as the others she lives amongst but struggles for a means to articulate that which is not usually articulated, latching onto being 'born and bred in Bristol' perhaps as an imperfect proxy for local accent and, therefore, class. When her parents are asked if they feel they have much in common with the people they live amongst, they reply in the negative (and recount their horror at hearing racist comments from neighbours), prompting their daughter to triumphantly retort – now mobilising an intuition of the space of foods and its homologies to convey her point, and an assumption of her superiority within it – 'Exactly, because they'd never have like a casual piece of Roquefort in their fridge and stuff like that, would they, or a casual avocado.' Her father finishes by stating there are a few families 'similar to us' who live in some of the streets, but his daughter adds, to his agreement, that 'they're just dotted around', like oh-so-rare oases of 'good taste' in a mire of perceived vulgarity.

If current location is vilified by these fishes out of water on account of its class composition, then other locations within the city, housing those perceived to be more 'like them' or higher in the social space than them (who, given the current misrecognition order, they aspire to be like), are idealised to greater and lesser degrees, presented to consciousness as places they would like to live in but know are unattainable, places they intend to live in one day, or places they have lived in (particularly before children put a strain on finances) and dream of returning to. Mr Buchanan, for example, when asked about places he might like to live in the city, recalls the days when he used to live in St Andrew's, which sits between Redland and Ashley, and says 'It'd be lovely to live in Redland or St Andrew's.' His wife adds: 'Cotham would be nice. Big house, massive garden.' But an awareness of limits, a sense of the feasible attuned to their intermediate social location, kicks in:

MRS BUCHANAN: Well, yeah, if we had loads of money and money wasn't an issue, I suppose. If we could share a lovely house and we could afford it and it was money's no object, then yeah.

MR BUCHANAN: If I had half a million pounds. Yep.
MRS BUCHANAN: Possibly, yeah.

But then they close with what seems to be a *call to order*, a bringing of oneself back to one's place in the world, thus revealing a libido somewhat different from that of the typical residents of these irenic areas and an effort to turn what one has into what one wants, needs, and desires:

MRS BUCHANAN: It's not a driving thing, is it? Not really driven, are we, by making loads of money or anything.
MR BUCHANAN: No, got a house. It's big enough for us. There's no reason to go and get a bigger house.

However, when it comes to dreams of return no one seems to be quite so desperate, or so literal, as Ms Kent, currently living not in Lockleaze but in an area just down the road, Fishponds, which fairs marginally better on the usual deprivation indices.[8] Ms Kent appears to originate from a family located toward the economic pole of the intermediate class: her father was a supervisor of manual work, while her mother managed a launderette. It was, in fact, the launderette job which landed them in their place of residence, Redland, as the family occupied the flat above it when Ms Kent was growing up; and so, despite their less comfortable economic situation relative to their neighbours' and their divergent modes of mastery of the world, they found themselves in one of the more exclusive areas of Bristol, shopping in its shops, walking its streets constantly, mixing with its residents and, in Ms Kent's case, attending the nearby school. Such was the social discordance that Ms Kent was always haunted by a gnawing sense that she was 'not good enough to be there' and forever 'embarrassed about where I came from' (in terms of social space location), finding it difficult to make friends and staying 'lonely' as a result. Yet now that she lives in Fishponds, due to a combination of economic necessity and social capital (they bought her partner's brother's house because it was cheap), that past, and all that she used to know, is cast in a different light. A misfit in her place of origin on account of class differences she may have been, but now she feels like a misfit all over again. 'After growing up in Redland,' she says, 'I really, really didn't like it over here,' whether in terms of housing style, shops or (with her children and social reproduction in mind) schools:

MS KENT: I don't know, it's just…I don't like how most of the houses look, I don't like the shops, I don't like the cafés. For example, the vegetable shop, you won't find basil or something like that in it; it's just tomatoes, potatoes and cucumber – it's like really nothing slightly interesting, really. The bread shop, you know, you won't get olive bread or something, which I used to go up Gloucester Road [in Redland] and get the olive bread or something else like that, and it's just….it's got no character to it, really. So no, don't really like it here. […] The senior schools are awful, so that's a….
Q: Senior schools are awful?
MS KENT: Yeah.

Overall the area is, she says, 'not really me', and while the current disjunction between her social location and spatial location is part of that – having gained a degree in education later in life (though she does not use it in her work) she is a little unlike most of the Fishpond residents anyway – the ill-fit is exacerbated by the original disjunction between her social location and spatial location. She had, quite simply, *come to take for granted the dominant-class tastes, practices and orientations which had always been around her,* i.e. part of the texture of her routine lifeworld, even if her orientation toward them was always slightly different from everyone else's in some way (seeing bread in the bakery as less affordable, for example), and, being surrounded by people espousing and assuming these tastes and lacking many real-life models for other forms of recognition, she imbibed to a greater extent the sense that these were worthy, desirable, normal or 'natural' modes of being – a form of embodied social capital, perhaps – and thus fell prey to a mismatch between objective probabilities and subjective expectations. So difficult, in fact, was the enforced transmutation of her lifeworld upon relocation that, like the Michaels' daughter, she initially found herself pacing trails to and from Redland for her bread and other groceries as a means to hold onto the old and ameliorate the new, but the movement between domains proved unsettling:

> It annoys me that where I grew up I can't afford to live now, and that upsets me. You know, you think…you go over to Redland and Clifton, which is where I grew up, I'd go and play around there, and you think, 'Who are these people? This is where I was born, where I grew up, and you're in the house that I grew up in and I can't afford it, but you're there.' So I do find that a bit sad, really.

With time, however, the subjective field of possibles has begun to realign with the field of objective possibilities, and the initial shock and despair has given way to general discontent:

> But yeah, I do feel that now, like I said about getting my head around things, I have got my head around the fact that, yes, we are going to stay here, we can't afford to move, we're never going to afford to move anywhere else […].

Even though she is trying now to 'make the most of it', she adds: 'Do you know what, when I dream, I dream that I'm back in the launderette. Yeah, that's probably…. I never dream about [Fishponds]. I've had a couple. But yeah, I think I still feel more rooted over there, you know.' The Freudian discourse in which a 'dream is the (disguised) fulfilment of a (repressed) wish' (Freud, 1924: 28) may well construe the Redland launderette as a cipher for some kind of family romance, but we might instead simply take it as evidence of the deep sedimentation of the earliest experiences and the fact that Redland will always be carried within Ms Kent, framing all subsequent experience and judgements no matter where she goes and no matter how long she lives distant from it.

Redland: battleground of the dominant class

So what of this neighbourhood of dreams and desires? Redland is an old housing area, having nineteenth-century origins, and, as is apparent from the size and splendour of its buildings and streets, was built not for dockers and factory hands but merchants and professionals. Much of its housing stock, centred around imposing architectural landmarks like Redland Court (now an independent girls' school), comprises rather grand detached, semi-detached and terraced houses built in local grey rubble-stone with limestone details, some of which are Grade II or Grade II★ listed.[9] Many of these villas are large enough to have been partitioned into multiple flats still commanding relatively exclusive prices, sometimes filled with well-heeled students, but the majority of homes are complete houses. The streets themselves are generally spacious and leafy, some perfectly straight and others more meandering, but there are no bleak grassy spaces plonked in the middle of avenues here, only a speckle of picturesque and often busy parks and woods (40 per cent of residents say they visit such green spaces at least once a week) with huge mature trees formed around natural features of the landscape. Local amenities include public tennis courts (meeting a demand, no doubt, but then providing a specific *enablement* for practice), a health club, bowling clubs and, toward Henleaze (its even more expensive northern neighbour), a small cinema, while clusters of independent shops and cafés are dotted here and there to save people having to travel too far for their goods and services. The bulk of shopping is provided, however, by the long and bustling Gloucester Road. This thoroughfare marks the western boundary of Redland, beyond which lie St Andrew's and then Ashley (each a successive perceptible notch down in exclusivity and grandeur), and teems with independent stores, cafés, restaurants of varying nationality, delicatessens, artisan bakers, greengrocers, bars and bookshops as well as a few supermarkets and charity outlets, at least until it stretches beyond Redland, northwards and southwards, where it starts to become a little more rundown.

The area is well connected to the city centre by local train services, but it also sits close enough to the core for many key employers of the dominant class – not least the University of Bristol – to be within easy cycling or walking distance. Hence the high proportion of Redland residents reporting their routine journey to work to be by bicycle or on foot (13 per cent and 25 per cent respectively), neatly facilitating any environmental concern or desire to 'keep active and healthy' (Mr Tanner) they may have. As to the inhabitants of Redland themselves, other than being very wealthy and highly educated, they are predominantly white British, and what ethnic minorities there are tend to fall into the 'other white' category, made up particularly of Irish, German and 'other EU' nationals with a little money taking advantage of the accessibility of the city centre and employment or educational opportunities. Moreover, while doubtless many living in Redland were born and raised there or nearby, and saw no need to move too far away in adulthood since their capital possession and their capital-accumulating projects plug snugly into the local landscape, the area draws in an endless stream of newcomers from across Britain pursuing educational and employment strategies and thus boasts a variety of accents and experiences among its residents. Unlike the longer-term Lockleaze inhabitants, these appear to be people for whom staying within the area of their birth and youth was never an option, principally because of more or less early commitment to studying at university. This is a venture of capital accrual which, for those with the distance from necessity to consider perceived position within the field of educational establishments above all else, usually obliges geographical mobility, thus inscribing it into perception of the time to come and thence generating an assumption post-graduation that, to use Schutz's phrase, 'I can do it again', i.e. relocate, this time to wherever desired jobs are available.[10] Mr and Mrs Williams, he originally from Hampshire and the son of a sales manager and a clerk, she from Belfast and the daughter of an academic and a nurse, express this most clearly of all. For his part, he 'always considered that I wouldn't live in the area that I was brought up in', that 'I wanted to move on, there was more to see out there', and feels that

> it was the move away to university, and then that sort of opens up your horizons; and then, I think, if you have that move and you meet people from all over the

country and that sort of…yeah, that's a good stepping-stone for your sort of desires and aspirations to be more mobile.

His wife, meanwhile, adds that

It never felt a problem to me to go off. No one else in my family had sort of gone off overseas, but nobody had stayed in Northern Ireland; everyone had been sort of edu-…everyone went to university over in England. So maybe in that respect it kind of opened the doors for me.

She continues: 'I was never brought up with the idea that I was going to live down the road from my parents', with university and the move it entailed all being 'very accessible to me, I just felt like I could'. In other words, significant geographical mobility was always inscribed in her perception of the future as probable, and her sense of achievable reach encompassed the British Isles at least, since it was co-given with the assumption, built up through experiences within a familial microcosm rich in cultural capital and rich enough in economic capital, that university attendance was normal and desirable. Yet, while Redland is the new resting place of the Williams family and others like them, the new spatial bounds and experiential texture of their lifeworlds through which their paths weave, far from universally professing a desire to quickly 'move on' once again in pursuit of more pay, better jobs etc. – some did, admittedly, conceive a move in the future as possible if the circumstances were right – they often envisage themselves now staying put, berthed for the long run, their motility curtailed above all by commitment to children's schooling (cf. Savage *et al.*, 2005).

On top of all this, and in direct contrast to Lockleaze, levels of obesity and smoking in Redland are well down on the city average, while just 7 per cent of people feel their life to be affected by the fear of crime and only 12 per cent believe anti-social behaviour to be a problem in their area – compare those figures with those from Lockleaze cited earlier. There is, therefore, a very different experiential environment here – a sense of security, of safety, of trust, of distance from the social ills reported in the news and proximity to the events and opportunities of Bristol's centre – and no doubt a somewhat divergent sense of what is normal or typical. *In nuce*, Redland is an area of the (white) dominant class, and if one happens to have come to live there from elsewhere in the country, and to have one's lifeworld now largely confined to it, as Mrs Williams has and does, one could, like her, make the claim that Bristol 'is not very culturally diverse' – an effect of *allodoxia*, conflating the city itself with the city as one experiences it, since it would take only a relatively short walk, but a radical departure from one's routine world, to find a plethora of cultural influences.

Like anywhere, though, Redland is hardly hermetically sealed off from other classes, and not just because Gloucester Road attracts an assortment of *habitués* from neighbouring areas. People pass through, people work in its corner shops, people live in its cheaper periphery and sometimes particular strategies spearheaded by local powers can throw the socially distant into geographical proximity. In all cases, however, the sense of displeasure or even disgust at repeated encounters with (or stories about) the select few in the locale from the lower echelons of social space is palpable. Mr Williams, for example, describes going to his local grocery shop as 'grim' for no other reason than he dislikes the woman who works on the till there. 'She is,' he says, 'without being too judgemental of somebody's appearance' – a qualification soon to be well and truly buried – 'her appearance is absolutely dreadful. She's enormous, with really big greasy hair and just the most unfriendly approach. And for someone who's in sales you just think, "Come on love, really?"'. Having a large frame is not normal or commonplace in this part of town, but noteworthy and unsightly, and the sight of someone not having spent time and money on their appearance for work is shocking and repulsive. Or again, Mr Yates was horrified when a bail hostel opened up near his street, bringing with it people and practices deemed not just objectionable but, unlike in Lockleaze, *out of place* – raising the question if, following Mary Douglas' famous definition of dirt as matter out of place, these people are equivalent to dirt for the Redlanders – and, therefore, to be cut out as quickly as possible by concerted mobilisation:

> We were forever getting cars' wing-mirrors kicked off, and a couple of incidents where I had a bit of a row in the road because I saw people doing stuff, and it got a bit nasty and we got burgled when it was all happening. So it was, it sounds classic 'not in our back yard', but it turned the area really sour a bit, so we kind of got onto the landlords and got it, um, moved. If you can't control it, then can't have it, so. But there was stuff happening all the time and it was coming from the people in there.

For the most part, however, class differences and class struggles within Redland are rather more localised in social space. It may well be a more or less homogenously dominant-class territory, though not without some from the intermediate class clustered in certain zones, but because of its particular geographical and architectural features – its large and expensive houses and its proximity to the University of Bristol – it brings into close proximity the opposing *fractions* of the dominant class, with their divergent orientations and practices, and the latter become the salient points of comparison and contrast in everyday existence. With the primary axis of social difference more or less neutralised by spatial clustering, in other words, the second dimension, i.e. the greater or lesser possession of cultural capital relative to economic capital, comes to the fore of experience in one way or another.

So, on the one hand, there are those who, being further toward the cultural pole of the dominant class, react against the ethos and lifestyle of those further toward the economic pole. A diabolised image of *laissez-faire* parenting, producing rude and boisterous children, comes in for particular scorn, though often wrapped up with distaste for other symbols of social position. Mrs Yates, for example, says: 'I think being a fairly sort of middle-class area, I get quite irritated sometimes when I see some of the children, the way they talk to their parents, and their parents just put up with it. I think *there's a lot of people living round here who have got more money than time*' – she halts for fear that her 'judgements' may leak out, but when reassured of the confidentiality of the interview she continues – 'Yeah, I think there's a lot of children with really bad attitudes. And I see some of the boys' friends, who are nice kids but they talk to us as if *they're looking down their noses at us*. And I just think that's really shocking' (emphasis added). The Newcombe/Oliver family, moreover, sensing that Redland is maybe a little more 'upmarket' than they would like (they bought a house there with inheritance money, but feel they need to economise on heating it) and lamenting the paucity of fellow Labour supporters nearby (tapping into the homologies between class, place and politics), comment to the researcher during a family excursion to a café on Gloucester Road (which they nevertheless see as 'less pretentious' than Redland as a whole):

MR NEWCOMBE: Just a word about where we're going. There are loads and loads of cafés and this is one of the more sort of stuffy and middle-class ones. It happens to have a very nice ambience which – and nice coffee and nice cakes and stuff – but we don't feel at home with the typical people that use it. But the café that they use, the coffee isn't so nice.

MS OLIVER: [correcting Mr Newcombe] The cafés that they don't use, yeah.

MR NEWCOMBE: Yeah. So we, we keep trying to experiment with other places that we find more homely in, but it is the quality of the taste of the coffee and the food that we like.

MS OLIVER: Yeah, and it is nice decor, it is a nice café.

MR NEWCOMBE: You should see it if you're not going to stay.

Q: Oh no I'll come in, definitely. I don't think I should run off.

MR NEWCOMBE: Well, let's see who's around. They're slightly pushy, the conversations about, you know, where they're going on holiday or what they've ordered or bought.

MS OLIVER: Well, for me it's also, it just feels a bit self-satisfied, whatever I mean by that.

DAUGHTER: And they let the children run wild.

Notice how, just like Mrs Yates, Mr Newcombe uses the label 'middle-class' to refer to a set of people whose practices would indicate a placement toward the specifically *economic* pole of the dominant class, bracketing them off as 'not like us' (they 'don't feel at home' with them), despite their obvious privileges (their postgraduate qualifications in social sciences) and shared taste for 'quality' coffee. Notice also that the term 'pushy' is being deployed here to refer particularly to the perceived conspicuous consumption corresponding with the top-right section of social space. Conversely, continuing their conversation and after digs at prosperous 'kept women' and their 'consumer talk', the parenting they often witness comes under fire for being, in their eyes, anything but pushy:

MR NEWCOMBE: On a weekday morning at about 9.15 it's [the café] full of kept women who have dropped off their kids.

SON: The kids have gone to school, yeah.

MR NEWCOMBE: Coming down here, talking consumer talk or holidays. [...]

MS OLIVER: [A friend] and I were in here one day and there was a bloke sitting there, having a nice chat with a bloke sitting here, the whole time on his mobile phone while his toddler got more and more frustrated, louder and louder screaming, and the more that she was screaming for attention, the more he was, was [inaudible] so he could have a decent conversation and she was being neglected. And [my friend] and I were getting more and more irritated by his neglectful parenting.

Of course, we have no way of knowing where the flesh-and-blood targets of these contemptuous remarks are actually sited in social space, but they are all nevertheless taken together in this narrative as part of the same phenomenon: as emblematic of the typical, anonymous 'middle-class' Redland resident, who is, in this family's eyes, leading a less desirable and justifiable life. The necessary implication, even if they would not say it so openly, is that the Newcombe/Oliver family think their orientation worthy of greater recognition, that one should be more attentive to children's demands, nurture them, teach them 'manners' and humility and so forth.

On the other hand, those Redlanders positioned closer toward the economic extremity of social space, or in possession of less cultural capital at any rate, see things differently. In a remarkable reversal of values, the parenting practices of those richer in cultural capital, focussed on the transmission of their primary capital and the reproduction of social position through schooling, can be painted as overbearing or – to mirror the accusation slung at them regarding their own conspicuous consumption – 'pushy'. Mr Richards, for example, notes that Redland

> is a bit of a professional get-up…you know, I was going to say professional and managerial, but it's not even that. I think I'm about the only person up here who works in industry; I think everybody else is a professional of some kind.

His wife adds, in relation to their children's schooling (and despite the fact their children do an abundance of extracurricular activities):

> Because I don't think we're pushy parents. You know, a lot of parents round here are very pushy. Well, we try very much with the kids as well to make them do… because this area of Bristol is very pushy. There are a lot of very, very pushy parents, especially on the academic side.

Moreover, inverting Mrs Yates' sense of being looked down on by wealthy neighbourhood children, those with less cultural capital can come to feel, to use Mr Daniels' words, 'a bit inadequate and stupid' compared to their fellow residents. Elaborating on this, Mr Daniels and his wife – an engineer and primary school teacher respectively, and thus, while not devoid of cultural or technical capital, holding less than the archetypal local – typify the people on their street:

MR DANIELS: Yeah, lots of doctors.
MRS DANIELS: Lots of people from the University.
Q: What was your comment about that? [referring to something said during one of the observations]
MR DANIELS: Can't remember.
Q: You said 'a bit intimidating' or something.
MR DANIELS: Yeah, I feel a little bit intimated. When street-party time comes, because there's so many kinds of professional people here, you know. And there are a couple of very academic types, aren't there, two doors up, [neighbours] a, I didn't realise he's a professor, someone said he's a professor. Lectures in UWE [University of West of England], I think. There's another one a few doors up.
MRS DANIELS: There's a scientific author as well.
MR DANIELS: There's a scientific author, I mentioned before. There's a lot of very clever people on the street here.

In this case vertical as well as horizontal difference (especially in relation to Mr Daniels) comes into play and the principle of intimidation – and thus domination – is the very nub of cultural capital rather than one of its numerous lifestyle manifestations: symbolic mastery.

For all the local symbolic struggles, however, Redland residents tend to maintain they are 'lucky', 'blessed', 'fortunate' or 'privileged' to live in the area, extol its amenities and shops (which they visit often) and even, where their street and their interactions have cemented a sense of social similarity rather than difference – perhaps because of objective proximity with consociates, or because events and interests focussed on shared dispositions among the dominant class rather than divergent ones have prevailed – report a sense of 'community' and 'fit'. Ms James, for example, seems, on account of her and her children's specific networks of association, oblivious to the laissez-faire versus pushy parenting divide picked up by others and instead senses only that

> there are a lot of like-minded parents to us around making sure the school stays on its toes in terms of what it does and the way it does things. And a lot of their friends are involved in taking learning seriously, and their parents make sure they understand that, and to some degree the girls [Ms James' twin daughters], just by osmosis, get that message.

This does not, however, stop some denizens from *still dreaming of living elsewhere*, like the ill-fitting Lockleaze residents idealising Redland. For some – particularly those possessing and being more inclined toward accumulation of economic capital – this takes the form of fantasies of inhabiting the most affluent mansion-lined streets in Bristol, such as Grange Park in Henleaze for the Tanner/Upson family, or Sneyd Park in Stoke Bishop for the Patricks, or even just the most luxurious streets of Redland for Mr Allen, and is testament to the fact that what one has can be so easily taken for granted and that, given the nature of the misrecognition order in contemporary capitalist society, no matter where one is one can desire to be higher than one is, to accrue more economic capital and to access the goods and spaces associated with it. Symbolic capital ensures relative deprivation often persists right up to the apex of social space, in other words, and even there one can yearn to widen the distance from others. However, where cultural capital – symbolic mastery of the world and the forms of culture, cuisine and so on it inclines one toward – is the primary possession and principal desire, a different reverie can take hold. Certainly this is the case for the Newcombe/Oliver family, who we know feel a little ill at ease about Redland on account of their opposition to the ever-present trappings of economic capital: they claim, intuiting a homology between their social location and physical location, that one place that would have been 'more to our liking', as 'the ambience suits us better', is Bedminster. To make full sense of that assertion, however, we now need to bring into focus the final area under investigation.

Southville and Bedminster: the friction of social tectonics

Southville and Bedminster sit on the southern bank of the River Avon, to the west of Bristol and close to the city centre. Today, insofar as there are no natural or human-made boundaries or barriers between them, they appear to run into one another seamlessly, Southville to the west and north, Bedminster to the east and south, separated only on paper by official boundaries drawn out on maps and in people's minds according to their schemes of perception. Yet this classification of space, and the relational comparisons inhering in it, is rooted in a series of historical developments. For a long time Bedminster existed as a village outside of Bristol proper, while Southville started life as a small collection of large villas facing Clifton. Industrialisation, however, transformed the former into a sprawling and unsanitary Victorian slum for dockers, miners, labourers and their families not unlike those chronicled by Engels (1892/1987) in Manchester, eventually reaching and enveloping the larger abodes known as Southville. Then, in the twentieth century, Bedminster was subject to a slum-clearance programme that etched a long-lasting social fissure into the urban landscape. While the most squalid properties were bulldozed and their inhabitants shipped out to the freshly built Hartcliffe and Knowle estates (Lockleaze equivalents south of the river) or rehoused in new tower blocks piercing the sky where slums once stood, the tidier and sturdier housing to the north and west remained.

Toward the close of the century, as Clifton, Redland and their like became too expensive for the mounting numbers of increasingly educated and relatively affluent families populating or moving to the city, the north-western area known as Southville began to rapidly gentrify, at first primarily drawing those flush in cultural rather than economic capital, attracted by the modest prices attached to spacious period-architecture houses and proximity to the city centre, but then, as they began to remould the area, those rich in economic capital too (Bridge, 2003). Older and poorer inhabitants died off or moved out, their terraces were snapped up and renovated to match the tastes of their purchasers, the vestiges of industry were transformed into theatres and bars and North Street, the main through road of Southville, has come to boast a collection of neat delicatessens, artisan butchers and bakers and cosmopolitan cafés and restaurants reminiscent of Gloucester Road. Bedminster, meanwhile, stagnated in the face of disinvestment, and its main avenue of consumerism, East Street, teems with low-price chain stores, thrift shops, budget eateries, battered amusement arcades and boarded-up properties. Since East Street is at the terminus of North Street, this yields a jarring shift in the character of experience – a shift from the symbols of one section of social space predominating to those of another fairly far removed preponderating – within a short geographical distance and, therefore, ample material for drawing symbolic boundaries and casting judgements. To give just one instance, Ms Barnes, from her vantage point in the heart of Southville, asserts:

> Bedminster is a different prospect, really. I mean, you go quarter of a mile down the road and it starts getting a bit shabby and shopfronts have closed and you see people pushing [baby] buggies holding a can of lager and a fag in one hand, and everyone's so much younger. Like the average age around here of having children is probably about 34, 35. Down there it's probably about 22 […]. I suppose it's a bit snobby, but I'd much rather be here than in Bedminster.

A number of binaries homologous with the social and symbolic spaces, as viewed from a particular point of view within those spaces, are present here – shabby/not shabby, young parents/older parents, bad parents/good parents, vulgar/tasteful, unworthy/worthy – but they have been accreted through experience of, and have thus come to be ineluctably co-given with, the *local* perceptual binary of Bedminster/Southville.

Yet the patterning of people and their time-space paths between the two patches of turf is far from absolute. To be sure, the gentrifiers of Southville, or 'urban colonialists' to adapt Atkinson and Bridge's (2005) provocative appellation, tend to stick to a circumscribed territory and, knowing what is 'for the likes of us' and what is 'not for the likes of us', frequent only the revamped eateries and outlets nearby and consistently avoid those with a contrasting aesthetic and clientele (cf. Atkinson, 2006; Watt, 2009). On a routine walk around the area, for example, Mr Quinn lauds a nearby pub on the harbourside he uses often, The Pump House, with its shiny decor and 'family-friendly' approach, yet when asked whether he ever uses a weathered-looking pub nearer Bedminster he gives a blunt 'No, never', indicating a distinct symbolic-spatial-practice boundary. Likewise Mr Anderson extols a pub near the terminus of North Street as a 'nice pub' but describes another, just metres away and within the line of sight of the first tavern yet standing at the end of East Street and thus just within Bedminster's perceived boundaries, as a 'scary pub' not to be entered. Yet there are still significant pockets and fringes of the geographical space known as Southville where those possessing less sym-bolic capital than the typical inhabitant continue to dwell, either because they bought (well or just) before house prices rocketed following gentrification or as renters, and members of the dominated class residing in the heart of Bedminster pass through North Street and other Southville thoroughfares regularly. Hence the Southville ward reports higher levels of the kind of practices and problems typically associated with deprivation than somewhere like Redland, though obviously much lower than Bedminster: 26 per cent of Southvillians believe anti-social behaviour to be a problem in their area (36 in Bedminster), 18 per cent say their daily life is blighted by the fear of crime (28 per cent in Bedminster), 82 per cent believe litter is a problem (compared with a city average of 76 per cent), 63 per cent believe graffiti is a problem (again compared to a city average of 42 per cent), 39 per cent of the population are overweight (though that is still con-siderably less than the 62 per cent of Bedminster), and so on.

Many of the residents we spoke to, while evidently thankful that the gentrification they spearheaded (described as 'clearing up' or 'tidying up', again recalling the dirt analogy) has pushed 'nutters', 'idiots' and 'drunks' further from the routine pathways of their everyday lifeworlds, also describe the area as still 'rough around the edges' for this reason and report mild fear of or distaste at 'incidents', 'druggies' or 'youth' in the parks and shops, graffiti on the walls or behaviour deemed transgressive in one way or another (Mr Anderson, for example, says he 'almost fell off my bike' when a young girl he was cycling past told him unceremoniously to 'fuck off'). We might say, developing the famous analogy of Robson and Butler (2001), that if social-spatial rela-tions are indeed to be likened to the subduction of the Earth's tectonic plates, this is not only because it captures the practical segregation of geographically proximate but socially distant human beings, as the two London analysts have it, but also because it encapsulates the niggling friction and potential eruptions when the residents of two adjoining areas populated by divergent zones of social space regularly bump and chafe against one another – frictions which, it seems, furnish a sense among at least some Southville inhabitants that they are not quite like Redlanders, who they describe as 'higher-ups' and 'snooty' compared to the 'down-to-earth' 'middle-class profession-als' of Southville (Mrs Quinn), or as the privileged party in the saying 'how the other half live' (Ms Evans), despite the fact that their particular capital holdings and typical occupations *are no different* from those prevailing in Redland. This, perhaps, puts the Newcombe/Oliver family's earlier comments on their sense of fit in context: having previously lived in an area in Worcester that was 'very mixed' – a ring of fire, perhaps, just like Southville and Bedminster – they feel more at home with daily encounters with the dominated than the economic dominant, i.e. with those 'below' them socially than those above or adjacent, and the comforting sense of not being quite so dominant and 'closed-minded' that can yield.

There is, of course, another side to any story of gentrification: that of the people not only witnessing the steady transformation of elements of their lifeworlds to match the tastes of incoming others but increasingly feeling out of place and denigrated in their own neighbourhood – i.e. the dominated class (cf. Savage *et al.*, 2005; Paton, 2015). Take, for instance, the Lyon family, who live just to the south-west of North Street, within the official bounds of Southville but a part less characterised by large housing or colonised by the dominant than north of the thoroughfare, who have lived in or around the general area all their lives (Mr Lyon grew up in Hartcliffe, just to the south, and Mrs Lyon was raised in Bedminster) and who, with a little technical capital and a mod-est household income, are firmly situated within the dominated section of social space.

When taking the researcher along a regular time-space path up to North Street from the family home, Mr Lyon indicates a clear symbolic boundary homologous with the spatial organisation of his lifeworld. While his particular territory has, he claims, 'always been like a working-class area, it's always had, like, that's where its roots are', 'anything that side [i.e. to the north] of North Street, I mean, that's Southville. And there's obviously been a huge influx of, you know, like working but middle-class, you know, people'. In his eyes, then, 'working-class', *his* geographical area, *established* residents and, ultimately, himself are categorised together – within the horizons of one category of thought, that is, lie the others – and are done ineluctably in contrast to 'middle-class' (albeit 'working-middle-class'), *their* area (he even distances himself from the label 'Southville') the *newcomers* (or we might say 'outsiders', to use the terms of Elias and Scotson, 1990) and, ultimately, 'them'.

When it comes to the mutation of the high street's physiognomy, this 'di-vision' per-vades experience and leaves a somewhat bitter taste in his and his wife's mouths. On the one hand, they readily use and 'appreciate' the new shops and facilities that have sprung up to serve the needs of those rich in cultural capital – such is the nature of symbolic capital: the trappings of the dominant are perceived as 'better' or an 'improvement', at least amongst sections of the dominated who, like the Lyons, are not totally excluded from accessing them. Hence Mr Lyon says they like to frequent the delicatessens and fishmongers ('love the stuff'), to 'chill out' in the coffee shops and renovated gastro-pubs, to see the local art hanging in the Tobacco Factory café and to visit the Sunday market in its car park where fresh-baked bread, locally made chutneys and cooked dishes from various national cuisines are on offer. And yet the whole experience is laced with a vague, difficult-to-articulate sense of not fitting, of it all being tailored to the tastes of others not like them and of being looked down upon by the usual patrons. The art in the café is, to his mind, 'a bit pretentious, I won't lie', the delicatessen is marred by 'a little bit of pretention' as the owners are 'catering to a market where there is a lot of pretention around', there are 'too many' coffee shops in the vicinity and he and his wife find the market 'too cliquey'. He expands upon the last comment, spontaneously framing it with the discourse of 'class':

MR LYON: It's like, how can I put it, there is an air of snobbery about the whole thing. I mean, I don't know whether that's just because I'm a working-class kid, but obviously most of my customers are all middle-class, I mean working-middle-class people; but sometimes, I don't know, I get the impression that – it's probably just me, but I get the impression that sometimes there is an air of, I don't know really what the word is for it, like a slight feel – I'm not explaining myself very well at all.

Q: It's all right, carry on.

MR LYON: So yeah, I think [Mrs Lyon] just basically – I like it because I just like that general going-to-the-market type feel, you know, and I think [Mrs Lyon] thinks it's a little bit, yeah, a little bit snobby.

In short, the family feel out of place in their place of everyday activity, not because they believe themselves to be in some way 'better' than those around them, as with the people we spoke to from Lockleaze, but because they feel themselves being looked down upon – and increasingly so, we might posit, given the area's direction of travel.

It would be wrong, however, to think that gentrification is always and every-where a two-bloc struggle and that there are, therefore, only ever two views on the gentrification of an area (cf. Blokland, 2012). The patterning of social space over geographical space is more complex than that, not least because members of all sorts of other class fractions are dotted about here and there within the transitional zone and experience its transformation through the particular lens provided by their specific position. This is most evident, perhaps, among those falling closer to the intermediate zone of social space, whose perception of local change and struggle is framed by their peculiar position 'in the middle', or among those with a statistically less-typical trajectory who may see both sides. Amongst families we talked to, the Kings seem to fall into this mould somewhat: both working in finance, they have a sizeable household income but fairly low stocks of cultural capital and, especially, inherited capital, having travelled through social space from the dominated class (all parents and grandparents were manual workers with little formal education). They therefore earn a lot more than the typical dominated resident of the area (the Lyon family, for example), but their paucity of valued cultural resources, and the tastes this generates (swimming, football, sport in general, television-watching, pubs, rock and pop music but with a little popular classical and jazz), sets them apart from the typical incomer. On top of that, their experience is compounded by the fact that while neither was *born* in the area – Mr King started life in Birkenhead and Mrs King in Saltford – they both moved to the Southville/Bedminster area when fairly young and were *bred* in it.

All this conspires to give the Kings a very particular viewpoint on the mutation of Southville over recent years, one in which they perceive two major sides of the struggle and fully identify with neither. Mr King, while taking the researcher through the streets near his house, describes it in terms of a divide between 'younger, trendier people' who have 'moved in' and 'what I call old South Bristol people'. It is hard to judge whether age is being fully grafted onto this perceptual division or just length of residence, but the former are, in Mr King's mind, associated with 'handmade posh bread' from the bakers on North Street, 'organic this, organic that' in the delicatessen, Asian restaurants and cultural venues which 'ten years ago you would never have dreamt that it would be here, really,' and a certain domestic aesthetic – Mr King recounts once walking down his street on an evening, seeing through the windows of newcomers' houses, noting all the stripped wooden floors and Ikea furniture and thinking, 'Blimey, this road has really changed.' The 'old South Bristol' folks, on the other hand, are characterised by their 'pretty simple views' and being 'fairly crude in their language', with Mr King recalling their numerous clashes with incomers having late-night house-warming parties proving a 'shock' for those buying into the area. Clearly, from the way Mr King talks about the two antagonists and their tastes and how he sees himself (as 'kind of in between'), he distances himself from both, and his overall evaluation of the changing face of Southville is rather ambivalent: he does describe it as a 'regeneration', seems to appreciate that it is a little more 'culturally diverse' in its cuisine offerings and is happy that his house value has risen, yet he bemoans how 'bloomin' expensive' the new shops are, laments the disappearance of the skittle club and local pubs (where 'there might be a pie-warmer and a packet of crisps and a packet of pork scratching' rather than the detailed menus of the new gastro-pubs) as 'sad' and describes the growing preponderance of Ikea-outfitted homes as 'scary'.

A similar point of view is articulated by Ms Floyd, though from a social location slightly richer in cultural capital and poorer in economic capital than the Kings' – she is a degree-educated former teacher of English as a foreign language currently doing bar work, her partner is a design technician and they have a household income of around £32,000 per annum – and a perceptual-geographical position situated more thoroughly within Bedminster. She uses more abstract terms to depict the major schism south of the Avon, distinguishing the 'working-class' from the 'middle-class' newcomer and situating herself somewhere 'in between', yet the tear she evidently feels between the two warring orientations is harder to articulate and comes out in oscillatory and sometimes contradictory affiliations and disaffiliations. On the one hand she is drawn toward elements of the transfigured Southville and North Street, describing it in positive terms as 'thriving now', having 'come up', 'fantastic' and full of 'lovely shops' and venues (delicatessens, organic butchers, the theatre) which she travels through the streets of Bedminster to get to (bypassing East Street and other avenues which she sees as 'a bit horrible'), yet, on the other hand, she exalts Bedminster's 'salt of the earth' feel and its 'familiarity' (she was brought up not far away). Conversely, on the one hand:

> There's like the really middle-class, really middle-class mums, that I feel like I probably don't relate to – their values are very different. 'Oh, my darling son' and 'my darling this', and you hear them in the playground at [her child's school], erm…. 'my precious boy'. And they get very involved with school, with what the teacher's doing.

'Some of the newcomers', she says elsewhere, 'I get on well with. Some, we're worlds apart.' On the other hand, however, there are:

> A lot of sort of *Daily Mail* readers and racism. And a lot of sort of Union Jack flags, and you can tell it's a bit – and English flags painted on doorways and stuff. We're just at the cusp of where Bedminster gets a bit – I don't want to sound snobby – bit more up, with, sort of, you know – I'm being really, sound really stereotyping – the sort of more skin-heady, football fans.

She recounts two clashes with the latter: one, with a neighbour who was going to vote for the British National Party, to Ms Floyd's horror, and another at a town council meeting over the planned opening of a new chain supermarket (competition for all the local, 'environmentally friendly' delicatessens and shops favoured by those rich in cultural capital) in conjunction with a revamped football stadium in the area. Regarding the latter she says they had

> very different values that I would call quite right-wing myself. You know, they were more concerned about the football stadium than the environment. You know, more concerned about their football than the neighbourhood, the environment and…a lot of people thought.

So she does not feel she fits with the incoming 'middle classes' of Southville, those higher than her in social space, on account of modes of speech and childrearing, though she does share elements of their consumption tastes, and distances herself from the 'working class', those below her in social space, on the basis of political position-taking and pastimes, even if she vaunts a lack of airs and graces. 'I'm kind of an in-betweener,' she concludes, saying she probably feels most affinity with some long-time residents in western Southville, where the Kings hail from (they are 'on my wavelength', 'I can chat better' to them), before reflecting – as a pithy summation of some major themes in this chapter – 'It's so class–divided, actually, just in this neighbourhood.'

Dialectic and differentiation: conclusions on class and place

In this and the last chapter we have seen that the physical, geographical locus of lifeworlds, both in the nation and in a contemporary British city, corresponds to some extent with class – volume of capital most notably in the first case, but composition of capital too in the latter case. We have observed indications, however imperfect, that movements around and away from that locus, routinised and less routinised, are differentiated by social position, and that the means by which those movements are realised are dependent to some degree upon possession of economic capital, cultural capital and the ethos they generate. We have uncovered signs that the phenomenological sense of reach, of movement potential, is anchored in the conditions, projects and past experiences attaching in differing degrees of probability to different sections of the social space. And, finally, we have been witness to the effect of class differences, including final differences, in setting people against others residing in close proximity.

These relationships, however, represent not a one-way class determinism – not, as some Bourdieu-inspired studies (for all their many insights) seem to imply, a case of capital possession and class habitus pre-existing and simply driving one into and around certain ready-made locales and determining all interaction (e.g. Rosenlund, 2009; Jarness, 2013) – but, rather, a *dialectic* between social space and physical space (cf. Fogle, 2011; Bridge, 2013; Benson, 2014). Yes, etched in the horizons of any perception of space or potential movement is a sense of the possible and desirable as furnished by capital possession; but as other Bourdieusians specialising in urban studies have begun to broach (e.g. Butler and Robson, 2003; Savage *et al.*, 2005; Benson, 2014; Bacqué *et al.*, 2015), and as ecological psychologists and phenomenologists have indicated in their own limited ways for years, the spaces, objects and people populating lifeworlds – flowing through variegated spatiotemporal circuits of symbolic power generated by struggles and strategies within so many fields which those experiencing them are not necessarily situated in themselves – have their own specific effect on (class) habitus, practice and even position. Conditions of existence, for instance, are given their concrete form through the buildings, avenues and acquaintances encountered, and the perception of the possible and the desirable, the thinkable and the unthinkable and daily practice and projects are negotiated in dialogue with them. Domination can be written in redbrick or breezeblock, and privilege wrapped in rubble-stone or sandstone, but they will each instil *particular* complexes of associations within the minds and bodies of the perceivers; and while the differences and distances of social space and its various homologies provide the conditions of possibility of class sense, when, where and how that sense is activated – and thus the symbolic battles one must face on a routine basis, the nature of experience leaving its everlasting sediment in the habitus and the kinds of views and outlooks one develops – is shaped by the specific nature of the place in which one comes to live. Hence members of the dominant class in the North are more likely to see themselves as 'working-class', and the dominated in the South more likely to describe themselves as 'middle-class'. Hence a person possessing few resources but living among the dominant can develop a very particular sense of what is 'normal', even if they fail to match up to or attain it. Hence local struggles with socially distanced and denigrated others can spur specific mobilities, be they the circumscription of routinised circuits or specific strategies of 'escape', whether short-term or permanent. Yet there is still one more layer of spatial experience and practice to explore – one which, being a prime site for not only the display, formation and clash of class tastes and ethos but, for many, the relatively autonomous, yet still entwined, struggles for recognition constituting (part of) a familial field, showcases the multiple determinations of the lifeworld: domestic space.

Notes

1 All figures cited in this chapter are drawn from the Bristol City Council's repository of area statistics for the year 2014 at www.bristol.gov.uk/page/council-and-democracy/ neighbourhood-partnership-statistical-profiles.

2 Acorn is a method of classifying areas on the basis of selected demographic features and consumption behaviours of typical residents. Being a profit-led, market-research-oriented approach rather than a tool of proper sociological construction, it is largely descriptive, limited in its choice of variables, homogenising and uninterested in power relations, so its findings always have to be used with caution.

3 Although, after our research had finished, Bristol City Council had committed itself to redeveloping some parts of Lockleaze by building affordable housing on waste ground and re-landscaping public spaces. It remains to be seen what the impact of that will be.

4 This is a small point of difference with Wacquant *et al.* (2014), who depict intra-class struggles and strategies as almost trivial and misguided defences against territorial stigmatisation rather than, more straightforwardly, products of geographical proximity to the socially distinct (at the level of class *fractions* if not *classes*). Labelling of the area, in other words, becomes the key causal mechanism of struggle rather than the interplay between the structural relations of social space and interactive relations of physical space – which is not to say that reactions to labelling have no compounding effect, of course, particularly in areas more infamous than Lockleaze.

5 This is a recasting of Merton's (1938) classic 'anomie theory', with the 'cultural goals' being understood as the predominant forms of recognition, or capital, imposed by the dominant class as legitimate and the 'institutionalised means' of attaining them the legitimated modes of reproduction, i.e. the education system, lawful business etc. (cf. McKenzie, 2012).

6 For readers not familiar with Anti-Social Behaviour Orders, these are legally binding behavioural orders applied to those deemed to have been indulging in 'anti-social behaviour', a notoriously capacious classification. Introduced by New Labour in 1998, they soon became known as ASBOs and a pejorative prefix ('ASBO kids/youth/area') reserved for those members of the dominated tending to turn toward, or perceived to be oriented toward, non-legitimated forms of recognition (low-level crime, violence, intimidation, etc.) as a means to attain worth.

7 Chiefly due to money: Mr and Mrs Michaels may be culturally rich but their combined gross income of £51,000 per annum is not enough to buy them into the area where their children go to school.

8 Her family was recruited through a school serving both areas.

9 The UK government's Department of Culture, Media and Sport, continuing the practice of its past equivalents, routinely places certain buildings deemed significant enough on a Statutory List of Buildings of Special Architectural or Historic Interest, graded by significance, which accords them special protections (e.g. they cannot be demolished or altered without special planning permission). Needless to say, this is itself an act of symbolic consecration produced by players within the local and national fields of power (especially the bureaucratic field) in tune with the interests and tastes of the dominant class.

10 To be more precise, the decision to relocate after university to a particular site for work is often shaped by a multitude of interacting forces pulling on the socialised libido, not least commitment to new-found or long-lasting amorous relationships, i.e. affective recognition.

References

Atkinson, R. (2006) 'Padding the Bunker: Strategies of Middle-Class Disaffiliation and Colonisation in the City' *Urban Studies*, 43(4): 819–32.

Atkinson, R. and Bridge, G. (2005) 'Introduction' in R. Atkinson and G. Bridge (eds.), *Gentrification in a Global Context: The New Urban Colonialism*. London: Routledge, pp. 1–17.

Bacqué, M.-H. *et al.* (2015) *The Middle Classes in the City*. Basingstoke: Palgrave Macmillan.

Benson, M. (2014) 'Trajectories of Middle-Class Belonging' *Urban Studies*, 51(14): 3097–112.

Blokland, T. (2012) 'Blaming Neither the Undeserving Poor Nor the Revanchist Middle Classes' *Urban Geography*, 33(4): 488–507.

Bridge, G. (2003) 'Time-space Trajectories in Provincial Gentrification' *Urban Studies*, 40(12): 2545–56.

Bridge, G. (2013) 'A Transactional Perspective on Space' *International Planning Studies*, 18(3–4): 304–20.

Butler, T. and Robson, G. (2003) *London Calling*. London: Berg.

Elias, N. and Scotson, J. (1990) *The Established and the Outsiders*. London: Sage.

Engels, F. (1892/1987) *The Condition of the Working Class in England*. London: Penguin.

Fogle, B. (2011) *The Spatial Logic of Social Struggle*. Lanham: Lexington Books.

Freud, S. (1924) 'An Autobiographical Study' in P. Gay (ed.) (1995) *The Freud Reader*. London: Vintage, pp. 3–41.

Jarness, V. (2013) *Class, Status, Closure: The Petropolis and Cultural Life*. Bergen: University of Bergen.

McKenzie, L. (2012) 'The Stigmatized and De-valued Working Class: The State of a Council Estate' in W. Atkinson, S. Roberts and M. Savage (eds.) *Class Inequality in Austerity Britain*. Basingstoke: Palgrave Macmillan, pp. 128–44.

Merton, R. (1938) 'Social Structure and Anomie' *American Sociological Review*, 3(5): 672–82.

Paton, K. (2015) *Gentrification: A Working-Class Perspective*. Farnham: Ashgate.

Reay, D. and Lucey, H. (2000) '"I Don't Really Like it Here but I Don't Want to Be Anywhere Else'" *Antipode*, 32(4): 410–28.

Robson, G. and Butler, T. (2001) 'Coming to Terms with London: Middle-Class Communities in a Global City' *International Journal of Urban and Regional Research*, 25(1): 70–86.

Rogaly, B. and Taylor, B. (2009) *Moving Histories of Class and Community*. Basingstoke: Palgrave Macmillan.

Rosenlund. L. (2009) *Exploring the City with Bourdieu*. Saarbrücken: VDM Verlag Dr Müller.

Savage, M., Bagnall, G. and Longhurst, B. (2005) *Globalization and Belonging*. London: Sage.

Schutz, A. (1970) *Reflections on the Problem of Relevance*. New Haven: Yale University Press.

Wacquant, L., Slater, T. and Periera, V. (2014) 'Territorial Stigmatization in Action' *Environment and Planning A*, 46: 1270–80.

Watt, P. (2009) 'Living in an Oasis: Middle-Class Disaffiliation and Selective Belonging in an English Suburb' *Environment and Planning A*, 41: 2874–92.

Young, M. and Wilmott, P. (1962) *Family and Kinship in East London*. Harmondsworth: Penguin.

7   Domestic space I
Decor and regionalisation

Bourdieu (1990) famously saw in the organisation of the Kabyle house the whole cosmology of the encompassing social order. In contemporary Western nations, however, with dispersed social spaces, multiple fields competing for any one individual's desire and attention and a certain pre-eminence bestowed upon affective recognition, domestic space reveals a rather more complex array, and play, of forces. Any one entity or space within it can hold significance in relation to a multitude of struggles conferring justification on our singular existence, enveloping, for example, elements which might appear in an analysis of correspondences between the social space and symbolic space within a mist of personal significance. As Bachelard's (1994) celebrated phenomenology of domestic space illuminated, the tiniest elements of home – its corners and drawers, its smells and stairs, all of which will vary in form by class – can reverberate, lingering in one's memory ready to be awoken in the present, filling in the horizons of perception with a *sense* of 'home' when certain phenomena enter the sensory field and shaping desire.

The objects we accumulate around us in our place of residence, too, on the walls and mantelpieces, adorning dressers and shelves, not only symbolise what we like and value in *class* terms – as markers of our *taste* – but also bind us to specific people we care for and love, and prompt nostalgia or reflection about, or at least reawaken awareness of, relations with others past, present and future, even if the inclination for that to occur is itself specified by taste (cf. Halle, 1993, Painter, 2002). Ultimately, when it to comes to the section of the lifeworld enclosed within the walls of our domicile, class and its allied fields are deeply entwined with the web of relations specifically anchored, due to particular sociohistorical developments, within domestic spaces: the family – not simply, as Bourdieu sometimes cast it (e.g. 2005: 20ff), as an integrated unit, but as a *field of force* (or a section thereof at least), where *love* and *care* amongst other forms of recognition are striven for, bestowed and diminished in the *durée* of daily action and interaction, and where knowledge and practice oriented around this struggle can become so taken for granted as to become nothing less than doxic (for details see Atkinson, 2016a). I want to explore this entwinement, as it manifests in the lives of Bristol families, in relation to three themes. The first two, decor and regionalisation within the home, the latter leading into a consideration of the evening meal as a particular site of intermingling social forces, will be explored in this chapter. The next chapter will then take up the third and final theme: the nexus between the spatial boundary of home/outside and the phenomenological boundaries between the familial field on the one hand and the social space and associated fields (i.e. of cultural, economic and ideological production) on the other.[1]

Class taste and family significances

We have already seen the statistical differentiation of domestic aesthetics according to class – clean and tidy for the dominated, distinctive homes for the dominant – and decor, as an element of that, was famously examined by Bourdieu (1984), and others after him (e.g. Silva and Wright, 2009), as a site for the display of the goods their residents' capital and attendant schemes of perception have drawn them to, symbolising their social position and, in some cases, facilitating the reproduction of capital between the generations. In this regard alone there is little to add here except confirmation and illustration. It can easily be shown, for example, that the number of books in a household follows cultural capital (Figure 7.1), and observation reveals that the tomes in the homes of families rich in this particular fount of recognition (particularly the Allen, Carlisle, Evans/Francis, Illsley/James, Newcombe/Oliver, Quinns and Samuels households) take the form not only of consecrated literature old (e.g. Jane Austin, Albert Camus, Fyodor Dostoyevsky) and newer (e.g. Zadie Smith, Salman Rushdie, Monica Ali) but volumes more directly oriented toward building, consolidating and/or signifying symbolic mastery. Reference books on art, music history or astronomy; popular history/philosophy/science/social science texts (Alain de Botton, Stephen Hawking, Andrew Marr etc.); encyclopaedias, dictionaries, books of quotations, atlases and travel books – all are rampant, opening up possibilities for the inculcation of valued modes of knowledge (as with Mr Carlisle, who states that if he does not know the answer to a question his children ask them from their homework, he will pull out an encyclopaedia and look it up for them) and display of items believed to signify their possession (as with Mr Illsley, who has on his shelves books from art exhibitions he has visited still in their cellophane wrapping).[2] Ownership of copious volumes can also have a particular effect on the look and feel of

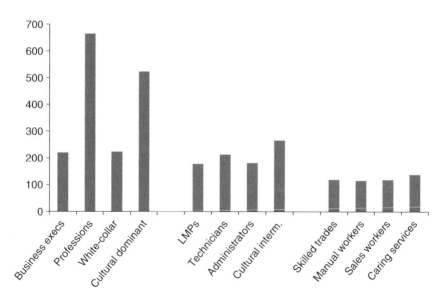

Figure 7.1 Average number of books owned

a house via their seeming omnipresence – in living rooms and kitchens, bedrooms and hallways – and the use of tall, imposing floor-to-ceiling bookcases filled with these slips of varying girth and colour, sometimes overflowing, stacked sideways on top of others or, in some instances, colonising and cluttering various surfaces and contending with other objects and ornaments (which are themselves often small replicas of artworks, i.e. sculptures, possessed for their aesthetic qualities, or objects signifying travel, 'brought back from America/Australia', and thus money and a certain taste).

Art, too, seems to follow cultural capital: prints and posters are more numerous in homes where capital is ample (where there is often more wall space to fill…), and these tend to take the form of either reproductions of works by consecrated modern artists – Picasso, Chagall, Matisse, Van Gogh, Klimt, Hokusai, Mackintosh etc. – or original works by local, more obscure artists. Posters in children's rooms, meanwhile, while often related to films, TV programmes, cartoons, sports, music and so on, sometimes include explicitly pedagogical prints – a chart of clouds with their Latin names, for example, the periodic table, times tables, a world map or a diagram of animal classifications. The furniture around which books and pictures weave, finally, is more likely – though far from exclusively – to be antiquated, solidly built and well-travelled, in the sense of having come from a different part of the globe, or else bought second-hand for the same qualities, giving a mismatched feel to many of the rooms.

Books are rather less ubiquitous in the homes of those with less cultural capital, and where they are present they tend to be popular fiction, joke books, biographies of various 'personalities' or reference books on gardening and cooking lined up neatly on modest bookcases or shelves, sometimes tucked away in the bedroom (as with the Collins/Taylors) or utility room (e.g. the Arnold/Jeffers family) since they are not possessed as a display of, or to-hand means of augmenting, symbolic mastery. Much more in abundance on shelves and other surfaces are various knickknacks – matching urns, vases, candles and orbs of the kind purpose-made and vended by stores to 'fill a space' and give the room a clean and ordered aesthetic – as well as, in some cases, collections of particular items – 'Tatty Teddy' bears for the Greens, dolls for the Nash family – and, most frequently, DVDs. Indeed, the CCSE data reveals that ownership of films (presumably DVDs) follows not cultural capital but, if anything, economic capital, with those richest in this resource but less so in symbolic mastery having the largest collections (Figure 7.2). The walls, meanwhile, are less bedecked with reproductions from the luminaries of the history of art and more likely to display realist pictures of romanticised pastoral scenes or professional photographs of sentimentalised animals or local landmarks (e.g. the Clifton Suspension Bridge), while furniture tends to be coordinated and bought new from large shops like Argos.

The binary division between dominant and dominated class households, while useful for conveying the key oppositions structuring domestic decor, should not be overdrawn, however: all manner of variations and shades of difference appear on the basis of even just precise position and trajectory within social space. The Richards family, for example, being richer in economic than cultural capital, though far from without the latter altogether, do have bookcases full of tomes in the hallway and the study, though these are mainly fantasy fiction and religious volumes, and Mrs Richards has a collection of model dragons displayed on a set of shelves, while Mr Cavendish displays all the orientations of an autodidact between the upper-dominated and petite bourgeoisie – in his own words, a quest to 'achieve higher', a desire to 'escape' his deprived neighbourhood of origin, a 'questioning mind' and so on – manifest not least in the sheer number and variety of books piled up around his modest family home covering topics as diverse as poetry and astronomy.

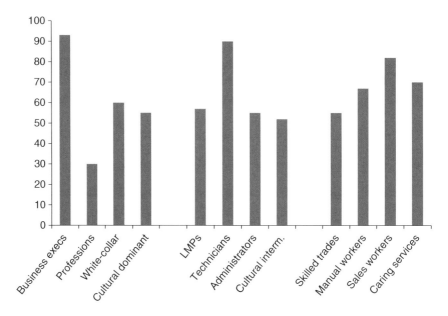

Figure 7.2 Average number of DVDs owned

None of what has been said so far is out of step with what would be expected from a reading of *Distinction* or of Chapter 3, even if it provides a trans-Channel update in one case and further flesh in the other. What I want to bring front stage, however, are some of the ways in which, in everyday consciousness and practice, the markers of position in social and symbolic space dotted around the house are interwoven with, merge with and compete with relevances, significances and forces from the *familial* field, whether those implicated in the consolidation or realisation of the family and its doxa or those sparking tension and struggle. To begin with there are, of course, all sorts of items around the home with an overt familial significance. Returning to pictures on the wall or on shelves, for example, in all households there are plentiful photographs of family members – whether present and past members of the household, i.e. the domestic subspace, or more distant relatives; whether in some combination or singularly; whether naturalistic shots encapsulating a shared experience or specifically posing; and whether framed and mounted to catch attention or catalogued in albums ready to be pulled out. Some houses even have whole doors or walls dedicated to pictures of family in various situations, sometimes alongside specific standardised and commercialised textual maxims on family life, or use them as screensavers on communal computers in the house. As Bourdieu *et al.* (1990) indicated long ago, and as scholars exploring family 'displays' continue to emphasise (e.g. Finch, 2007; Gomila, 2011), such photos serve the purpose of reinforcing the belief that this thing called 'the family' exists, that these people are bonded together in a specific way, that they have a certain 'heritage' or 'lineage', insofar as they prompt memories of 'togetherness', of events 'we' did and enjoyed, and make us think 'where we came from' (see also Rose, 2010). Certainly many of the families talked of them in terms of 'triggering a memory', and possibly a co-constructed story of 'good times' or 'lifetime experiences' together – their presence within the perceptual field, in other words, injects into consciousness specific relevances grounded in a specific bundle of relations and solicits further action.

More than that, however, photographs function to indicate the distribution of love as a form of (mis)recognition, demonstrating that these people 'matter' to one another, that they are important, that they care about one another enough to want to have pictures of them together on display. This means, of course, that the display of family photographs can also become a *stake in the struggles* within the family, or a key practice through which love, care and attentiveness are (perceived to be) shown or not shown, and (perceived to be) received or not received, to greater and lesser degrees. Who decides which photos are displayed, and the degrees of discontentment and resistance to the display ('I hate that photo'), perhaps viewed as a sign of diminished standing in need of challenge ('If you know/love/care for me you'll take it down'), become key. For instance, the Carlisles have a whole wall dedicated to family photographs on the landing between the ground floor and first floor of their large house: holidays, Mrs Carlisle when she was pregnant for the first time, moments from the children's younger lives, family 'reunions' and so on all jostle alongside one another for the eye's gaze. This is, it seems, the product of the conjunction of specific parental dispositions to integrate the family. Mrs Carlisle did it 'one afternoon' to fill the space, and nearby is a wall-mounted silver dish with a motto on love and happiness which, when put up, was accompanied by 'a little ceremony' and a speech by Mrs Carlisle on love, but it relied on the fact that Mr Carlisle is (in tune with his position in social space) an avid photographer for purposes of chronicling family life – he says 'we're keen photographers', projecting (or imposing) his practice onto the domestic field as a whole, but he seems to be the primary photograph-taker (when his daughter's friends come around to celebrate their school exam results during one of the observations, he is quick to get out his specialist camera to capture the moment and make the girls pose). Yet while Mr Carlisle tells me he often proudly shows the photo wall to visitors, his second daughter (17 years old) is more ambivalent. She appreciates having lots of family photos on display, but the particular ones of her mounted in plain sight lead her to dub it the 'wall of shame':

DAUGHTER: When people come over and they say, 'Where's the loo?' they have to come past this wall and spend ages 'Oh yeah, look at you [daughter], when you were like a boy in primary school. Isn't that funny!'
MR CARLISLE: You never looked like a boy!
DAUGHTER: Literally, that [one of her school photos] is the photo that one of your patients thought was a boy. That picture up there with me in the blue shirt, the third one from the right, is the one where your patient said, 'What lovely sons you have' and it's a picture of me and the boys [her two brothers].

She would evidently rather not have these particular pictures on view to others since they show her in what she sees as a worse light than she would like – as not as feminine as she desires. Yet she takes it in good humour, and does not seem to challenge their display openly (though she may have done before, or since), perhaps because she does not feel she has the symbolic capital within the family relative to her father, or perhaps because the sense of recognition generated by their display outweighs the wish that they were absent or alternative pictures.

Indeed, perhaps potentially more damaging for self-worth in the family are instances when there appear to be few photographs of oneself relative to others within the family field, and especially the domestic subspace. This was the case, for example, with Ms Morgan's younger daughter, aged seven. The context here is a particularly fraught struggle for love due to Ms Morgan's separation from her children's father, who now seems semi-absent and unremorsefully forgets birthdays and weekend visits, usually sending his children into fits of emotional trauma which rebounds back on Ms Morgan. During a tour of her home with the researcher, Ms Morgan pulls out a photo album and leafs through the pages with her daughters, commenting on its contents. There are pictures of Ms Morgan's family and friends, of her former partner, and many of her elder daughter (aged ten) as a baby and toddler ordered chronologically. As the folios turn and the pictures of her sister stack up, the younger daughter gets increasingly anxious, beginning to interject, accompanied by turns with sad whimpers and angry shrieks: 'Where's me?', 'When am I going to be born?', 'Mummy!', 'Why aren't there any pictures of me!?', 'There's no pictures of me', until, eventually, she gets very upset. Ms Morgan tried to placate her by telling her there were photographs of her elsewhere in the house, but the sense of lack of recognition relative to her sister had already set in, feeding back, in however minute a way, in to the maintenance of the structure of affective relations within this particular familial field.

Yet family photo displays are not divested of classed (or other) significances. Where the pictures are taken, what the subjects are doing in them and the kinds of poses they strike all bear the imprint of class tastes and dispositions, as do the number and position of family photographs relative to other pictures, paintings and objects around the home (as more or less 'tasteful' or 'vulgar'). We already know, for example, that within households richer in cultural capital family photos are more likely to have to compete for attention with painting reproductions. Photographs have, therefore, *multiple pertinences* – within the horizon of consciousness when they are attended to are their place (as indicators of relative standing, of position-taking or of what is done) within more than one system of relations – and therefore represent *multiple plays* – a statement of (*inter alia*) class taste as well as love. This multiplicity of field relevances, and their mingling in everyday life, however, is even clearer in relation to the elements of decor described earlier. Paintings, ornaments and furniture are not *just* expressions of class taste and travels, they are not *just* symbols of class position, they are not *just* affordances for building certain masteries in children; they are also 'souvenirs' of times together as a family, paintings of or from favourite holiday destinations, gifts from one to another and individual preferences imposed on others – they too are, in other words, also elements of the realisation of the family spirit and objectifications of symbolic capital, and the exchanges which sustain it, within the family field.

The small pastoral painting of Victorian children hanging on the Nashes' wall is not just, therefore, a vector of class taste – Mrs Nash says she likes the rural background, the look of the children and (somewhat unsure) the 'way the picture is', seemingly appreciating the realism of the artistry and the emotive sensations it can evoke, such that it 'took her eye' and she thought 'Ooh, that's a nice picture.' It is also, and perhaps primarily, a symbol of her 'nan', from whom she took it when the latter was moved to a care home, such that when asked about the artwork her first response was: 'That came from my nan's house' (this is, indeed, where it took her eye), indicating, without saying as much, that this is the primary relevance attached to this artwork, since it was only when pushed that she offered the hesitant aesthetic comment. Similarly, the print of Matisse's *Les Oiseaux* that hangs in the Allen family's kitchen is a product of Mrs Allen having (in her words) an 'interest in art' – the abstract field *per se*, in other words, its movements and developments rather than just the resonance of specific pieces – after having studied it at A level, no doubt bolstered by the inherited cultural capital that comes from having a father competing in a field of cultural production (architecture). Yet it also has particular significances in the familial system of relations. On the one hand it symbolises Mrs Allen's domestic dominance in matters aesthetic, perhaps given her greater cultural capital than, and parity of economic capital with, her husband: all the pictures on the wall are hers, and Mr Allen explicitly distances himself from them ('They're Mrs Allen's', he says, and he is 'not too keen' on the Picasso in the dining room). On the other hand it also plays a specific, recognised function in the daily inter-generational power struggles within the family:

> Mrs Allen: Yeah, it's quite good – you can see the reflection, so you can actually see the reflection of the stairs [in the picture]. So they [the children] can spy on us but equally we can spy on them, so it's kind of a handy tool without being an actual mirror. So you can see, when they're fighting, who hit who first! [Laughter]

If seen by another – an outsider to the domestic subspace of this familial field – this picture might be read only, or at least primarily, as a symbol of class taste, of being 'cultured' or 'pretentious'. But for the residents of this house it is inescapably polysemic, symbolising Mrs Allen's specific interests and history, and their place relative to others' within the house, but also acting as a practical tool, mobilised through motor schemas, deployed in the maintenance and exercise of parental symbolic power (as well as its subversion by the children, since they evidently use it for counter-espionage), and, therefore, also symbolising specific events, tactics and possibilities in the struggle for recognition within the family. Which significance presses upon consciousness as relevant at any one moment will depend on the solicitations of the situation, but, since its observational function was the feature first reported, one might suppose that its role in reproducing the structure of relations in the household is the most frequent manner in which it finds its way into the phenomenal field of at least some members.

For parity it is perhaps worth noting that posters and pictures in children's bedrooms or dens embody the same (at least) double significance. We have already seen that they can sometimes take the form of aids in the nourishment of symbolic mastery and cultural capital in capital-rich households, but there are others, even in these homes, referencing youth/popular culture (*High School Musical*, football, cars, TV programmes or films), sometimes displaying alternative (heterodox/subversive) values or models to those found in the home, and acting as means of asserting the child's own taste as worthy of recognition (with greater or lesser parental approval). Even the pedagogic posters, including those bought for young children, are the product of an interplay of class and familial forces: parents insist they are buying them and putting them up only because the children are 'into' numbers, birds, or whatever – and hence they are recognised by the children themselves as acts of recognition, a sign of being loved and cared for, by others they themselves recognise, and constitute one element in the system of exchanges maintaining the distribution of capital within the field. Yet – as will be explored in greater depth later – what the children are 'into' is shaped significantly by classed parental tastes and practices. To give just one example at this juncture, Mrs Quinn has adorned the walls of her five-year-old daughter's bedroom with anime figures representing Japanese culture (in traditional dress, etc.), providing conditions of possibility for building knowledge and awareness (i.e. symbolic mastery) of different national cultural styles, because, she says, her daughter is 'really into Japan'. An initial spark of this interest seems to have been Mr Quinn's cousin marrying a Japanese woman, but Mrs Quinn (who teaches media studies to A level pupils at a secondary school), rather than let it go, encouraged, channelled and – as the Vygotskians would say – 'scaffolded' it through watching not just any old Japanese cartoons with her daughter, but the output of Studio Ghibli specifically (the attachment to the named studio signalling mastery of and taste for specific *styles* of filmmaking), including films such as *Spirited Away* and *My Neighbour Totoro* (not the Disney remake), critically acclaimed for their exploration of social, cultural and spiritual themes as well as showcases for distinctly Japanese folkways.

Furniture, too, interlaces classed aesthetics and affordances with specific familial memories and events, inherited or gifted furniture in capital-rich homes representing a particularly obvious case. It may well be perceived as 'good quality', 'solid', 'beautiful', and 'valuable' in money and cultural/historical terms (symbolising a particular time and place at far remove), as opposed to furniture which looks 'cheap', 'generic', etc., thus contributing to a certain classed ambiance in the home. Yet it also, like the Nash family's paintings, awakens memories of specific family members, narratives and events, thus building into the overall family spirit, or speaks of specific affective-power relations. The baby grand piano that the Illsley/James family used to have, for example, was not only a 'beautiful piece of furniture' according to Ms James, and not only an affordance for valued musical masteries (her children said they wanted to learn to play it, and they did), as *Distinction* would emphasise. It was also, indelibly, an objectification of both Mr Illsley's father, from whom it came, and family times together in this home; and so when, it being deemed too costly to maintain, they finally opted to dispose of it, they found it 'very sad' not simply because a symbol and tool of cultural capital was lost but because a visible symbol of affective capital, and an instrument for gluing together and upholding a certain musical family ethos, perished.

The large, old wooden table in the Carlisles' dining area, moreover, is valued not simply for aesthetic or functional reasons – for instance, its usefulness for the children's revision for school exams since it offers enough space to lay out large volumes of books and paper. It also has its specific place within family lore – it is, for example, also the table where Mr Carlisle revised for his A levels, giving him 'flashbacks' to his own youth (i.e. prompted by the present was a specific recollection of the past on account of shared features) and cementing a sense of 'the done thing' within this family – and within family power relations. Mr Carlisle sits at the head of the table, just as his own father used to and so, he says, 'where, in my imagination, the parents would traditionally sit'; but also, interestingly, there is an intense competition between the children for specific seats at the table at mealtimes: when the eldest child left the home to go to university, the next-eldest child assumed her place, but when the former returns in vacations there is, the latter admits, an intense 'rivalry' for the seat, revealing that places at the dinner table, at least in this home, are etchings of the power relations within the family into the organisation of domestic space.

Finally, just to show that class and familial significances are not always concordant, a small table stands in the Newcombe/Olivers' living room, its worn condition, which some might take for 'shabby chic' or at least a sign of valuing older furniture, a source of aesthetic discontent for Ms Oliver, who tells me she 'would love to be able to get a sander and take the surface off and have it polished or polish it'. Yet this is not just any table, but the table Mr Newcombe had his nappy changed on in his first days of life, cherished by his mother, from whom it came, and so Ms Oliver admits, regarding the desire to polish it, 'I can't possibly do that whilst Mr Newcombe's mother is alive. She'd be horrified.' In this instance, then, the state of play within the familial field – specifically, Ms Oliver's recognition of Mr Newcombe's mother's wishes (which is also recognition of Mr Newcombe) – has *frustrated* class taste, situating within this abode where cultural capital is in abundance at least one item at odds with at least one resident's class dispositions. Doubtless many households are filled with such items, making them mosaics of compromise and tension, to greater and lesser degrees, rather than 'pure' paradigms of class taste.

Dispersion and concentration

The second modality of interplay between class, space and familial forces in the domestic sphere is the distinct *regionalisation*, as Giddens (1984) would dub it, that takes place within the home, that is to say, the carving-up of material space into distinct zones associated with different activities, times (mealtimes, bedtimes, etc.) and people ('my room', 'your room', etc.). The notion that dwellings should consist of multiple rooms with different functions and affordances for privacy, rather than be one large space open for everyone to use interchangeably, is a scheme of perception with a wide geographical span and long genesis, traced by Ariès (1990) and Elias (2000), and is continually perpetuated and objectified by the fields of architecture and building in the form of doors, thresholds and so on, as well as all the players within the economic field commodifying a scheme of thought (in the form of stickers or signs humorously declaring or naming a space or warning 'Keep Out') and the media fields constructing 'family life' in various ways. Subtending wider familial doxa of 'who (i.e. which family members) lives where' and the paths between abodes, it is, of course, refracted by gender – as was the more open Kabyle house – insofar as men often colonise certain spaces (offices, 'dens', sheds, spare rooms and so on) as their own (cf. Hunt, 1989) – the full significance of which will be unpacked in Chapter 8 – but it is also dispersed by, and in turn reproduces, class in at least two ways.

First, the number of rooms or size of a house, as well as the thinness of the walls, limits the degree to which back regions, in Goffman's sense, can be formed and privacy taken for granted and valued over communality. Where families have enough economic capital to purchase large houses and, on top of that, build loft or garage conversions and extensions, not only are there greater possibilities for individuals – particularly children – to colonise and decorate specific spaces in line with their own divergent or convergent tastes, with some parents rich in cultural capital encouraging their off-spring to 'personalise' bedrooms and dens as 'their spaces' (Mrs Allen) or their 'own little empire' (Mrs Quinn), celebrating individuality and initiative (within limits). There is also a sort of *dispersal effect*, as residents (at least adults and older children) occupy discrete parts of the house to undertake their own activities. The Kings – perhaps because, being upwardly mobile into the intermediate class, possession of an amply sized house (relative to what they otherwise know) is less taken-for-granted, and more of a perceived achievement and break from the past (and indeed something they may 'talk up' to some degree in order to make themselves 'look bigger', in Bourdieu's words) – acknowledge this effect most explicitly:

MRS KING: I think there's enough room here, we can all have our space, we can do our own things. You know, so if [Mr King] wants to watch something on the telly and I'm –

MR KING: Rebuild his iPod on a Friday night!

MRS KING: Or, say he was doing that, I can go off on the computer or watch TV in a different room. 'Cos we don't – we're all human, we don't always watch the same things, you know. We just…

SON: Most of the time I'm up here, on the laptop, PS3…

MR KING: Sometimes doing schoolwork. […] To me, it's about, you know, the house is big enough, everyone can have their space if they need it.

As telephone conversations, listening to music, television-watching and suchlike go on behind closed doors, at different degrees of remove from one another, no one is necessarily disturbed by the activities of the other; fewer intra-familial struggles over what to watch/listen to or over one person's activity (e.g. listening to music) hampering another's (e.g. reading) need occur, and the hallways and corridors can fall quiet. For example, the Richards have converted part of their attic into a 'den' for the children, containing a games console, television, DVD player and drum kit, the sound of which barely registers on the ground floor. Their daughter in particular spends much of her spare time at home here, on the grounds that it is 'quieter' than her bedroom, since it is further away from her mother's 'rubbish' music playing in the kitchen, and roomier, allowing her to spread out her art homework – her everyday projects of accumulating cultural capital – and concentrate on it fully, though it is also a space where she can talk candidly to her friends on the telephone without parental intrusion (one can hear only occasional distant laughter emanating from the den in the lower floors of the house).

Contrast this to the situation of Mrs Atwell, living on social welfare, whose small Lockleaze house is filled with grown sons who have little choice but to all sit in the cramped living room together – whether talking or trying to do their own thing, both sharing in and disrupting one another's activities – and where any movements in the creaky and thin-walled small house are known by all because the noise ricochets around the building. Or again, take the domestic context of the Duncans, whose 16-year-old twins share a single bedroom:

MR DUNCAN: We got twin sons, they're still at home; we got an older son, 20 years old, still at home; and if we could have a four-bedroom house they could have their own bedrooms and their own independence.

MRS DUNCAN: 'Cos it's a problem at the moment, innit? When they got their girlfriends round.

Q: Are they sharing?

MR DUNCAN: They share a bedroom.

Q: The twins are sharing?

MRS DUNCAN: Yeah.

MR DUNCAN: Two single beds – not a lot of room in there – and then one of them got a girlfriend and it's like…

MRS DUNCAN: [One of them] shares this [living] room, he [Mr Duncan] sits in the backroom and I stand in the kitchen all night [laughter]. Every night's the same.

MR DUNCAN: Very difficult, those relations, very difficult.

Q: Not very good for privacy?

MR DUNCAN: No, it's not, no.

MRS DUNCAN: No, definitely not, but the worst thing is the one who got the girl-friend, that was the other one's girlfriend before! [Laughter] Which also causes problems.

This inevitably has consequences for the doxa and dynamics of the family field, not only by decreasing the facility for individuality, privacy and empire-building at home seen among the more privileged classes but by increasing the likelihood of clashes over uses of space and specifying the kinds of actions that must be taken – the unequal exchanges of mutual recognition (I do this so you can do that, but in return you must…) enacted – to maintain the balance of symbolic power within the domestic microcosm, such as Mrs Duncan standing in the kitchen all night.

There is not, however, a mechanical relationship between size of house and possession of 'a room of one's own'. The Geoffreys, for example, in a bid to save and accumulate extra money (in line with their intermediate position in social space), have opted to lease out some of the rooms in their house to students and sleep in the same room as their young children – something they describe as a 'sacrifice' as it hinders the capacity to be 'on your own with your family'; yet, attempting to make a virtue of necessity, they also describe it as 'fun' as 'it's sort of quite enjoyable waking up with your kids around you'. The affluent Carlisles, too, take in lodgers, though less as a strategy to accumulate money so much as to fill emptying rooms as children leave for university, particularly the converted attic room, at the top of their large house, with its own bathroom area, which allows for greater spatiotemporal separation and experiential remove to the extent that Mrs Carlisle admits she often simply cannot tell if her lodger is in or out.

There is a second discernible impact of class on regionalisation of the home. Specific people may well be paired in perception with specific spaces, the decoration of which can act as an expression or outlet for the expectations, positions and strategies within the abstract space of domestic relations (posters on the wall, colours chosen, and so on), but specific regions of the home also serve as gathering spaces for the residents, that is to say, as distinct *hubs* of individual time-space paths – the 'places to be' where everyone congregates, particularly on a weekday evening (and where refusal to be constitutes a clear subversive strategy) – and this appears to differ by position in social space. In households richer in both economic capital – meaning the room could be large, with multiple seats around islands and breakfast bars, filled with items of sociability (music players, laptops etc.), elevated from a functional to an aesthetically pleasing and show-piece space – and cultural capital – where there was a premium on conversation rather than joint television-watching as a primary mode of being-with-others – the hub was often the *kitchen/dining space*. Obviously this is where the cooking of the evening meal (nearly always by the women) took place, with men and children often helping out or 'keeping them company' (while in other houses they would be changing clothes after work or watching television in a different room), and where eating together and clearing up took place. The space is thus layered with a gendered significance, as evidenced not only by the phrases and slogans, playing on and perpetuating stereotypes, sometimes pinned up around the room (e.g. Mrs Carlisle's 'Motherhood Isn't For Sissies'), but also Ms James' bald statement that, while her kitchen is the 'hub of the house', it also happens to be 'the hub of all those domestic tasks that I don't really like'.

Yet, even if people tended to disperse around the house later in the evening, the kitchen was also where internet-linked computers were stationed, where guests and family were entertained, where glasses of wine would be drunk together, where conversations about each other's days would occur, where children would do their homework or activities (e.g. practising musical instruments) under supervision, and so on. Indeed, in some cases (especially the Allens', Quinns' and Carlisles'), the researcher barely left the kitchen from entry into the field until the family went to bed on weekdays, as even if one or two members vacated it for a period this was still where the majority of the domestic group spent the majority of their time. Families themselves described and actively encouraged this use of kitchens as 'hubs'. The Newcombe/Olivers, for example, admit the kitchen/dining space 'is the room we use most' when leading the researcher in, and tell of their recent renovations to open it up so it could be a more 'sociable' space where children and adults can talk together without hindrance. Similarly, the Allens exclaim 'It all happens in here' and that it is 'the most important room' when talking about their kitchen, and Mrs Allen recounts her plans to extend the kitchen further (it has already been enlarged in the past) so that 'we'll all hang out in [it] without being on top of each other'. Mrs Carlisle also acknowledges the kitchen is the 'most frequently used room', and, indeed, was determined to make it so when the family moved in. The kitchen/dining room in their old house

> was where it all happened. We'd all be in there most of the time together, so I didn't want a kitchen separate from dining, I just wanted it to be the hub. And this has been, again, the hub, hasn't it [to her husband, who nods in agreement]?

There is, evidently, variation depending on precise resources possessed, the internal contours of the home, number and ages of children and so on, but as the cultural capital and economic capital stocks of the respondents decrease, the kitchen – which shrinks drastically in size in smaller homes, often to the exclusion of a dining table (perhaps replaced by a breakfast bar, which encourages transience) – becomes less likely to be the time-space hub, or even the place where meals are eaten together, compared to the living room, where television can be watched, computer games are played together or people can sit on snug sofas to converse. The Collins/Taylor household, for example, did not have a space large enough for a dining table in their kitchen and tended, instead, to eat their meals quickly while sitting on stools at a breakfast bar before moving to the living room to play with the children, surf the internet on laptops or talk while watching television or films – 'putting their feet up', which Mr Collins described as a 'perfect end to the day'. The Green family meanwhile, their modest kitchen/dining area being dominated by Mr Green's DJ decks (he has no space for a room of his own where he could put them), ate their food sitting on the sofas in the living room, their children perched at a small table there, while they watched television programmes.

Teatime talk

The evening meal – known as 'dinner' by some, 'tea' by others – offers, in fact, a particularly sharp focal point for unravelling the intricacy and complexity of the phenomenology of class at home: that is to say, not only the myriad ways in which consciousness and practice during its course are underpinned by a habitus forged in a certain position in social space, but also how determinations and dispositions of class contend or dovetail with the sense of the possible and desirable in other fields too, the familial field most prominently. For the act of eating a main meal together – fusing, as Simmel (1910) saw, recognition of individuality, symbolised by separate plates, with submission to the collective order, via accepting one's portion from a shared preparation – is crucial to maintaining the doxic sense of mutual orientation binding distinct individuals into the same web of relations (the 'realisation' of the family and maintenance of field boundaries); to sustaining the doxic or orthodox sense of the 'done thing' in relation to this field; and to reproducing on a daily basis the structures of symbolic power and misrecognition between partners, between children and between parents and children insofar as it comprises so many exchanges (cooking, washing up, laying the table, saying 'thank you' etc.) signalling care, a sense of obligation and expectation (Murcott, 1982; DeVault, 1994; Charles, 1995; Kaufmann, 2010), as well as struggles and strategies to maintain or augment worth in the eyes of these others (arguments, demands, etc.).

Yet the domestic division of labour, the food prepared and eaten and the form and content of conversation bear the stamp of social class too. We know, for example, that the gendered allocation of tasks at home maps with possession of capital – with greater cultural capital comes a more pro-egalitarian *attitude* among both men and women (plus men doing more visible and creative tasks like cooking), but real egalitarian *practice* actually tends to come only with lack of economic capital in the household as a child of necessity (Usdansky, 2011; Lyonette and Crompton, 2015). We also know, on the basis of earlier analyses, that the food eaten in the household, and the orientation toward diet, the body and consumption underpinning it, correspond with class (Atkinson and Bradley, 2013; Atkinson and Deeming, 2015). What I want to explore further here, however, is the evening meal (whether eaten at a table or breakfast bar or while sitting on sofas) as a key spatiotemporal site of sustained familial interaction and conversation – linguistic exchanges of mutual care, interest and censure – about diverse aspects of one another's lives (work, school, other family members, etc.), at some junctures blending with pertinences related to the social/symbolic space and at others competing with or departing from them. With just one word – never mind the flux in people's heads that goes without verbal articulation – the stream of consciousness and attendant flow of conduct can surge from one structural space to another, or from one field alone to two or more, though in ways very different depending on one's class position.

Let us begin with those families where the major forms of symbolic capital in the contemporary misrecognition order are relatively scarce. Conversation in these instances was, first of all, often concise and to the point, existing as short bursts between periods of quiet yet relaxed eating and, while the effect of the gaze of an observer has to be taken into account, it seemed to be part and parcel of a functional orientation toward mealtimes – focussed on 'getting fed' and resting after a strenuous day – and to reflect the more economical approach to language, as a manifestation of practical mastery, generally observed in these families.[3] As to the content of that conversation, talk (and with it, we surmise, consciousness) tended to flow back and forth between several core topics. In households where the television was on, first of all, there would be comments or noises in reaction to the programmes – whether the twists and turns of a gambling show like *Deal or No Deal*, or a news feature on cake decoration prompting fantasies ('I'd like to do that'). Second, prompted by a particular flavour or behaviour, there were comments on the food and the manner in which it was being eaten. These could be vehicles for parental recognition of a child's tastes ('You don't like mushrooms, do you?') and desires ('Do you want some more mayonnaise?'), and thus exchanges of care, or they could constitute practical pedagogy steeped in parental symbolic power ('Look, get a bit of pizza, dip it in [the mayonnaise] and eat it', 'If you mix it [pasta] in sauce…[otherwise] pasta goes cold quickly…see that?'). They could also, however, take the form of parental censures of a lack of concentration on eating as children squabble, talk and play with their food. 'Sit down and eat your dinner', 'You turn round and eat your dinner', 'Hurry up and eat so I can do the dishes', 'Son, just leave it, eat yours and let him eat it', 'Eat!', 'Stop being silly', 'Sit up, please', 'You're not listening to me!' – just some of the injunctions, delivered with varying degrees of frustration and attached in at least one case to an allusion to physical capital ('Daddy's going to slap you'), puncturing the air, though there is less regulation of the manner in which the children are eating (that they *are* eating is enough).

Third, and most substantially, there is talk about one another's work or school days, sometimes laced with humour and often signalling mutual care. Colleagues getting stuck in lifts, whom children played with and in which games they participated in the schoolyard, what younger offspring made at nursery that day, where partners have been during their work day, what other family members have been up to and so on – all fodder for dinnertime talk cementing the familial field and its balance of affective capital. Occasionally these blend overtly with pertinences related to the social and symbolic spaces, in the form of discussion of certain favoured practices. The Nash girls converse with their mother about street-dancing, for example, talking about which friends do it and which class to join, while the Greens' eldest son mentions his ukulele recital, pleading for his mother to come and watch – she answers in the affirmative, an act of care pairing affective capital with this particular musical instrument somewhat dominated in the space of instruments. Yet class is always there even when homologous practices are not discussed, dovetailing with the specifically familial pertinences, insofar as these conversations, like those revolving around food, are oriented toward the practical, the immediate and the concrete – what has been and what will be done – rather than the abstract or transcendental, since that depends on a level of symbolic mastery denied to these families.

The contrast, therefore, is with those families where cultural capital is in greater abundance. Their dinner-table conversations are not only, thanks to their linguistic dispositions, much more elaborate and incessant – though once again we also have to factor in that these families may be more comfortable with a researcher in their presence since the university world is more familiar – but, even if they start from the same points as the conversations among the dominated class (the food or events in one another's days), constantly mobilising symbolic mastery and, moreover, are replete with attempts to instil that symbolic mastery in children (a captive audience) via acts of explicit pedagogy. This is not to say that pedagogy expressly aimed at nourishing symbolic mastery was absent within dominated families, but – as we will explore further in Chapter 9 – it was either somewhat fraught or kept noticeably separate (spatiotemporally and, thus, phenomenologically) from 'relaxing' family times, such as the evening meal, as an unenjoyable necessity (cf. Tizard and Hughes, 2002). In families rich in cultural capital, on the other hand, it was woven into this most intimate of familial, domestic activities, entwining the structures and strategies of the family field – the symbolic power of parents or siblings, the exchanges of affective recognition and so on – with the reproduction of that key fount of misrecognition in contemporary Western social spaces, cultural capital.

Take, for example, the Yates family, whose three young boys are of similar ages to the Green and Nash children. Just as for the dominated, there was the talk of what happened (or is going to happen) at school or work functioning to maintain affective capital, the disciplining of recalcitrant children resting on familial symbolic power (though it also included admonitions to 'talk properly') and the field-binding gossip about non-resident family figures. Just as for the dominated, pertinences and possibles from the symbolic space blend with familial practice to penetrate consciousness in the form of talk about specific favoured practices – in this case rugby and reading. Yet such talk often transitioned seamlessly into moments of explicit pedagogy aimed at cultivating symbolic mastery, as when a discussion of how many pieces of naan bread everyone had eaten with their kedgeree – specifically whether someone had taken more than they should have done, violating the parent-sanctioned distribution – becomes a maths question for the eldest son designed to reveal the truth:

> Mrs Yates, turning to her eldest son, states 'There were four pieces [of naan bread], I cut them into quarters. How many would there be?'. He replies 'Eight?' In a correcting tone, Mrs Yates repeats 'How many?'. This time he replies sixteen. Mr Yates then asks each person how many pieces they have had and tots them up. 'Ten', he finishes, 'so there should be six left. Was everyone telling the truth?'. 'Yes', says Mrs Yates, her husband then concluding 'So everyone is telling the truth'. After the youngest pleads for more bread than he was allotted, Mrs Yates notices her middle child has been drawing on his hands at school and gently upbraids him as it looks 'horrible'.

Similarly, mention of a more distant family member losing a lot of weight quickly after having their stomach stapled prompts amazement and jokes, but also seems to elicit an explicit test on the articulation of years, months and weeks for their middle son:

> Mrs Yates asks 'six months is how many weeks?' Her middle son responds 'Twelve'. Trying to find a way to correct him, Mrs Yates then asks 'how many weeks in a year?' He doesn't seem to know, so she asks how many months there are in a year. 'Twelve,', he correctly responds, leading Mrs Yates to follow up with 'Then how many weeks?' He replies 'Fifty-one?', prompting his mother to say 'Close' in a tone encouraging another answer. 'Fifty-two', he follows up. Before Mrs Yates can go back and now correct his guess on how many weeks are in six months, however, Mr Yates asks who would like to play on the Wii after dinner, beginning a different exchange.

In both cases, we see the way in which the flow of attentive consciousness around the dinner table is drawn by pertinences stemming from more than one structural space. Parental symbolic power – that they should be listened to, and their questions answered – but also affective recognition – that they want 'the best' for their children and act to secure it – dovetails with class ethos/strategy – 'the best' for children is defined as gaining what the parents possess, symbolic mastery – and, insofar as even pertinences stemming strictly from the familial field are framed by a halo of pedagogic potential, class dispositions.

The shifting relative balance of consciousness in the *durée* of activity between structural spaces – class and other things, in other words – can be glimpsed in another example. The Yates' youngest son breaks parental conversation about the national government's spending review, with all its pertinences for their capital and its interest to them on account of their classed political dispositions, as the meal is drawing to a close by dancing a little jig to amuse his parents, winning their smiles as tokens of recognition. This prompts Mrs Yates to approvingly show him an 'authentic' Irish jig on the internet using the laptop permanently stationed in the kitchen – an act of mundane pedagogy – but this, in turn, prompts Mr Yates to ask his wife if she 'remembers the Irish dancers' they saw. Alluding to a shared memory, in no need of further elaboration given their mutual knowledge, this is itself one of the million ordinary acts operating to glue the familial field together, sustaining mutual recognition, but it also refers to an event which may itself, we can conjecture, have blended familial strategies and class tastes. The conversation then returns to the spending review, which was only ever in mental abeyance, with Mr Yates saying he needs to 'unpack' it to work out its consequences for the family – and so the flow of conduct and consciousness continues, surging between and melding relevances from a variety of fields in the wake of all sorts of external and internal stimuli.

The prevalence of explicit pedagogy at the dinner table, and its linkage to everyday familial talk, was even greater in dominant-class families where children are older, to the extent, in fact, that it is fruitful to report it in a different form. The conversational sequence, as it was captured in fieldnotes, is given verbatim, and juxtaposed to it is analysis of the way in which it instantiates multiple field forces in various ways as it unfolds. In the Richards family, for example, an exchange begins when the 15-year-old daughter, who tends to dominate the discussion, suddenly remembers she received her mock exam results that day and tells her parents and her 13-year-old brother.

Fieldnotes	*The flow of field pertinences*
Daughter: I got my French mock result today.	This is premised on the perception that her parents will care (family field).
Mr Richards: What did you get?	At once an act of care (family field) and class interest (social space).
Daughter: A B, in Listening.	
Mr Richards: That's brilliant!	Familial recognition of symbolic mastery, fusing affective capital and cultural capital.
Daughter: I might actually pass French! It was all about animals playing games – like even if it was in English I wouldn't have known what was going on.	
Mr Richards: But is there a learning point here? Is there something you can talk to your tutor about concerning comprehension?	Class interest in improving symbolic mastery (social space) wrapped up in paternal care and authority (family field).
Daughter: What, about animals playing games? That doesn't make sense in English!	
Mr Richards: [firmly] Don't be obtuse.	Paternal authority deflating resistance.
Mrs Richards then starts to tell a story about a friend who went to Madeira, where cows are played music.	This has been brought to consciousness through analogical association with the animals playing games in the French test.
Son: Where is Madeira?	
Mr Richards: The middle of the Atlantic Ocean.	Explicit pedagogy aimed at fostering symbolic mastery begins.
Daughter: It's in Spain, isn't it?	
Mr Richards: No, it's an island. It's Portuguese. Madeira means Isle of Wood. I think there's more than one island there, actually.	
Mrs Richards: How many?	

Fieldnotes	The flow of field pertinences
Mr Richards: I don't know.	
Daughter: Can we go to Lanzarote?	An indication of the classed field of possibles (social space), as this question is delivered with sincere belief in its feasibility.
Mr Richards: That's the Canary Islands.	
Daughter: How many Canary Islands are there?	
Mr Richards: At least four. There's Lanzarote, Tenerife – that's the tackiest one, I think…	An act of class judgement (symbolic space).
Mrs Richards: [Some friends] went there.	
Mr Richards: What did they say?	
Mrs Richards: 'Don't go!'	
Daughter: Is Majorca a Canary island?	
Mr Richards: No, that's a Balearic island, Spanish, in the Mediterranean. Majorca, Minorca and Ibiza.	Explicit pedagogy resumes.
Daughter: [A friend] went to Ibiza. Can we go to Lanzarote? It sounds sooo Spanish.	An indication of the classed field of possibles (social space) again, including a taste for authenticity (symbolic space), but also a demand for recognition of a suggestion for family practice (family field).
Mrs Richards: I don't know. Daughter: We could go in the Easter holidays. Mrs Richards: We're not going anywhere in Easter with your exams. Son: We could go in February half–term.	A struggle begins in the family field… Maternal authority re-emphasising the priority of symbolic mastery acquisition.
Daughter: Will it be warm?	
Mrs Richards: Probably still about 28 degrees then.	
Daughter: Let's go in February!	
Mrs Richards: We'll see.	A concession to end the struggle.
After talking about the volcano on Lanzarote, and a lull in exchanges, the conversation then churns between:	
1. The son being teased for having a girlfriend, and the daughter for having a long-distance boyfriend.	So many plays within the familial field, reproducing heteronormative assumptions.
2. The daughter being teased for her tendency to cry at weddings and sad films.	A play within the familial field based on gendered dispositions.
3. The daughter commenting on clothes in a catalogue being 'soooo cool' and (with irony) 'only £200'.	An indication of class and gendered tastes as well as the sense of limits (social space).
4. The daughter complaining about leaks at her school, and how it undermines the teachers' positive vision of the school.	A pertinence from the school as a micro-field, told to the family to elicit care.
5. Mr Richards telling a story about a 'vivid white' company car, which prompts his son to ask 'What does that [vivid] mean?' The Richards' daughter responds 'It means really bright, like the sun or something.'	An act of sibling pedagogy.

Or again, a long conversation winding between fields is begun during the evening meal in the Carlisle household – where cultural capital is even greater than in the Richards family – by their eldest daughter (for ease called G1), who tells her parents, two teenage brothers (B1 and B2) and 17-year-old sister (G2) that she heard caesarean-section operations can be very violent affairs.

Fieldnotes	*The flow of field pertinences*
Mr Carlisle explains this is because 'the uterus is surrounded by very strong muscle. I'd have to ask [his colleague] more about it'. Mrs Carlisle: It's the rectus abdominis sheet, it's like a wall of muscle.	Explicit pedagogy begins, drawing on not just generic cultural capital but its specification by Mr and Mrs Carlisle's participation in the medical field (current for Mr Carlisle, former for his wife).
G1: Is that like a six-pack? What happens, when you get pregnant, to your six-pack?	
Mrs Carlisle: The individual muscles move apart as the stomach expands, so it stretches.	
G1: Wait, where's the muscle and the fat and the uterus in relation to each other?	
Mr Carlisle: The uterus is underneath, then the muscle, then the fat over the top. Everyone has a six-pack, it's just that there's usually a layer of fat over it. When you can see the six-pack, it just means they've got less fat.	
Picking up on the theme of strength, G2 then tells of a story she read in *New Scientist* about a strong toddler, and the family tease her that it sounds more like it was from the *Metro*. This then leads into stories each has read in the *Metro*, including one about a person losing weight after getting a gastric band. This prompts Mr Carlisle to explain that weight issues are often linked to mental health problems and that gastric bands can be adjusted, which variously elicits a 'really?', 'what?', 'gross' and so on from B1 and G2.	An indication of class taste (symbolic space), including disparagement of a 'light' newspaper (The *Metro* is a tabloid usually available for free on public transport) even though they all admit to reading it. Explicit pedagogy resumes.
Meanwhile G1 has attempted to help her mother out by serving up the pudding (pineapple upside-down cake), but when it starts to break apart unexpectedly she admits 'I'm not capable of this,' prompting Mrs Carlisle to jump up, saying 'I'll do it.' At the same time, G2 has poured herself a glass of milk from the fridge. Mr Carlisle tells her she needs to stop drinking so much milk, but G2 kicks back:	A play within the familial field: an act of affective exchange with Mrs Carlisle maintaining capital distribution, but its execution falters.
G2: What? I had like some milk on my cereal this morning, orange juice with lunch and now a glass of milk. That's hardly excessive. B1: You drink it all the time.	A struggle within the familial field: Mr Carlisle tries to exercise familial symbolic power (using *reason* to do so) *vis-à-vis* appropriate food consumption, perhaps underpinned by a classed relation to the body and visions of 'healthiness' (see Vandebroeck, 2016), but this meets with resistance (again on the basis of *logic*) which Mr Carlisle does not counter.
Mr Carlisle: You'll get too full. [firmly]	
G2: You all say I don't eat enough, now I get told off when I do eat!	

Fieldnotes	*The flow of field pertinences*
They then talk for a while about how G2 is going to keep up her exam revision, leading into stories from others about school lessons and then back to G2's biology exams. Mr Carlisle lists the Latin names of muscles to B1, prompting B1 to ask G2: 'What is science then, would you say?', to which she responds: 'I know this from psychology: the pursuit of objective knowledge through reason and empirical methods.' The conversational topics then flow as follows:	Experiences of the effects of the school field. Explicit pedagogy. Sibling pedagogy.
1. The price of stethoscopes and how blood-pressure gauges work, with Mr Carlisle explaining the relationship between blood pressure and heart rate. B1 asks if there are bigger sizes for 'fat people' and people using steroids, which then leads to Mr Carlisle being playfully teased for the way he pronounces 'steroids' ('steeroids'), which he insists is correct.	Explicit pedagogy. Judgements of body size, which are not unrelated to class (again see Vandebroeck, 2016). Plays within the familial field: teasing as an affective exchange resting on reciprocal typification (see Atkinson, 2016).
2. The grade a friend achieved at university, leading Mr Carlisle to explain the degree-classification system, remarking that 'some clever people get a first'.	Explicit pedagogy. Valorisation of symbolic mastery.
3. G1 talks to G2 about what she is going to study at university; G2 is astonished that G1 does not know. G1, in defence, says 'I bet B1 doesn't know,' only to find out that he does.	Plays within the familial field. This is contextualised by the fact that G1, now studying at university, has been non-resident for the last year.
4. The family begin to talk about holidays, with Mr Carlisle stating they're going to stay with his friends in France over summer, asking the rest if they mind this. G1 is on jury service over summer, though, which leads to a conversation about how trials work, with Mr Carlisle explaining to B1 why they cost so much (lawyer fees, building use, and so on). They then begin exchanging multiple comical holiday stories, co-constructing their narratives, before G1 says she dislikes going where there are 'beautiful people' as it makes her feel bad. Mr Carlisle responds: 'Don't be so insecure, be happy with yourself and your family.' 'I am,' she replies.	Assertion of paternal authority regarding classed holiday tastes (symbolic space). Mrs Carlisle confirms when interviewed that her husband always chooses the holiday destinations. Explicit pedagogy. Family field bonding. Reference to the sexual field (see Atkinson, 2016).
5. This leads to a discussion about tall women, including Miranda Hart, who B1 derides as 'fat' yet G1 describes as her 'idol', telling B1 to 'leave her alone'.	Struggle in the familial field over the legitimacy of judgements and taste, re-animating B1's derision of certain body shapes.
6. Finally, there is talk about which film they are going to watch on television together after dinner, with Mr Carlisle suggesting *Senna*, the film about F1 racing-driver Ayrton Senna. This prompts horror from his daughters, who deride it as 'boring', 'horrible' and 'not a proper film' before G2 jokingly exclaims, 'Don't you know us at all?!'	Family bonding time, but there is a clash and struggle on the basis of gendered tastes which leads to an apparent lack of recognition within the familial field.

Explicit pedagogy among families relatively rich in cultural capital has been observed *in situ* before, of course, most famously by Lareau (2003), and the *implicit* pedagogy at work here – the everyday use of certain words (like 'obtuse'), more elaborate sentences and logic by parents, for instance – must also be underlined. Yet what these cases illuminate so vividly is the place of class in the phenomenology of everyday life – the way in which, that is, the variety of interests and dispositions rooted in the social space and the symbolic space (taste, judgement, possibilities, reproduction) interplay with one another but also with interests and dispositions rooted in other fields, principally the domestic subspace of the familial field. This is not only insofar as the success of pedagogy rests to some degree on children valuing and therefore listening to what their parents say (which is nothing other than misrecognition within the family field).[4] On top of that, the ceaseless back-and-forth between field pertinences in the stream of consciousness and practice, with one thing leading seamlessly into another on the basis of some association and class dispositions not necessarily manifesting in *thematic* consciousness at all times, the world horizon of those parents rich in cultural capital, and therefore oriented toward fostering symbolic mastery in their children as the road to recognition and justification, fringes even the most prosaic play or practice within the familial field with a pedagogical pertinence and prompts moments of tutelage.

Pedagogy in these households does not start and end at the dinner table. There are moments before and after – particularly at other times when children are a captive audience, such as on car journeys or on walks together – when parents will turn the conversation toward some way of cultivating symbolic mastery in a manner not observed among families where cultural capital was less plentiful. Yet the evening meal, as a routinised spatial concentration of household members, is its prime arena within the domestic space, transforming the humble dining room or living room into a site where the work of reproduction of the largest national social structures gets done, but also where the battle or alliance of fields for structuring attention and practice is played out. Indeed, while we will return to the union or disharmony of family and class in the process of social reproduction in Chapter 9, if we are to fully understand the relative place of class and all the smaller-scale fields homologous with it in structuring the experience of domestic space we must now leave the dinner table and explore the spatial articulation of fields in individual lives.

Notes

1 In pursuing these themes a debt is owed to the work of Nippert-Eng (1996) on the phenomenology of home/work boundaries, though she is not especially sensitive to class and, ultimately, remains trapped in a subjectivist orientation in which work and home/family are simply cast as Schutzian 'provinces of meaning'. Without instead conceiving them as so many structured spaces of struggle, i.e. fields, there is no means for adequately grasping why the different 'provinces' matter to people in the first place (*illusio*), why boundaries between them are imposed or negotiated as they are (as [the effects of] so many cross-cutting *strategies*), why there would be conflict and negotiation between partners over them (given their relative *positions* and *interests*) and what the effects are of boundary struggles (securing, maintaining or diminishing *capital*).

2 For the broader picture to which these examples add flesh, see Atkinson (2016b).

3 The kind of 'convivial indulgence' and sociality of the working-class meal identified by Bourdieu (1984) was not really witnessed, though it may well appear at larger family meals, 'get-togethers' and parties.

4 Though we have no way of knowing if or how well the children remembered what their parents said.

References

Ariès, P. (1990) *Centuries of Childhood*. London: Pimlico.

Atkinson, W. (2016a) *Beyond Bourdieu*. Cambridge: Polity Press.

Atkinson, W. (2016b) 'The Structure of Literary Taste: Class, Gender and Reading in the UK' *Cultural Sociology*, 10(2): 247–66.

Atkinson, W. and Bradley, H. (2013) *Ordinary Lives in Contemporary Britain*. SPAIS Working Paper No. 02–14, University of Bristol. Available at www.bristol.ac.uk/spais/research/workingpapers/.

Atkinson, W. and Deeming, C. (2015) 'Class and Cuisine in Contemporary Britain' *The Sociological Review*, 64(1): 194–201.

Bachelard, G. (1994) *The Poetics of Space*. Boston: Beacon Press.

Bourdieu, P. (1984) *Distinction*. London: Routledge.

Bourdieu, P. (1990) *The Logic of Practice*. Cambridge: Polity Press.

Bourdieu, P. (2005) *The Social Structures of the Economy*. Cambridge: Polity Press.

Bourdieu, P., Boltanski, L., Castel, R., Chamboredon, J.-C. and Schnapper, D. (1990) *Photography: A Middle-Brow Art*. Stanford: Stanford University Press.

Charles, N. (1995) 'Food and Family Ideology' in S. Jackson and S. Moores (eds.) *The Politics of Domestic Consumption*. Hemel Hempstead: Harvester Wheatsheaf, pp. 100–15.

DeVault, M. (1994) *Feeding the Family*. Chicago: University of Chicago Press.

Elias, N. (2000) *The Civilizing Process*. Oxford: Blackwell.

Finch, J. (2007) 'Displaying Families' *Sociology*, 41(1): 65–81.

Giddens, A. (1984) *The Constitution of Society*. Cambridge: Polity Press.

Gomila, A. (2011) 'Family Photographs: Putting Family on Display' in R. Jallinoja and E. Widmer (eds.) *Families and Kinship in Contemporary Europe*. Basingstoke: Palgrave Macmillan, pp. 63–77.

Halle, D. (1993) *Inside Culture*. Chicago: University of Chicago Press.

Hunt, P. (1989) 'Gender and the Construction of Home Life' in G. Allen and G. Crow (eds.) *Home and Family*. Basingstoke: Macmillan, pp. 66–81.

Kaufmann, J.-C. (2010) *The Meaning of Cooking*. Cambridge: Polity Press.

Lareau, A. (2003) *Home Advantage*. Berkeley: University of California Press.

Lyonette, C. and Crompton, R. (2015) 'Sharing the Load? Partners' Relative Earnings and the Division of Domestic Labour' *Work, Employment and Society*, 29(1): 23–40.

Murcott, A. (1982) "It's a Pleasure to Cook for Him': Food, Mealtimes and Gender in South Wales Households' in E. Gamarnikow, D. Morgan, J. Purvis and D. Taylorson (eds.) *The Public and the Private*. London: Heinemann, pp. 23–34.

Nippert-Eng, C. (1996) *Home and Work*. Chicago: University of Chicago Press.

Painter, C. (ed.) (2002) *Contemporary Art and the Home*. London: Bloomsbury.

Rose, G. (2010) *Doing Family Photography*. Farnham: Ashgate.

Silva, E. and Wright, D. (2009) 'Displaying Desire and Distinction in Housing' *Cultural Sociology*, 3(1): 31–50.

Simmel, G. (1910) 'The Sociology of the Meal' in D. Frisby and M. Featherstone (eds.) (1997) *Simmel on Culture*. London: Sage, pp. 130–35.

Tizard, B. and Hughes, M. (2002) *Young Children Learning*, 2nd edition, Oxford: Blackwell.

Usdansky, M. (2011) 'The Gender-Equality Paradox' *Journal of Family Theory & Review*, 3(3): 163–78.

Vandebroeck, D. (2016) *Distinctions in the Flesh*. London: Routledge.

8 Domestic space II

The spatiotemporal articulation of fields

We have seen that items and events within the home can have pertinence in relation to both class (social space and symbolic space) and the familial field, and that domestic spaces are differentiated by class, but it is also true that time-space in and around the domicile is zoned according to which field's forces tend to press into the stream of consciousness there. Some spaces and pathways, occupied or traversed at specific times, are where one's mind tends to turn or be turned to thoughts of family, i.e. to the solicitations and state of play of the familial (and especially domestic) field, while others dovetail with phenomenological manifestation of the determinations of the social space and allied fields (of production but also specific firms, organisations etc.) – thinking about (or even doing) work, studying, earning money, how to get ahead and so on, in other words.[1] Evidently the general architectural and infrastructural projects produced by the local, national and international fields of power are responsible for providing the landscape in which this correspondence between space and thought is worked out, and the overarching sociohistorical context is one of flexibilisation and intensification of work and reorganisation of boundaries in the wake of neoliberal employment policy, feminisation of the workforce and technological developments (see e.g. Daley, 1996; McNay, 1999; Burchell et al., 2002; Wajcman, 2008; Agger, 2016). Yet there is also a major division with distinct class and gender tints.

Home as multi-field site

First of all there are those for whom the home has a specific region within it where attentive consciousness is encouraged or demanded to turn to the significances and effects of fields other than the family, specifically the fields structuring their employment or education. Members of the dominant class are particularly likely to possess such a space, casting it as the physical site in which certain mundane and radical strategies within fields comprising the field of power (the legal field, educational field, religious field, publishing field, economic field and suchlike) are forged and – via checking emails, reading documents, making telephone calls and so on – learned of too. The dialectic of social structure and physical space thus presents itself once again: this region of the home offers affordances for participation in field struggles, and its particular character and contents stand in phenomenological association with (and may even contribute in some way to) the moves and counter-moves of some social game, even if possession of economic capital and a libido channelled strongly enough toward the field's stakes underlay the original colonisation of this space for this purpose.

In many cases the region assigned to extra-familial field practice is a specific room, sometimes large, sometimes modest. It may be dubbed an 'office', after the Latin *officium*, the execution of a task, or, more fittingly perhaps, a 'study', derived from the Latin *studere*, meaning to concern oneself with, devote oneself to, strive after and concentrate on something – capturing, it seems, the illusio of a field, luring one toward it in the first place and continually in everyday life, and the thematisation of its effects in consciousness. For some this allows a sense of relative isolation and insulation against familial forces; of enclosure and total dedication, for some period of time, to other fields. Mr Illsley, for example, has a study at the top of his large house where, in his capacity as a lay preacher – as a very minor player in the religious field, in other words – he prepares his sermons (and the room is filled with icons he has collected from various places, items likely to pull attention in one way or another to determinations of the religious field) and where he sometimes undertakes tasks associated with his paid employment as a tax lawyer, such as writing commentaries on cases. This he does particularly when his partner, Ms James, is away from the home yet their 12-year-old twin daughters are in and need an adult to look after them. Standing in his study, he tells the researcher: 'That's when I'll come up here, so they can have the run of the house, really. I just lock myself in here and work.' Ms James, for her part, has her own study at the bottom of the house where she works on assignments for the master's degree in social work that she is undertaking – an exercise in accruing cultural capital – and states that 'unless, you know, I can't concentrate or I've, I've really got to do something, I spend my life shut in the study with the door shut'.

Yet any sense of insulation from the effects of the family field is only ever relative: when the respondents are in their studies working there are constant, more-or-less welcome, pulls toward the family field, shaking them away from their situated participation in the other fields momentarily or more long-lastingly, and these pulls can be imposed (an email, phone call or physical entry of another) or emerge more spontaneously, including via the family pictures and objects many people keep in their offices, which can awaken a sense of the state of play and one's place, as well as pertinent projects and practices.[2] Ms Oliver, a business development consultant to the third sector (i.e. she tells charities how to make job cuts), reports in her diary that while preparing on Sunday evening for a client meeting in Birmingham the next day (which will have some kind of effect on an organisation's field, and perhaps even encompassing fields), her daughter comes in to give her a cup of tea – a humdrum act nevertheless expressing the structure of affective recognition and symbolic power within the family field – 'popping down' to see her son doing his homework – a demonstration of care but also a moment in the reproduction of cultural capital – and talking to her partner, who was away on work in Europe, on the telephone. Another time she reports attending to 'domestic emails' in between working in the office, these mundane intrusions in the inbox re-channelling her attention to practices related to the family and calling forth a response.

Similarly, Mrs Samuels, an editor for a small publishing house, reports that, while trying to talk to a typesetter on the telephone in her home office – a routine act structured by the demands of, and contributing in its own small way to the dynamic of, the field of publishing (cf. Bourdieu, 2008) – there was a demand from the familial field battling for thematisation. 'All I could hear,' she says, was her ten-year-old daughter's constant cries of 'Mum, I'm hungry.' Her response, she continues, was to firmly state: 'Could you be quiet, I'm working from home' – a signal to her daughter that the latter's demands will not always be fulfilled, that Mrs Samuels is not at her beck and call, expressing the distribution of the capital of love, and, insofar as it was heeded, a demonstration of the symbolic power of Mrs Samuels within the domestic subspace of the family field. Also worth mentioning, perhaps, is that the office is also the site of laundry storage, thus constantly putting within Mrs Samuels' perceptual field phenomena carrying in their horizon eminently domestic chores manifesting a part of the system of mundane mutual obligations – and, she tells us, laundry is primarily her task – through which the balance of forces within the family is reproduced.

Lastly, Mr Patrick, a barrister, because his study is where he prepares for cases but also where he attends to family-related tasks, reports in his time diary that 'sitting down to do extra stuff' – in this specific case, on a Sunday evening, buying train tickets to London on the internet for his daughter so she can attend an audition – 'reminds me of all the other things I have to do [and] makes me a little stressed – work [and] dealing with my role as Chair of Governors of the children's school'. The list of such instances in diaries and observations where work or study are disturbed by family or domestic matters is almost endless, and in all cases we glimpse not only the competition for attention within consciousness, instances in which the mind turns from participation in one field to participation in another (which will, of course, be weighted by the strength of libidinal investment in each), but also how stress and anguish are generated by the demands of fields conflicting or piling up on top of each other, not simply what goes on in one.

The pull between the family and other fields can also have effects on what happens, and one's place, within each – less time or attention on one may diminish one's (or another's) standing, or effect the strategies one has to mobilise to maintain one's standing (buying presents to compensate missed time together, for example), in the other. The Patricks provide a good example of this: Mr Patrick's long hours locked in his study preparing for court (even if he often does family-related activities in there too) – he often works in there until past midnight on an evening and through the weekend – appear to have a detrimental effect on his wife's sense of recognition. 'We don't tend to talk much,' she says to the researcher, adding: 'A lot of weekends I'm just like a single mother because he works so hard. But, you know, he's the one who earns the money, really, you know, and these girls' – they have four daughters – 'are very expensive.' The assumption here is that if he did not work so hard, and spent more time with his family, he would not only be less effective within the legal field but would decline in the social space, and drag his family down with him. 'It's hard,' she laments another time, compounding her existing sense, communicated with melancholy, that Mr Patrick 'loves them [their daughters] more than he loves me,' i.e. that her position in the field relative to others – in terms of the capital of love if not symbolic power by other means – is not what she would like it to be.[3]

Others mobilise strategies to try to avoid letting the determinations from non-familial fields impair the desired balance of affective recognition within the family. For example, though we have already seen that both Mr Illsley and Ms James regularly spend time 'locked' or 'shut' in their studies at opposite spatial poles of their house where they can undertake practices that maintain or augment economic and cultural capital, both of them have made the decision to work more often in *shared* household spaces, including spaces shared with their daughters, such as at the dining-room table or in the living room. After making the earlier comment on shutting herself away, Ms James says: 'If it doesn't have to be, I try not to be like that, because otherwise it'd just be, Mr Illsley would be upstairs, I'd be downstairs, the girls would be in their rooms.' Mr Illsley adds:

> I tend not to come up here [to the study] and shut myself away unless I really have to, 'cos it just seems more communal if we can both work downstairs or if the girls – 'cos the girls read a lot, so we often joke about what a wild family we are,

because we're all sat there reading in the living room. And it's absolutely silent. And that's something we do together quite a lot.

This move toward communal work is, in itself, a play within the family field, contributing to the realisation of the category of family via 'spending time together' and maintaining the structure of affective relations, since spending time together is a demonstration of affective recognition, even if their minds are explicitly elsewhere at the time. Yet it also has effects for the reproduction of cultural capital insofar as it fosters an environment – one might say a domestic doxa – in which sitting and reading, and having jobs or studies requiring attention on an evening, is not only seen as normal but paired in perception with positive affectivity (see the next chapter, and cf. Atkinson, 2010: 82).

Working in shared spaces can, however, have its own effect on the balance of and flow between family and other fields in the stream of consciousness, as witnessed particularly among those who work from home but do not have 'a room of their own' to which they can retreat if they 'have to'. They instead requisition, for the pursuit of strategies in other fields, a desk within a room with an overt familial function (a kitchen or bedroom, for example), or a dining table, in the latter case folded within a particular temporal ordering since the table is a site of family practice, and struggle (e.g. over table manners), at other times of the day. The major consequence is a greater potential for the stream of consciousness to course between fields at a rapid and frequent rate – sometimes less so, if the study space is in the bedroom, but more so when the desk is in the kitchen, and especially when children and partners are milling around the vicinity. Mrs Allen, for example, is a sales representative for an academic publisher – another low-key player in the field of publishing, probably even lower-key than Mrs Samuels, whose form-filling and correspondence with clients contribute in their own way to the shifting forces and positions of the field. She has a modest desk in her kitchen – the hub of the house, as we have already seen – described by her daughter as 'Mum's space'. It hosts a computer, which she employs for home-based computing such as internet-shopping or arranging her children's extracurricular activities, but also a laptop and fax machine, which she uses when she works from home. However, the children, she states, 'wanna be close to where I am' when at home after school, reflecting the configuration of affective recognition, meaning they often entertain themselves on another laptop at the nearby breakfast bar. The following fieldnotes start at 3.30pm on a Friday:

> Mrs Allen, wearing a grey top, black skinny jeans and brown boots, lets me into the house and, when I ask how she is, she says 'cold' as 'I've been sat in the kitchen all day' working from home. We go into the kitchen, where her 12-year-old son, in a blue t-shirt and light-brown cargo pants, is sitting at the breakfast-bar laptop looking at a website whilst munching on something. Mrs Allen sits down at the laptop on her computer desk, next to the PC, and begins looking through emails. Mother and son don't talk for a few minutes, and the only noise is mouse-clicking and typing at computers. Suddenly, Mrs Allen initiates a conversation:
> MRS ALLEN: Have you got much homework?
> SON: Not too much. I'll do it over the weekend.
> MRS ALLEN: Don't save all of it.
> SON: It's not too much.
> MRS ALLEN: Okay. Well, I guess you won't have much time tonight, anyway [they are going to a relative's birthday party].

She then switches from her laptop to the PC before deciding to make a cup of tea whilst something is printing. She rubs her hands together for warmth, and whilst the kettle boils she goes upstairs and then into the dining room, collecting first a Lego box set and then some wrapping paper – this is the present to be given to the relative whose party they are attending this evening.

In a short span of time, because her workspace is where it is, attentive consciousness and practice have turned from the field of publishing (emailing, printing, typing documents) to quotidian concern with the reproduction of cultural capital (her son's homework), which also manifests Mrs Allen's symbolic power within the domestic microcosm (since she is policing the homework) and contains within its horizon the family event that evening, to the preparation of a birthday gift – a key act in maintaining the family as a group and its balance of power (cf. Bourdieu, 1998; 2000: 191–202) – and this is not to mention how thought may also have been turned toward the social and symbolic spaces via judgements of the researcher's appearance and manner on meeting. During the family interview, after complaining that having her desk in the kitchen yields a sense of constriction (hence making that extension to the house desirable), she acknowledges this splicing of participation in the fields of family and work that it brings:

> I guess the other downside of having it in terms of my work is the fact that I'll be logged on whilst cooking tea or whilst – whereas I guess if I had an office upstairs I'd kind of switch it off at the end of the day and it'd be that's that. So, because it's here in the kitchen, I would be more inclined to quickly check my emails [laughter]. I spend my life checking my emails!

In other words, there is a to-and-fro in practice between an activity plugging into the field of publishing (and the social space) and an act not only displaying and reproducing class taste but fundamental to the reproduction of the family group and its structure of recognition. Feeding the family is, after all, a major element of the system of unequal exchanges comprising the familial space (both Mr and Mrs Allen work, yet she does all the cooking and housework; but she also gets to impose her class tastes on the children by insisting they eat vegetables with every meal whether they like it or not). Though Mrs Allen seems to handle the balance between fields with cheer, one can imagine how attending to one could potentially compromise the other and effect positioning: burning food while emailing might be read as a sign of how little one cares for others within the family, or failing to respond to an email and close a deal builds a negative impression of what kind of employee one is and what kind of publisher one works for.

Likewise, diaries and observations reveal that Mr Yates frequently sends and receives emails, makes telephone calls and undertakes paperwork for his private physiotherapy practice – all activity related in however minor a way to the medical field – at the table in his kitchen (the hub of the house again) while also helping his sons with their homework, talking about their days and cooking their evening meal – acts of care as well as acts of reproduction, the former reinforcing the latter. His attention and his practice move backward and forward between the fields, crossing and even blurring their phenomenological boundaries repeatedly – he himself describes this 'very typical' situation as one of 'multitasking' – and, reminiscent of the Illsley/James household, this is a conscious strategy: the family used to have a study, but they found it too 'inconvenient' to trudge up and down stairs to transition between employment and domestic matters and instead opted to demolish the spatial (and mental) distance.

However, both Mr Yates and Mrs Allen seem to compensate for the looser spatial boundaries between work and family practices by drawing firm *temporal* boundaries. After 6.30pm and on weekends, Mrs Allen considers answering work emails 'beyond the call of duty', and, though she may well think about work, refuses to engage in any further activity related to it. Practices fusing interest in the familial field and tastes and values derived from the social space move centre stage instead: clearing up after the evening meal, helping her son with his homework and his Spanish guitar lessons and watching *Ugly Betty* before bed, for example. Mr Yates, though he often works into the evening after his children have gone to bed, draws a sharp perceptual boundary around Friday evenings, declaring, after the evening meal, 'No more work tonight' and clearing everything away. These nights have been allocated specifically to spending time with the family, playing games together, so as to avoid what Mr Yates sees as the invidious alternative, prevalent among some of his friends with what he calls 'high-powered jobs' who 'don't get to see their children much': sacrifice of time dedicated to the familial field, and the affective recognition it can bring, speaking of the balance of his libido between the multiple structural spaces in which he is positioned.

Home as sanctuary

The second group are those for whom the home as a whole is perceived to be a site dedicated solely to family activity. There is no region of the house colonised for focussed participation in a field of cultural, economic or ideological production, or for everyday practices of accumulating economic and cultural capital, for them (even if that is not the case for their partners); the spaces devoted to paid employment are all elsewhere, at remove from the home.[4] There is, therefore, a relatively clear phenomenological split, with the home often being described as a 'haven' or 'sanctuary' in which the pressures of the social space (e.g. earning money) and employment-based fields – though not class taste or reproduction, of course – are barred from thought, and family brought more to the forefront:[5]

> I close the door after work and I don't think about it any more […] I've kind of learned that when you've finished work it's like 'phew', you turn that part of your brain off until the next day and don't think about it. (Mr Babinski)

> I mean, there are times, depending what job I'm on, when I've been on big civic jobs or something, major building sites. You've got noise and dust, you know, all day long. It's nice to come home to a nice quiet – close the door on the world. There's that, I suppose. (Mr Cavendish)

MR GEOFFREY: We can shut ourselves away here and, you know, just be with one another. And that's, that's what also the back garden gives us as well – we've got that garden, our own little sanctuary away from the hubbub. [It's] a really good way to relax from the, what shall we call it, the furore of my job every day. You know, it's a real involved job, quite stressful job, so coming home here…
MRS GEOFFREY: You can just lose yourself in the garden.
MR GEOFFREY: I can just lose myself in the garden. I can come out here and potter, and just forget everything, get the girls out here with me.

Mr Lyons, commenting on the occupational hazard of bumping into customers in the streets around his home in Southville, and thus having to switch into a different mindset, adds:

> I mean, I think home is comfort, I'd say definitely comfort, security, a place where you can, you know, just literally walk in and flop out on the sofa and relax, chill out, and it's a place where I suppose really you can just completely be yourself and just, yeah, just relax and chill out, really. Because no matter where you are you've always got like 'work head' on, you know, you've always got to be – because – I'm a polite person, so if someone speaks to you, you're polite.

In some cases, the spatial and phenomenological split derives from the nature of employment: these people do not have the kinds of job where extra activity can or needs to be undertaken away from the designated site of work. This might be by formal decree, and therefore submission to symbolic power, or because, being excluded from significant decision-making and therefore effective participation within wider fields of production, and occupying subordinate positions and being less ensnared by the illusio in their organisational fields, they have less of a stake in their work beyond the acquisition of economic capital – the bare 'cash nexus', as Marx called it (cf. Bourdieu, 2000: 202–5). This is particularly the case for participants from the dominated and intermediate classes, whose lifeworlds are more likely to be spatially organised in this way. For others, however, the spatial segregation of work and home is the product of an explicit decision, or series of decisions, to prioritise family over career advancement, or at least to attain what is seen as a better balance between the respective pressures, in tune with the strength of the libido for each field. They could work from home, and others in similar roles may well work from home, but they do not – a decision bearing inevitable repercussions for their positioning within the organisational field and, insofar as it may affect promotion prospects and pay agreements, position in social space too.

Gender, though not the sole factor, is, as we know from Chapter 2, key in this regard. The feminine libido being channelled disproportionately toward the family field, or at least expectations of what women can and should do, including those institutionalised in law (e.g. maternity leave), defining the possible and the impossible, women are more likely to scale back their commitment to other fields, with likely consequences for their positioning. Mrs King provides a typical example of this: a banking and project analyst for an insurance firm, there is scope for her to work from home, but she opts not to – the office in the Kings' household is referred to as 'Dad's space' by their son during the home tour – and, indeed, she has arranged to work part-time, 28 hours a week, so she can finish at 2.30pm each day in order to pick the children up from school, take them to swimming practice, complete some domestic tasks and cook the evening meal. Despite receiving a promotion, she tells the researcher, 'I said I didn't want to work full-time because I wouldn't have the opportunity of being able to spend time with the kids.' Her career, after all, 'has not been so much important to me'. A little later, when talking about the future, she continues:

> I mean, my career aspirations at the moment aren't that strong because they're kind of…you know, we've got the kids, and the kids are still quite young, so probably until [daughter's] decided whether or not she's going to uni or anything like that. I probably wouldn't work more hours than I'm currently doing because it's not fair on family life – I need to be here with the kids. So it's kind of…you know, my career's kind of a little bit of a backburner more than anybody else's, you know,

than probably say [Mr King's] is, because I'm not the main bread-earner, I'm the... you know, mine is the supplementary income that means that we can have the lifestyle that we've got.

Yet this commitment to the familial field has distinct effects for her participation in her organisation's field:

> So there's lots of meetings to attend and stuff like that, so...and a lot of it is manag- ing the people. They arrange these meetings – because sometimes they arrange a lot of the meetings when I'm not there, so it's then sort of like reminding them, you know, 'Have you not looked in my online work calendar, that I've got a thing in there every day that says "'I'm not here from half-past two'"?, you know. But do you actually use the online calendar, or have you gone for a majority people can attend and, you know, "We'll accept that [Mrs King] can't go?"' So there are quite a bit... sometimes there's quite a bit that I actually miss out on because I'm not there in an afternoon, but that's a choice that I've consciously made, is that I want to work, you know, to be here for my kids. Because it's quite important that they have my time to be able to...you know, if they've got an issue with school or something like that, sometimes, you know, [daughter] will come out and say, 'Oh, they've all been horrible to me today at school,' and it's all raw in her mind and we can discuss it quite easily. So that's quite an important part of why I want to work part–time, is to...well, it's almost full-time, but it's quite an important part of why I want to be here on an afternoon.

In all this, then, there is clear indication of Mrs King's libido being more strongly channelled toward the familial field and its forms of recognition than her work-based field (also mobilising the justificatory trope of not being the 'breadwinner', itself loaded with gendered assumptions), and therefore her time and space, as well as her attention and practice, being dedicated to it to a greater extent than would be the case otherwise, though she implies that she continues working because she and her husband desire a certain amount of economic capital and the lifestyle it can bring – sources of recognition rooted in the social space and symbolic space, in other words. There is also indication that this decision, a multiple play since it constitutes a move in more than one field, has detrimental consequences for her capital accumulation within her employing organisation's structure of recognition and power as well as the social space more generally – a fate all too common for women in a social order where the players in the field of power continue to uphold, by various means, the orthodoxy that women should dedicate themselves to the familial field above all others.

However, while there may be no specific slice of domestic time-space assigned to the fields structuring paid employment, and while home may well, for the most part, be thought of as a sanctuary where family is the prime focus of attention – even if class is still there in the form of household consumption, taste and educational reproduc- tion – work-based phenomena still manage to bleed into consciousness while at home. Given that this often means a less desired form of justification is detracting from a more desired one, and invading the latter's space, the effects for wellbeing are usually, to greater and lesser degrees, pernicious. To begin with, there are those respondents who do not have a distinct space for working at home nor spend regular and sustained time periods engaged in activity related to it (i.e. reading, writing, planning etc.), but who are, thanks to the so-called 'wonders of modern technology' (especially smartphones), extending the chains of symbolic power linking field participants across the globe, always 'on call', i.e. making and receiving work-related telephone calls, or sending and receiving work-related emails. At any moment, or at a pre-planned moment, they can be hooked into a field whose participants and practices are at great spatial remove, while sitting among their children, having previously been engaged in, and subsequently returning to, family practices, and this might be seen as an unwelcome distraction by oneself and others. Mr Williams, for example, is an executive with a large multinational company who needs, from time to time, to liaise remotely with colleagues in different parts of the world, particularly the US, and this means that the most convenient time for telephone calls is often after his 'nine to five' is done, when he is at home, since he must talk to someone eight or more hours behind, even though there is no study or office in his family's flat. The result of this inability to spatially contain field effects, he says, is that it becomes harder to *mentally* 'departmentalise' work:

> It's up there [in his head], still, a bit hard to sort of departmentalise it. And sometimes I'm aware that – I'm a bit distant sometimes from the family because of what's churning on work-wise up there when it's all quite busy. Because it will go on in the evening as well because of the States, you know: BlackBerry will be going and the phone will sometimes go as well.

There is, therefore, a negative effect on his participation, and potentially his standing, in the familial field as his stream of consciousness regularly floats away from it to a different field, despite being among, and in the site usually dedicated to, family. He is, in fact, looking for a new role which will avoid this intrusion, such are the perceived ill-effects on his domestic relations.

Even for those who do not receive, respond to or check messages from work 'out of hours', however, there are all those moments – so many are recounted in respondents' diaries (among both men and women) – when, while being at home – making a cup of tea, eating breakfast, or whatever, usually at the start of a work day or (if they do not work weekends) on a Sunday evening – they are 'thinking about/stressed about/not looking forward to/dreading work'. Sometimes it is described as being in the 'background' – or, we might say, cycling between the periphery and theme of consciousness in antagonism with other tasks. Innocuous enough, it might seem, were it not an unwelcome incursion of field forces into the mind in a space from which they are intended to be excluded, and (since it inevitably knocks family thoughts out of one's head) the overrunning of one field in which one is heavily invested, and more or less dominant, by another in which one is sometimes less so. Mr Richards, a tax director for a multinational company, provides an elaborated account. 'I fight pretty hard to keep work at work and home at home,' he says, meaning that though he does occasionally have to undertake some work at home this is not the general rule, the house's study being instead more of a family space where the internet can be surfed, computer games played, family letters written and so on:

> If there's a lot on, you could end up working into the evening, over the weekend. And I do that, have done it, and I would do it if there were a short-term need, but I wouldn't do it generally. In the normal routine it's just got to wait.

In other words, Mr Richards tries to maintain a clear spatiotemporal cleavage in his lifeworld corresponding to commitment to his organisation's field (itself nestled within the economic field), rooted in his workplace, and his familial field, or the domestic sub-field thereof, anchored in the home. Underpinning this is an effort to dedicate more space and time to practices within the family field, indicating, perhaps, a greater investment of his libido in the latter compared to his work, and certainly a strategy within the family field not only adjusted to boost affective recognition there but forged in opposition to his own father's practice, since Mr Richards reports somewhat resentfully that he 'didn't do a lot with us' (Mrs Richards displays the same orientation in her stated antipathy to having been a 'latchkey kid' in her youth, cementing the subversion of former orthodoxies). In fact, reminiscent of Mr Williams, Mr Richards is looking for a new job with fewer demands 'cutting across things to do with the children' – i.e. meetings clashing with family activities – and is willing to take a pay cut to that end, but states he would not leave Bristol to take a new job on account of his children being settled in the city. He continues, however:

> But I think the other pressure is a sort of softer psychological pressure to be con-stantly thinking about work. And there's not a lot you can do to positively manage that other than, I suppose, get on with doing other things. Then if you're doing other things you're not as likely to think about work.

His wife confirms this: 'You need to actively do something in order to take the mind off the other stresses that are going on, and you get quite frustrated, don't you, if you're just not doing anything?'. The tussle between the different sources of recognition for headspace within a physical space intended largely for one of them is, therefore, something both he and others in the family field are evidently conscious of, and only by plunging into domestic activity is he able to suppress work-related relevances while at home. Quite apart from the subtle effects this might have on his standing at work, and in turn the position of his employer in the economic field (he may get less done for them, after all), this shapes his mode of participation in the family field and nuances his lifestyle – he spends little time sitting and watching television, instead doing the gardening, playing guitar, completing crosswords, playing rugby with his son in the park or going for evening walks with his wife.

In fact, the evening strolls are not quite so segregated, since Mr Richards often uses them as opportunities to talk through problems and strains at work, his wife acting as a sympathetic ear and a sounding board for events and strategies related to a field she does not directly participate in (her apparent care integrating the familial field at the same time), but they do still fulfil the function of keeping work-related thoughts outside of the home as much as possible. Indeed, there are others – including those who do work from home occasionally – for whom routinised time-space paths beyond the home serve as outlets for work-related thoughts, keeping their invasion of the home space to a minimum, though more often these are solo jaunts. Some – from certain sections of the social space, of course – go for runs in the morning or evening to get things 'sorted in my head', to 'plan for work' and suchlike, for example, like both Mr and Mrs Yates. There are others for whom the ritual journey to and from work (especially if it is a walk) serves as a useful *transitional* pathway, the movement from one spatial hub to another corresponding with phenomenological movement from concerns related to one field to those of another. Mr Geoffrey, for example, wrote in his diary that while travelling to work in the morning he is typically 'thinking about work', and conversely, when travelling home, he is 'looking forward to seeing [the] family'. A policeman with a pastoral role for drug addicts, he elaborates on his walk to work as a spatial spur for gearing into the bureaucratic field, in which he is a minor player and node in its circuits of symbolic power:

> I sort of just get going, think about what's going to be happening that day; try and plan my day as I'm walking along. Sort of, quite an intense role that I carry out at work, so…yeah, it's good to have a plan for each day, really, so you know how to actually start going about it when you get there.

Mr King, meanwhile, explicitly acknowledges that his own walk home from work served as a useful spatial and mental bridge between there and home – 'all the stress levels would go just with the walk home', he says – but that since his employer relocated their premises beyond walking distance, forcing him to drive to and fro, now 'you can bring the stress into the house a little bit'.

Others are less able to fend off the invasion of work into their headspace, thanks to the specific state of play and pressures of their organisational field, the social space and, indeed, the familial field. Mr Tanner, for instance, is a contract delivery manager for a housing organisation, and finds himself earning a salary (over £50,000 per annum) of the kind he has never earned before, yet the insecure nature of his job has instilled a fear of redundancy:

> I just think like, you know, I have to work at this level for as long as I need to for the family, basically. I haven't been earning this sort of money for very long, have I [he asks his partner], so it's relatively new for us […] I could easily in a couple of years find myself out of this post, maybe out of a job from redundancy and maybe I'll have to sign on to an agency or something. […] if I can keep this job and this income going for as long as possible it's going to contribute to our retirement.

First of all, let us note that 'keeping this job' combines pressures from both the familial field – doing it 'for the family', a typically masculine disposition to derive position from being the main 'provider' – and the social space – doing it to maintain a certain standard of living, i.e. economic capital, particularly into retirement, with the fear of redundancy being induced by the insecure work arrangements facilitated by machinations in the political and economic fields. His attitude is, therefore, to 'make hay while the sun shines', that is to say, to do whatever he can to improve his chances of maintaining his earning level. Yet, ironically, the serious stress he acknowledges this produces comes at cost to his participation, and perhaps standing, in the family field. Not only is it likely to persist in the periphery of consciousness, frequently threatening to become thematic, while at home with the family, and even to frame experience of his partner and son with a nagging negative horizon (of the order 'I'd enjoy this more if I wasn't so stressed'); he often finds himself unable to sleep at night due to stress, and gets up in the small hours, but this means he often falls asleep in the early evening, truncating his interaction with his partner and son – once he even fell asleep while in conversation with his partner's mother, which did not go down very well.

Leading on from this, there are all the admissions in the diaries, or at other points during the research week, to physical exhaustion from work, particularly at the end of the day, a bodily sensation which, even if not thematic in consciousness, forms a negative horizon for home experience, dampening the enjoyment otherwise to be had there, not least by pairing it with a specific motor protention of 'I can', or rather,

'I cannot', e.g. play with the children as long or as heartily as I would like. Of course, it works the other way too: dealing with family can leave one tired for work, and therefore less effective in the organisational, or wider, field. Or both pile up on one another and encumber participation in the work-based *and* family fields. As Ms Evans, a hospital consultant, puts it, while she tends to keep her employment (in her case involvement in the medical field as well as the organisation field comprised by the hospital) and her home life (the everyday acts of housework and childcare generated by and sustaining the family field) spatially and temporally distinct, she finds the balance between the two 'tiring' and comments that 'the hardest thing is trying to do both and do them both well. And I think sometimes you feel like you haven't really done either very well'.

However, not only can stresses and strains, whether corporeal or mental, produced by non-familial fields still manage to infiltrate the consciousness of those who opt not to actively dedicate a region within the domestic space to paid work. Intra-familial struggles over the balance of time and attention allotted to employment and family, of the kind we saw with the Patricks, can still occur too, but in these cases the prime source of contention is the amount of time one partner – nearly always male – spends in the distant spaces assigned to work at the expense of spending time in the space zoned for family. This is, to be sure, a source of tension where working from home occurs as well – Mrs Patrick, for example, also lamented the frequency with which Mr Patrick had to attend formal and informal work-related dinners and events (as so many occasions for fostering social capital) – but as part of a larger package of discontent over time-space organisation. For those who do not work from home, in contrast, this is the sole frustration, and, indeed, is exacerbated by their firmer home/work spatial division since they may have to spend longer in the workplace hub(s) or traversing certain work-based paths to complete their tasks or (especially in the case of overtime) accrue or maintain a desired amount of economic capital.

Displeasure, however, can emerge in multiple ways from the spatiotemporal articulation of fields. On the one hand, there are some workers who themselves openly resent having to spend more time in the spaces of work than at home in order to reproduce their economic capital because it prevents them from partaking in the affective exchanges and basking in the recognition of the family, toward which their libido is more strongly channelled, to the extent that they would like. Mr Nash, for example, works long hours as a delivery-driver and admits, 'I don't see as much of the kids as I'd like,' indicating that the necessities generated by his conditions of existence stop him from dedicating time and attention to that which is, ultimately, more important for his sense of justification and self-worth in the world, though both he and his wife, like others in the dominated class, seem to accept this invidious situation as an inevitable imposition if they are not to sink in the social space (see Atkinson, 2012: 28). He has, he says with characteristic brevity, 'got to do it'.

On the other hand there are some (male) workers who seem to be less vexed by their time out of the home, but whose (female) partners vigorously contest it as a counter-strategy to what they perceive as a lack of recognition within the family field. They use what symbolic power they do have in the family to this end ('if you love me…', 'if you don't…'), but possession of relatively ample economic and cultural capital could well boost this contestation too insofar as they each increase the likelihood of being in a position to question the inevitability of the arrangement. Take, for instance, the Quinn family. Mr Quinn, a commercial manager, does not usually get home from work until around 7pm, sometimes later, after Mrs Quinn, who works almost full-time as a teacher, has made the evening meal for herself and the children and eaten. Mrs Quinn reflects in the interview:

> It's quite disruptive for family life because I'd like us all to sit down at half-six and eat, and that rarely happens, and it's always this kind of – and you [Mr Quinn] get grumpy sometimes because you're like, 'Oh, I haven't got any food,' but I'm like, you know. […] It's bad enough cooking two different meals – I don't want to cook a third one when you rock up, you know. I mean, that is an issue, isn't it?

Mr Quinn's decision to work later than he is strictly contracted, in his wife's eyes, not only hampers one of key everyday acts of 'togetherness' that bonds the family into a group and maintains its internal doxa, but also suggests a devaluation of her (and the children) by someone she values. Yet Mr Quinn himself perceives Mrs Quinn's refusal to cook a separate meal for him, or keep some of theirs to warm up for him, as itself a failure to recognise him and his needs, inducing over time a sense of diminished affective capital in the field.

The issue extends beyond the evening meal, however, to housework and childcare too. When asked about the division of household labour, Mrs Quinn replies that 'It's not completely equitable, I obviously do more,' and of food preparation for the children that 'It's basically me. I do like cooking, but it's – when you've got kids and work full-time it's a bit like grit your teeth and get through it.' Mr Quinn's customary response was: 'I'm not around as much. I'm not around, I have work, and that's the sort of friction – "you're not pulling your weight", but "I'm actually not here" was my answer.' A rigid version of the common, traditional gender segregation of the familial field – the woman's acts garnering recognition and reproducing the family involving housework and childcare, the man's involving earning money and, consequently, engaging less in everyday affective exchanges – seemed to be emerging. Yet when the female partner also earns essentially a full-time salary, and is highly educated, challenge becomes more probable – higher education is, after all, closely tied to progressive views on gender relations (Houtman, 2003). Hence, after having had 'quite big rows about it', Mrs Quinn 'put her foot down' – flexed the symbolic capital she had, in other words, in the hope of gaining more – and said she was 'doing too much'. Mr Quinn yielded to some extent, agreeing to undertake the weekly shop for his wife and to cook his own meals when he gets home from work – but he does not come home any earlier.

Finally, there are instances where neither partner in a household is happy with the arrangement – the one thinking that they are being neglected, the other thinking they must work long hours or go on trips away from home in order to provide adequately. Here is Ms Kent, talking about the situation which prevails between her and her partner, Mr Johnson, who works as a fitness instructor, security provider and competitive martial artist, the first two of which entail work away from home at all hours of the day and evening and the latter of which involves weekends or weeks at competitions across Europe:

> I really struggled because it was so difficult with him being away a lot. I used to sit down feeling sorry for myself when I'd want to take the girls out, and it was so hard, like if he was away for the weekend and I'd think, 'Oh, I can't go out because I've got the two girls on my own – because it's so difficult.' But I've really got my head round it now and the girls are easier to handle, and I've just kind of accepted, you know, 'this is how it is'. And a lot of the time I was feeling sorry for myself.

And we had had lots of rows about it, and then one day – I wish he'd told me sooner – he said, 'Don't you ever think I don't want to be at work on my own?' And I thought, 'Oh, he's got a point.' And he really…you know, I just wish he… because he's very quiet…I just wish he'd told me that years ago, because I suddenly thought, 'Well, yeah, he doesn't want to be at work on his own, I don't want to be here on my own, but this is how it is and I wouldn't want it any other way, so we've just got to accept things and get on with it, really.' So, yeah, I've got my head round it now, but when they were younger it was loads more difficult and I had to do… there was lots of…we had lots of rows and this and that, but I think it's all panned out now, really, and we sort of accept things as they are, really.

Initially, then, Ms Kent read Mr Johnson's constant absence, and its disruption of family 'togetherness', as a privation of affective capital, with all its emotional fallout ('feeling sorry for myself') and, like Mrs Quinn, sought to challenge it using what symbolic power within the field she had (it is perhaps worth remembering that she too has a degree). His response, however, suggested that his absences were, to his mind, necessitated by their conditions of existence, i.e. their relative proximity to necessity (which, Ms Kent notes, was somewhat exacerbated by the economic climate at the time of the research), bringing her round to acceptance of – though by no means satisfaction with – the spatiotemporal ordering of the articulation between fields in their lifeworlds similar to the Nash family's.

Home as hub of mundane multiplicity: conclusions on domestic space

Domestic space is not simply the domain for displaying class taste, enacting class dispositions, and undertaking practices of class reproduction – it is so much more than that. As a pivotal hub of people's everyday lifeworlds it is shaped by forces, dispositions and practices forged in a multitude of fields, sometimes competing, sometimes harmonising, not least those of their family and the specific cluster structuring their paid employment, while also having its own impact, in turn, on the possible and impossible in those fields. Objects, decisions and actions have thus been shown in this and the last chapter to be layered with pertinence in relation to many struggles for recognition, or, we might say, to have in their horizon the state of play and possibles within more than one social game, and to constitute plays – sometimes disadvantageous ones – in multiple quests for capital. People have not just a 'sense of the game', as Bourdieu had it, but a sense of the *games* they are positioned in, and practices are often, if not nearly always, *alloys*, driven by and affecting the structure of myriad fields. The size, shape and design of the home, meanwhile, have emerged as constraints and enablements, demonstrating that the dialectic of physical space and structural spaces occurs within the home as well as beyond it.

In relation to decor, for example, we saw that furniture, pictures, photos and knick-knacks are, indeed, structured by class taste, but that they also have significance, and are sources of struggle, in relation to quests for recognition from kin. They may well be objects of aesthetic judgement and even aid in the process of reproduction, but they are also symbols of heritage and togetherness, and of love, care and attention to the wishes of others – or the lack thereof – and the two aspects might dovetail or conflict. In relation to regionalisation within the home, moreover, we saw that class resources, via size of house and number of rooms, have a distinct effect on the way in which everyday family life is lived, playing into the content of the doxa, struggle and affective capital within the field and having knock-on effects for class reproduction insofar as they offer affordances for self-directed and parent-scaffolded accumulation of cultural capital. The differential capacity to possess and personalise a 'space of one's own' and the contrasting locations – kitchens or living rooms – and uses – focussed conversation or television-watching – of household hubs were the two key differences in this respect. This brought us to focussed analysis of conversation around the dinner table, or on sofas, while the evening meal is being eaten at home, which revealed not only the oscillation of consciousness between pertinences and forces from the familial field and the social space, as well as other fields, but their fusing and, amongst the dominant, transition via a disposition to foster symbolic mastery, or, more precisely, a world horizon appresenting (in Husserl's sense) pedagogical possibility in the most intimate of interactions.

Finally, in relation to the correspondence between the spatiotemporal organisation of domestic spaces within the lifeworld and direction of consciousness toward different fields, we have seen all manner of tensions, strains and conflicts. Broaching broader issues of 'work-life balance' and the gendered division of household labour, whether people have spaces at home dedicated to activities of capital accumulation in non-familial fields or not, mental incursions or time away from significant others can have specific effects on positionings within the familial field, and, conversely, time away from work in order to undertake family practices can have often detrimental effects on positioning in the fields structuring employment as well as the social space itself. Either way, it has to be acknowledged that – even if the experiences of social space are somewhat more encompassing – this is how participation in any one field, whether of family relations or of production or of an organisation, actually occurs, and what it feels like, for many people in everyday life: it is not total immersion, with attention focussed on it twenty-four hours a day, but moments of greater and shorter length in regular periods or snatched here and there, in competition with other fields, often while sited in certain physical spaces at certain times.

Notes

1   We can only talk of tendencies: it is impossible to capture the full fluidity of how, when and where consciousness turns from one theme to another, but we can identify certain structures of correspondence. Of course, there are also often multiple significances – thinking about a family holiday, for example, is relevant to both the familial field and the symbolic space, and children's extracurricular activities are bound up with the nurturing of cultural capital as well as symbolic power within the family – but some themes of consciousness plug more into one field than another.

2   It is also true that participation in a field of production, and the practice of capital accumulation in the social space, in one's study, and indeed anywhere, can be disrupted by brief or lingering phenomenological plugging-in to the symbolic space, as when a picture on the wall or a song on the radio prompts an aesthetic judgement, however banal ('I really do like those colours', 'this song's rubbish', etc.)

3   It is possible that Mrs Patrick compensates this sense of relative lack of affective recognition with other forms of symbolic power operative within the familial field, since she is quick to lose her temper and shout at the children throughout the observations as a means of patrolling the 'done thing', what is acceptable and so on, i.e. the orthodoxy, of the field.

4   This is not to say the determinations of the social and symbolic space are completely absent, not only because of decor, as we have already explored, but insofar as home can be a site of expenditure of economic capital, especially via the internet, or prompt one to worry about paying the mortgage or rent.

5 It must not be overlooked that those tending to describe the home in this way are often (though not always) male, recalling Lasch's (1976) assertion that family and home serve as a 'haven in a heartless world' and the feminist retort that while they may do so for men, who derive greater symbolic power within their familial and domestic fields, including as a compensation against the stresses and domination experienced at work, this is less the case for women, who are more likely to occupy relatively subordinate positions within the family field – and yet, as we will soon see, tend to be disposed to dedicate more of their time and attention to it thanks to the workings of masculine domination.

References

Agger, B. (2016) *Speeding Up Fast Capitalism*. London: Routledge.

Atkinson, W. (2010) *Class, Individualization and Late Modernity: In Search of the Reflexive Worker*. Basingstoke: Palgrave Macmillan.

Atkinson, W. (2012) 'Economic Crisis and Classed Everyday Life' in W. Atkinson, S. Roberts and M. Savage (eds.) *Class Inequality in Austerity Britain*. Basingstoke: Palgrave Macmillan, pp. 13–32.

Bourdieu, P. (1998) *Practical Reason*. Cambridge: Polity Press.

Bourdieu, P. (2000) *Pascalian Meditations*. Cambridge: Polity Press.

Bourdieu, P. (2008) 'A Conservative Revolution in Publishing' *Translation Studies*, 1(2): 123–53.

Burchell, B., Lapido, D. and Wilkinson, F. (eds.) (2002) *Job Insecurity and Work Intensification*. London: Routledge.

Daly, K. (1996) *Families and Time*. London: Sage.

Houtman, D. (2003) *Class and Politics in Contemporary Social Science*. New York: Aldine de Gruyter.

Lasch, C. (1976) *Haven in a Heartless World*. New York: Basic Books.

McNay, L. (1999) 'Gender, Habitus and the Field' *Theory, Culture and Society*, 16(1): 95–117.

Wajcman, J. (2008) 'Life in the Fast Lane? Towards a Sociology of Technology and Time' *The British Journal of Sociology*, 59(1): 59–77.

9 Struggles for love and social reproduction

That intergenerational reproduction of the social space is not the cold and mechanical process that some critics of Bourdieu imagine it to be – that it is, instead, bound up with love, affection, care, desire and, with that, immense joy and satisfaction as well as struggle, tension and distress – has already been broached in the preceding chapters. Let us explore this more fully now by bringing front stage the practices and exchanges within families through which children's class positions are forged and maintained. The focus is not so much going to be on so-called 'extracurricular' activities, though these occurred in abundance among the families participating in the research and fell roughly along class lines in number, variety and type. Others have explored these amply (e.g. Lareau, 2003; Vincent and Ball, 2007), and so we would only be providing confirmation of established phenomena. Some have even drawn out the entanglement of targeted activities delivering cultural capital with familial intimacy (Stefansen and Aarseth, 2011), though they fail to root that intimacy within the doxa and struggles of the familial field imbuing the activities with multiple pertinences within the world horizon and, of course, furnishing the explanatory principle for why parents and children would engage in these activities in the first place.

Instead the spotlight will be on the more mundane, subtle and pervasive actions and exchanges between family members in daily life continuously channelling children's libidos toward, or away from, development of the masteries misrecognised as legitimate in the education system and translated into cultural capital. For as Bourdieu (2000) broached, and has been detailed elsewhere (Atkinson, 2016), it is only through the constant, almost imperceptible interactions in which parents – the first major targets of a child's quest for value in the eyes of others, and thus the first others to whom they routinely submit – bestow or appear to withhold recognition from children do children see their activities and the associated symbolic prizes as worthy of, or in need of, pursuit. Whether it be through explicit gifts and rewards for performances, displaying examples of work or awards, or, more ubiquitously, through the frequency and intensity of verbal and gestural praise or admonishment (some examples of which we have already seen at the dinner table), the struggle for the specific form of capital generally operative within the family today – love, care, affection – is the conduit for initial capital accumulation outside of it. Of course it should not be forgotten that, the familial field and its domestic subspace being sites of contestation like any other field, the dominated – in this case usually (but not necessarily always) the children – are prone, depending on the particular state of play within the field (and thus their sense of the possible given by their position), to strategies of subversion. In some cases this can even, as has been found previously, engender a revolution within the field, tearing apart the otherwise uniting doxa, pitting orthodoxies against heterodoxies in an acrimonious clash and sending young people on divergent trajectories through the education system and social space (Atkinson, 2012). For the most part, however, including among the families taking part in the research presented here, conflicts and efforts to impose an alternative way of doing things, from the earliest years through to adolescence, are much subtler, infusing all the little resistances and protests about being made to do something disagreeable or reaction to perceived failure in the eyes of others, and still usually add up to what would be called, at the 'macro' level, social reproduction.

In the following I will focus primarily on a few case studies of families from contrasting zones of social space selected because they provide particularly clear illustrations of the way in which the emotion-laden minutiae of quotidian practice dovetail with the development of interests and capacities of differing worth in the contemporary misrecognition order and, therefore, the education system. They will each be unfolded in a two-step manner. First, I will present the parents' hopes and desires for children's futures as an indicator of what must be done, in everyday practice, for their children to attain parental recognition – or, more prosaically, to make them happy, proud, content, etc. and avoid causing disappointment, shame, and so on. After that I will recount instances of observed *in situ* struggles relating at one and the same time to familial recognition and accumulation of class capitals.[1] The dominant class will be considered first, including a report of instances when things do not go so smoothly, followed by the sharply contrasting examples from among the dominated class. Coverage of those falling into more intermediate positions will round out the analysis, though here the data is, unfortunately, a little sparser and complicated by the composition of the sample.

Learning for love

The first cultural-capital-rich case, encountered several times already, is the Newcombe/ Oliver household. Mr Newcombe, 63, is a policy consultant operating within the European Union. His father was an accountant and his mother a housewife and he possesses a master's degree, but while his expenses are all paid and he owns his large house outright due to inheritance, he earns a modest salary of £25,000 per annum. His partner, Ms Oliver, 52, is a business development consultant in the charitable sector. Her father was a civil servant and her mother a medical secretary. She too has a master's degree and earns a modest £10–20,000 per annum depending upon contracts, though that is a considerable drop in salary from her last job as a government researcher, meaning she occupies a not dissimilar social position to Mr Newcombe's. They have a 15-year-old son, Bobby,[2] and a 10-year-old daughter, Sophie, and Mr Newcombe has three adult children from a previous marriage (whom, interestingly, he says are always 'getting at' his younger children and criticising the way he is bringing them up). When asked what they want for their children, Ms Oliver responds that she wants them to 'get what they can from school' and that she will 'encourage them in whatever it is that they're good at' and seek to give them 'the chance to explore and be able to move on to anything that particularly grabs them', giving the example of organising a French exchange trip for Bobby when he expressed interest in the language. Already, then, it would seem that the kinds of objects or ends to which she would like her children to be oriented are closely bound up with the school and scholastic knowledge. But Mr Newcombe – professing to speak for the 'we' – interjects:

> I think that we steer them a bit more than that. So when you said you'd like them to be able to achieve in something that particularly grabbed them, if that was being a merchant banker we wouldn't necessarily....and I put it more strongly: I certainly have a hope that when they get of working age that they will be doing something to make the world a fairer place, or the fact that half the world are starving, that they will take an interest in those kind of things rather than becoming rich or living in a big house. […] We've definitely, by the programmes that we encourage them to watch, the newspapers we encourage them to read, and books and stuff, left of centre, *and it's quite important to us that they understand and appreciate what it is.* I mean, if [Bobby] does decide to become a Tory, then we won't cut him off, obviously, but *we are pleased that he is sympathetic to a left-of-centre point of view* (emphasis added).

Here the affective significance of not only cultivation of a certain symbolic mastery but a spurning of economic capital and development of a particular political position-taking, indicating a desire that their children reproduce not just their class but class fraction, is made clear, indicating the kinds of things Bobby and Sophie must do and be to give pleasure to their parents (or at least Mr Newcombe) and thus win recognition and affective capital. When the possibility of university is broached, Mr Newcombe says it is not strictly necessary for them to 'achieve' the kind of future he would like for them, giving his former boss as an example, but then Ms Oliver points out that university will ensure the level of 'learning' – i.e. embodied cultural capital – necessary to reach the desired site in social space. She continues:

> And I think that if they went to university and they got something that enriched their kind of learning and their thinking and then went off and became a social worker on whatever social workers get, you know, far lower than [Mr Newcombe's old boss] ever earned, that would be good for me because I'd think, 'Well, they got all that'.

In any case, their children's emerging masteries have facilitated a particular perception of the possible – 'Knowing their brains to the extent that I currently do,' says Ms Oliver, 'I think they've both got the capacity to' succeed through university, while their economic condition and practice – they have already saved the money to pay for their son's tuition fees – indicates that higher education is a more or less assumed destiny.

That Bobby 'loves' school, considers his sociology GCSE as more of a 'hobby' than work, sat his French GCSE early and tutors older children may be taken as indicators of the channelling of his libido in the direction his parents wish. But the actual *process*, the way in which development of symbolic mastery (and not just of social affairs) is bound up with the struggle for recognition from parents disposed to recognise certain practices, is observable in everyday life. One Saturday lunchtime, for instance, Bobby and Sophie are sitting in the kitchen/dining room while their parents prepare soup. The topic of conversation turns to mathematics, with Bobby announcing he had a maths test that week and, as if to impress his parents, that he 'did Pythagoras' theorem in one question, solved the volume of a trapezium'. He continues, with some measure of pride, to say, 'It was really easy. I answered all but one that I didn't bother about.' His sister, witnessing this boast, tries to show her mother an equation she herself did at school, on a piece of paper, with her mother telling her to show Mr Newcombe. Bobby tries to counter by interrupting and asking a question about his drama performance the next week, but Ms Oliver tells him to be quiet while Sophie explains her equation. Mr Newcombe asks if Sophie got her equation correct at school, and when she says yes he immediately and happily responds 'What a star!' – a clear act of recognition, a token of familial capital, bringing a smile to his daughter's face. Bobby, not to be outdone, starts trying to flex his mathematical muscles by telling Sophie, in view of his parents, that he can 'factorise' the equation. He takes the paper and performs his manipulation of symbols, showing his mother while goading his sister to 'write an algebraic one'. She does so, but both Bobby and Ms Oliver spot an error, forcing her to give a sheepish 'Sorry [Bobby], sorry, Mum'. Bobby then states, his eyes glinting with eagerness for recognition, 'I'll draw a Pythagoras question for you, Mum.' Shortly afterwards he asks what the area of a trapezium is, having drawn one, and Sophie offers to work it out for him. Bobby clearly does not want her to (it threatens to diminish his own standing) and scoffs, 'You don't know how to.' When she suggests splitting it into triangles Mr Newcombe exclaims, 'Well done, Sophie!', after which there ensues a physical battle over the paper and pen, with Bobby using his physical capital to muscle his sister away. Ms Oliver intervenes and tells them to do it on separate pieces of paper. As they perform their operations Bobby sounds out technical terms as if to present his mastery publicly ('parallel one, parallel two by convertible height') while Sophie splits the trapezium into triangles. Everyone concludes that Sophie has done it 'the easy way' and, to her visible pleasure, Mr Newcombe congratulates her. As one last act, however, when then talking about working out the area of a circle and the need for pi, and Sophie says pi equals seven and Mr Newcombe corrects her to say it is 3.1416, Bobby interjects with a boastful 'Pi goes on forever.' 'You're making it up,' retorts his sister in a bid to counteract, but he self-assuredly responds: 'Theoretically you'll never know when the end is.'

Attaining or failing to attain recognition in the moment should not be mistaken for winning or losing significant amounts of capital, as if the structure of the family field were constantly in violent flux. Moments of recognition are only symbols of the deeper state of play; and domestic symbolic capital is accumulated and sustained only through the constant labour of these small, seemingly innocent, everyday strategies for parental attention. For the most part, and notwithstanding the effect of specific events, the structure of the field remains relatively stable, shifting only slowly through time, and provides the conditions of possibility for the kinds of strategies pursued. The rivalry between the Newcombe/Oliver children, for example, must be contextualised by the fact that the parents are aware that their son has in the past attracted and still tries to attract his parents' attention at the expense of his sister, who is often 'quietly interested in things' compared to Bobby's brashness and dominated by him in conversation, something which they are consciously trying to rectify.

The second exemplar among the cultural-capital rich is the Allen family. Mrs Allen, let us recall, is a sales representative for a publisher of school textbooks. Though she did not attend university despite initial intentions, she appears to possess ample inherited and embodied cultural capital (her father is a very successful architect, her mother a teacher, she speaks French and has a taste for Camus, Matisse and Picasso). Her husband, Mr Allen, is a highly paid telecommunications engineer with a degree. His father was 'in insurance' while his mother did secretarial work. Like the Newcombe/Oliver family, the Allens have two children, Jack, 12, with a precocious interest in architecture and engineering, and Olivia, 10, who 'loves' school and – idealising, in Chodorow's (1978) sense, and wanting to be like a much-loved and often-visited auntie – desires to be a teacher. Mrs Allen also reveals the entwinement of emotional stakes with educational success when asked what she wants for her children, though in this case it is less bound up with a particular site of social space and version of symbolic mastery so much as a generic desire for her children to 'do well' by accruing legitimated capital:

MRS ALLEN: But you do have your expectations and – maybe not expectations as such,
        but you do kind of want them to do well and be good at stuff, and it's quite hard…
OLIVIA: If they're not!
MRS ALLEN: If they're not. There are some things that you might be disappointed in.

Despite higher education not being mentioned in the question, she goes on to say: 'I mean, I didn't go to university, and I've come out fine,' and, with an evident hesitancy, 'If they don't go to university, it's not the end of the world' – indicating implicitly that attendance is the assumed and preferred course. She encourages Olivia's artwork, describing her as 'our little artiste' and displaying her works on the mantelpiece in what they jokingly describe as a 'shrine to [Olivia]', and has persuaded Jack to take up Latin classes, not through appeals to love or care but by giving him extra pocket money (a consequence of her symbolic power), in the belief that it will be 'good for him' – and, given the nature of the subject, that can only mean it will stand him in good stead for an academic future.

One evening, after the evening meal, Mrs Allen is helping Jack with his Latin homework in the kitchen, getting him to translate simple sentences and correcting his pronunciation (she obviously has some familiarity with Latin), while Mr Allen sits at the laptop on the breakfast bar. As Olivia enters with a hardback, thick-papered drawing pad and a book on how to sketch Victorian fashion, Mrs Allen reminds Jack that there is a website on his homework test where he can translate random sentences in a timed test. They go over to the laptop, Mr Allen moving aside, and Jack begins doing the test repeatedly until he gets ten out of ten in six seconds. Each time, Mrs Allen, standing closely over Jack's shoulder, exclaims 'Wow, look at that!', 'That's amazing!' and 'I don't think you'll beat that!', much to her son's delight (he grins broadly). Display of symbolic mastery has won esteem in the eyes of the esteemed. During the excitement, Olivia tries to show her mother a drawing she has done ('Mum, look…Mum!'), eager to be seen and valued as well, and Mrs Allen breaks away from the laptop to signify care and interest: 'That's good, darling, is it a new one?' Olivia nods and smiles at her confirmation of self-worth. Mr Allen, as during other similar events in the week (e.g. Jack's Spanish guitar practice), stays quiet throughout, suggesting his role in fostering this form of cultural capital is more limited, though he is observed at other points trying to nurture and encourage an interest in engineering and technology with his son (they talk intimately about gadgets and bridges, for example).

Hysteresis and counter-pressures

Of course, exchanges within these families may not always blend family-specific capital and accumulation of cultural capital so smoothly. There will be moments of greater and lesser disagreement and resistance, and different phases of the children's lives where other interests and idealised others shape practice, or when the sense of their place makes more subversive activity desirable, may bring long periods of tension and instability. For example, the Newcombe/Oliver family admit that, in the not too distant past, Bobby had for one reason or another gone through a stage of displaying 'challenging behaviour', frequently 'locking horns' with his mother in particular and generating 'considerable stress' within the house, but that, 'gradually and remarkably', he had settled down, becoming more 'sociable and work-oriented', even if he still has a 'quick temper' and can be 'rude and unpleasant' at times. Sometimes, however, a longer-running phenomenon can engender a much more disjunctive relation between class and family. Two cases illustrate different variants of this scenario: in one instance, discordance between parental expectations and desires on the one hand and a child's performance and perceived ability on the other, generating tension and conflict but also a difficult readjustment of the sense of the possible and desirable; in another, conflicting pressures within the lifeworld hindering frequency and duration of parental pedagogy.

Mr Tanner, whom we have already seen fretting over his job insecurity, is not deprived of legitimated capitals. We know he earns just over £50,000 per annum, on top of owning a house with almost no mortgage, and to that we can add that he has a degree and attended boarding school. His father was an economically successful grocer, and his mother a primary school teacher. His partner, Ms Upson, also works in the public sector, as an events officer, also attended boarding school and also has a degree (in humanities), though she comes from a line of globe-trotting diplomats and civil servants, suggesting a greater degree of inherited capital, and currently earns a much lower salary of £14,000 per annum. Their son, Billy, was adopted when he was aged 15 months and is now 10 years old. He was diagnosed with receptive language delay and attention deficit hyperactive disorder (ADHD), and it is through this lens that his parents define his conduct with them as 'challenging', self-centred ('me, me, me') and 'a bit more out of control' than other children's. However, indicating that this conduct is perhaps specific to or at least accentuated by the familial field, and thus key to Billy's field-specific habitus (which is only part of his overall social surface), they also acknowledge that

> when he's around other people, he's usually fine, very polite, but when it's just us, it can be a bit of a challenge. So with dinner, for example, he might be okay with Adam [the researcher] there, but it's a bit of a challenge for us […] he knows he can push the boundaries with us. (Mr Tanner)

It is also interesting that relations between Billy and Ms Upson have been tense from the very start, as this is bound to have fed into the structure and dynamic of the domestic subspace of the family field and, therefore, Billy's current habitus and behaviour. As Mr Tanner states:

> [Billy] sometimes used to drive her up the wall. I'd come home from work and find [Ms Upson] sat halfway up the stairs, the baby gate down at the bottom and [Billy] trying to get at her and she putting a physical distance between her and [Billy]. Just to kind of keep herself from damaging him in any way, 'cos he'd just driven her completely to distraction, which is, you know, I think a lot of small children can.

In any case there are two observable ways in which this tension colours the relationship between class reproduction and family.

The first is that efforts at pedagogy are particularly fraught, troubling any link between the quest for recognition within the family and the acquisition of cultural capital. Helping Billy with homework, for example, or even just getting him to do it, is a constant battle. As Ms Upson puts it:

I mean, both of us obviously want him to get the best education he possibly can within our means and within his capabilities, you know. So, I mean, with the homework, I find it incredibly stressful, and I could just say to him, 'just get on with it yourself,' and he would hand in an inadequate piece of work every week, which isn't going to do his confidence much good and isn't going to help him. [...We're] trying to make him do the work, trying to make him think more rather than just sitting back and expecting it to land on his lap.

She also describes aiding Billy with his homework as the 'low point of my week', and notes in her diary for the research that it is 'One of the most stressful jobs of the week – invariably involves raised voices and arguing. Very frustrating.' That they insist on helping and even, as they say, 'pushing' Billy, unlike families we will see later, is an alloy of their class dispositions – in which success within the education system is seen as 'the done thing' – and familial desires – committing themselves to assisting Billy is an act of care, a strategy within the family feeding into the structure of affective and power relations within it. The same multiple play can be witnessed in their investment of money and time in extra tuition for Billy and Ms Upson's efforts to secure disability living allowance to help pay for it. Yet parental assistance nearly always ending with tension and anger may well taint pursuit of cultural capital with a negative hue for Billy, hardening his already resistant attitude toward it.

The second consequence, inevitably entwined with the first, is not only that Billy's performance at school is deemed relatively poor, but that his parents' expectations and hopes for the time to come, otherwise attuned to the class future they would have expected given their resources, trajectories and familial doxa and wrapped up in a desire for their son to thrive (as they define it), have been shockingly dashed and slowly readjusted. The sense of the probable forthcoming – the subjective field of possibles – has been repeatedly challenged by events, transforming the horizons of perception attending thought and talk of their son's prospects, and since this *hysteresis effect* and the perceptual shifts it generates involve someone to whom they give and from whom they seek affective recognition – and not just someone they invest in as a continuation of the family project, as Bourdieu's language sometimes implied – this is not only disorientating but distressing. Mr Tanner recalls returning from a parents' evening at Billy's school, where the teachers 'slated' his son, 'absolutely devastated': 'It absolutely killed me. I mean, I was just so upset with the whole thing, and that's when we first got an inkling of the fact that [Billy] was failing pretty badly at school, basically.' Since then he has formed the judgement that his son is 'not going to be the brightest spark', and Ms Upson states that 'the way things are at the moment, I don't envisage that he would be going to university', though she has now reconciled herself to that future, comforting herself with the thought that, 'Well, actually it doesn't matter if he doesn't; that's not the be all and end all. You can actually have a career without going to university, you know.' Yet, importantly, this categorisation and halo of expectations feeds back into practice, discouraging Billy's parents from engaging in mundane peda-gogic activity – familial affective exchange nourishing valued capitals – with him and, perhaps, unintentionally *fulfilling their prophecy themselves.* At home one day Mr Tanner and Ms Upson are talking about whether Billy should be taught how the kettle works, with Ms Upson suggesting that he should know how to use it. Mr Tanner is direct and uncompromising: 'We're not letting [Billy] near a kettle,' he says, as 'we've always thought he's 18 months behind.' Ms Upson is unsure, but he states conclusively, 'I wouldn't be comfortable with it.'

The revaluation of possible futures may be in part a resignation to objective prob- abilities in relation to the social space, making a virtue of a previously unforeseen neces- sity perhaps, but it interplays with the specific forces – the illusio and stakes – of the familial field, or at least the domestic subspace thereof. For ultimately Mr Tanner and Ms Upson's greatest desire is that their son be *happy* in life, whatever future that may entail. In Mr Tanner's words:

> Well, I mean, we want him to be numerate and literate, but, I mean, the main thing at the end of the day, we want him to be happy in his life, you know. He doesn't have to go to university or be, you know, incredibly academic to achieve that. But, you know, if he's got the basic skills and we can guide him, you know, possibly at sixteen instead of going on to A levels he'll go on to tech college and do a more, you know, technical vocational-based course, you know. Even if he's a plumber, doesn't matter, as long as he's happy and he can earn a reasonable living.

Even here the future, and their role in producing it, is stubbornly conceived within certain limits – acquiring technical capital if not cultural capital, and earning a 'reasonable' amount of economic capital, with their guidance – but the giving of care, recognition of Billy's contentment as paramount, is woven through it and, in the end, trumps (or at least compensates) the original reproduction strategy.

The second instance of social reproduction being far from smooth – which may well reveal something of what goes on in other families, though it was certainly most evident here – comes from the Samuels family. Mrs Samuels, as we have seen previously, is a publishing manager, earning £35,000 per annum. She attended a private school in Bristol, at the behest of her father (a computer programmer), and has a degree in English and theatre, Brecht being her particular interest. Academic books on literature, poetry, women's studies and theatre – just one example of objectified cultural capital in the house, there to remind Mrs Samuels of 'what work I did' – are thus stacked up in tall bookcases in the living room. True enough, these resources may be more or less 'unac- tualised', as Lareau (2003) would put it, insofar as they are not obviously drawn upon in regular explicit pedagogy, though the very presence of these books and the names and words they have on their spines still plays into the sense of the normal, the possible and the familiar characterising the household and its inhabitants' lifeworlds, as well as providing potential resources for the future or unintentionally capital-building allevia- tors of boredom. Mrs Samuels' husband, a human relations advisor earning £33,000 per annum, has an undergraduate degree in sciences and a postgraduate diploma, and also attended private school, so symbolic mastery in relation to a variety of subjects is not short within the house. His father was an hotelier and his mother a French teacher, implying some degree of inherited cultural capital.

The Samuels' twin children, Max and Grace, are ten years old, and they struggle to help them with their homework. Proximity to necessity is not the problem here, nor is a dearth of symbolic mastery. Instead the issue appears to be the conflicting demands and effects of different fields structuring the Samuels' lifeworlds, particularly Mrs Samuels' lifeworld. We have, in fact, already seen in Chapter 8 the way in which relevances flowing from her position within the publishing field compete with those anchored in the familial field, but now we see how the lingering effects on conscious- ness and corporeality of sustained attention to the actions aggregating to form strategies within the publishing field – the phone calls, meetings, read-throughs and so on to get books published – drain time, attention and energy away from explicit pedagogical work within the family even when at home. Of her work she states 'mentally it's quite demanding', to the point where she simply cannot read a book for pleasure when she comes home (an interesting nuance in the genesis of her particular lifestyle setting her at odds with the general tendency of those within her neighbourhood of social space), but more pertinently:

> And I think if I've had a particularly busy day I'm a bit short-tempered with the kids. Obviously, you know, I find it hard then to settle down and do their home-work. I don't feel like I've got that kind of energy at the end of the day. It's nice to have a switch and do more practical things, like cooking or…you know, house-work things, but to then sit down with the children and read to them or do their educational things, I do find that quite hard, which isn't great for them. Pretty bad, really, isn't it?

She goes on in relation to homework:

MRS SAMUELS: I don't think we do anywhere near enough of it, really […] They get about an hour and a half homework a week, I think, and we never do it. […] We try and do their spellings with them, but they just don't seem to want to do it. So because they're not enthusiastic and we're not very pushy parents I don't think – are we?

MR SAMUELS: No, we're not.

MRS SAMUELS: Some of the parents at the school make sure they've done every single piece of homework and so on, but we're not really like that. But that partly is a time thing. By the time we've all got home and cooked and eaten and done all other things, that seems to go to one side, doesn't it?

There is need for a phenomenological buffer zone – not strictly between fields, since the tasks Mrs Samuels mentions as wind-downs are evidently relevant to the domestic microcosm, but between periods of mental exertion or focus relating to different fields (juggling contacts and schedules on the one hand, engaging symbolic mastery in order to foster it on the other). Though James (1950) used it to articulate something slightly different about consciousness, it recalls his distinction between the moments when consciousness is in 'flight' and the more restful, 'perching' moments. The trouble is, without those phenomenological resting points Mrs Samuels feels unable to 'settle down' to homework assistance – she finds it difficult to concentrate as her mind is invaded by the pressures stemming from another field despite apparently being engaged in a practice relating to the family and class reproduction – yet if she does have them they take up so much time that the homework does not get done.

Formally set schoolwork is, however, only a small element of the reproduction pro-cess as a whole. There are also all the extracurricular activities the Samuels encourage their children to pursue, for example: both Max and Grace play musical instruments (drums and cornet, respectively); both play a variety of sports (football, tennis, dodge-ball, fencing, archery, martial arts); Grace attends drama club; Max wants to attend sci-ence club, and so on. Then there is the regulation of television within the home: the children are not allowed to watch more than one hour per weekday, or two hours on a weekend day, and Mr and Mrs Samuels try to steer them towards 'educational programmes' like *Newsround*, *Horrible Histories* and *Natural World*, and 'more intelligent' programming of the kind they associate with the BBC, rather than 'American rubbish' which they find 'unbearable'. They are also pleased that their children are now – perhaps wanting to know what those who they seek recognition from value – 'more and more […] watching, or taking an interest in, the stuff we're watching', which includes the news (Mrs Samuels says she is 'obsessed' with it, admitting that she 'watches it all the time' and has developed a 'fairly good awareness of what's going on') as well as programmes such as *The Sopranos, Frasier, Curb Your Enthusiasm* and *The Wire*. Recalling the dissection of television tastes in Chapter 3, these are all programmes which, despite being American (!) and notwithstanding the different readings that could be applied by adult and younger schemes of perception, tend to be lauded by critics as humorous or dramatic commentaries on abstract questions of power, social relations or the state of contemporary society, are (in the case of *Frasier* at least) filled with 'highbrow' cultural references and which viewers rich in symbolic mastery construe as 'educational', 'more thoughtful' and so on, suggesting the possibility that they cluster in the section of the symbolic space homologous with ample cultural capital.

On top of that, Mr and Mrs Samuels can rely on even more subtle, implicit and pervasive means to ensure their children still acquire symbolic mastery and cultural capital. For one thing, the Samuels, their own trajectories and assessments of their children's emergent capital stocks establishing a certain vision of the probable and desirable future, *expect, want and work to make sure that their children expect, want and work toward university entry*. Mrs Samuels explains that her children are 'quite competent with their reading and writing and their spellings', 'quite creative' and that 'I think they are both easily capable of exploring whichever area they want to go into' – all so many typifications formed by someone possessing symbolic mastery and premised on routine observation of the signs of that mastery. She thus admits not only that 'we're expecting that they will go to university' and 'kind of trying to prepare for them to go to university' – including 'financially', a full eight years before they would actually be enrolling – but also something more:

> And we put that in their minds as well, that that's the route that you go through: kind of primary, senior, do your A levels and then go off to university. And their cousins, their older cousins are preparing for that route as well. So I think we're just *trying to make it seem like a natural progression* to go through that route (emphasis added).

The indication here is that a future in higher education is not quite doxic within the domestic microcosm in the same way as, say, the belief that there is such a thing as 'family', 'my family', and so on, since it is articulated and worked at in a way that doxa is usually not. It is, instead, an *orthodoxy* rooted in Mr and Mrs Samuels' class positions and familial heritages which they are – drawing on their plentiful resources – actively striving to *make* doxic for their children. The same is true for the Allens and Newcombe/Oliver families, of course, and may say something about the evolving relationship between subjective expectations and objective probabilities in an inflated education market (cf. all, 2003); but how successful this strategy will be – as with the regulation of television-watching and encouragement of extracurricular activities – depends on the structure of symbolic power within the domestic microcosm (in the context of competing or harmonising pressures from the wider familial field, like those older cousins and their parents). To what degree do their children value what Mr and Mrs Samuels say, take them seriously, do as they decree, strive for their love and attention and therefore struggle to acquire and display properties (capitals) indicating the parentally desired future? Mr and Mrs Samuels may struggle to help with homework thanks to time pressures, but does the nature of affective exchanges and implicit pedagogy within the household premised on their desire channel the libido toward accumulation of cultural capital nevertheless?

Certainly the Samuels admit their children are intensely 'competitive for our attention', often 'fighting', 'squabbling' and 'winding each other up' over it. In amongst the wide variety of arbitrary indicators of recognition over which they struggle – who gets a slice of cheesecake after dinner, who gets which chair in the living room, whom the guinea pigs belong to, etc. – are, moreover, a few persistent currents. There is clearly a gender dimension, for example. Just to give one instance, while their parents prepare dinner, Max mocks Grace for apparently not displaying the toughness associated with hegemonic definitions of masculinity, pretending to hit himself, make a great deal of it and whining, 'I'm [Grace] and I hurt myself!' in front of his father – though without any endorsement in response (a misfire, perhaps). Furthermore, at least from what could be gleaned from our limited time with the family, everyday struggles and jealousy in relation to affective recognition do also appear to revolve around the display of symbolic mastery. On one evening, for instance, Grace spends her time looking up what she deems 'interesting facts' on the computer and excitedly bounding into the kitchen with each one to tell them to her parents, leaving in a manner described by the researcher present as 'victorious' each time her parents engage her on them or look surprised by the fact. On another occasion, Grace, while making custard with her mother, eagerly tells the latter that 'for our writing assignment [the teacher] read mine out and said it was written by a lady genius'. Mrs Samuels congratulates her with a 'well done' – the token of recognition motivating Grace's utterance – but not before Max, who is present, has rather sarcastically mocked her by repeating 'lady genius' in a silly voice. Conversely, on the same evening when Grace is playing a computer game and is told by her parents – with a tone indicating not only positive appraisal but 'what you should be doing too' – that Max is watching 'something serious' and 'something intelligent' on television she quickly inquires, looking (according to the researcher) a little jealous, 'What is it?'[3] But it is too late to compensate: Grace is instructed to start getting ready for bed, and though she tries briefly to negotiate, she recognises her parent's symbolic power and relents.

The clash of affective capital and cultural capital

A very different scenario is observed in domestic fields where consecrated cultural capital is scarcer, such as the Greens'. Mr Green, 26, is a plumber's mate with several GCSEs and an income of around £300 a week. His father is a warehouseman and his mother a factory worker. His wife, Mrs Green, is 27 and a housewife, though she also runs Ann Summers parties on some evenings to bring extra money into the household. She has one GCSE grade C, her mother is a carer and her father has built up a moderately successful plumbing business (which employs Mr Green). They have three boys, Liam (aged seven), Ryan (aged three) and Jake (16 months), and their hopes and expectations for them, and thus what their children perceive they need do in order to avoid 'being a disappointment', are attuned to a somewhat different set of objectively probable futures to those seen above. Namely – and it should be made clear that the Greens, thanks mainly to Mrs Green's father, are relatively affluent compared to more impoverished sections of the dominated class, who may simply wish for their children to 'stay out of trouble' – there is a desire for their children only to *better their material conditions*, i.e. 'get on' by accumulating *economic* capital. Insofar as the education system is imposed by the dominant class as the sanctioned pathway to more highly remunerated positions, this can mean self-accruing a degree of cultural capital is valued as a means to that end, but it is not strictly necessary to achieve the fancied future, and so if children struggle at school or do not attend higher education it is less likely to diminish capital within the family. Mrs Green thus states that she wants her children to attain 'good grades' at school so they can earn 'good money' and be 'not like us', yet while she would *like* them to pursue post-compulsory education, and sees it as within the realms of the possible (but not taken for granted), she is adamant that

> I'd never push them to like 'no, you will go to college, you will go to uni, you will become a doctor or a dentist, or this and that' […] as long as they're happy with what they're doing. I'd never force them to do it but I'd just try and give them a gentle push in the right direction.

There is not, therefore, the same tangible sense of significance and disappointment attached to the cultivation of symbolic mastery and potential failures displayed by the Newcombe/Olivers and Allens, i.e. not the same entwinement of affective recognition with the attainment of cultural capital, because it is a future not intuited as likely or necessary to ascend in social space given their starting point.

Moreover, observation of daily practice reveals that, given the limits of parental cultural capital and the demands of everyday living attached to their class positions, the relationship between development of symbolic mastery and affective recognition is fraught and ambivalent if not unintentionally negative. On one occasion, for instance, Mrs Green and Liam are running through basic maths exercises, using a book which Mrs Green bought with the intention of boosting and encouraging Liam's mastery, in the front room where his other two brothers are playing loudly nearby and his father watching television – there is no separate space (e.g. a dining table in the kitchen) in their house where they could do it. His brothers' constant demands on Mrs Green's attention, jeopardising Liam's attainment of motherly recognition, visibly annoys him, but Mrs Green reminds him that she has to look after the others too and suggests they do it later. He persists, not wanting to cede recognition to his siblings, but when their rumpus continues to distract Mrs Green he reacts violently and lashes out at his brothers, only calming down when his attention is turned to a television programme. When he resumes later, Mrs Green, still attending to the other two children (changing nappies and so on), moans tiredly – but not unreasonably, since it might be assumed the school should do more – 'Why do I need to help?', indicating that this work, at first encouraged, is now seen as a burden, an extra pressure in a pressured life invoking displeasure and thus, potentially, loss of affective capital within the domestic space.

The resultant inability to supply the school with what it demands is perhaps why Liam describes the institution as 'rubbish'. His libido has, instead, been directed elsewhere and his and his brothers' *successful* struggles for love take a different form. Football, in particular, seems a source of shared joy and encouragement, not just in Mrs Green's explicit statements of support and congratulations but in the less obvious fact that Liam and his father frequently play the football-themed computer game FIFA 2011 together, with Mr Green giving Jake affirmative smiles when he mimics the movements of the game with his body. Or again, Mr Green, a keen dance music DJ with decks set up in the kitchen, holds Jake – wearing a set of headphone-imitating earmuffs to emulate his father – affectionately in one arm while playing and changing the records, and Mr and Mrs Green encourage Liam to dance, clap and nod to the beat of the music. Making a virtue, or desire, of necessity, bodily mastery and practice rather than symbolic mastery appears to be the source of affective recognition and value.

Another example of the troubled relationship between affective capital and school-work amongst the dominated is supplied by the Nash family. Mrs Nash, 36, works as a part-time cleaner and possesses a few CSEs. Her father is a prison guard and her mother, like her, a cleaner. Her 38-year-old husband, Mr Nash, is a delivery-driver who left school with no qualifications. His father is a semi-skilled manual worker and his mother a shop worker, and he and Mrs Nash between them bring in an income of around £20,000 per annum. Like Mrs Green, Mr and Mrs Nash state that their daughters, Zoe (aged eight) and Charlotte (four), 'need to do well' at school if they want to get on but are content for them just to 'do their best':

MR NASH: If you enjoy your learning, there's not much more you can do – just do your best, enjoy it. I mean, there's no point putting yourself under added pressures. You enjoy what you're doing, that's how I look at it. I'm not going to put pressure on her and say, 'Right, I want you to get grades up here and grades up there.'
MRS NASH: If you don't get it, you don't get it.
MR NASH: Do you know what I mean, 'I just want you to go out there and enjoy school, do your best at your grades and that's what I expect from you. Just enjoy it.' There's no point in added pressures. It could affect them later on, so….enjoy life while you can.

This instantly recalls earlier tropes among the dominated class (see e.g. Hoggart, 1957) that children should enjoy their childhood and not worry themselves with schoolwork ('kids should be kids', said another participant in a similar position), premised on an expectation that the time to come, adult life, is one of compulsory drudgery. The interview continues:

Q: So, you know, whether they go to college or whatever, that's not so important to you?
MR NASH: No.
MRS NASH: No, as I say, it's like once they leave senior school it's what they want to do.
MR NASH: If they feel comfortable, they can go down to college.
MRS NASH: If they want to carry on, they carry on. If they don't….if they want to go out and work, they want to go out and work. You know, I've been telling that to them.

In other words, Mrs Nash articulates to her children that her evaluation of them, her sense of pride and happiness, and thus the accumulation of familial capital, is less tied to developing the specific modes of mastery or scholastic achievements demanded by the dominant that their class position renders objectively and subjectively less probable.

Misrecognising the authority of the school and its demands, the Nash family still remind their elder daughter to complete her homework and Mrs Nash states that she will give her children 'any help they need'. In practice, however, their positions in the class structure mean that, just as with the Greens, homework as a prime vehicle for develop-ing symbolic mastery at home tends to works *against* recognition within the domestic subspace of the family field, this time much more clearly due to the limits of parental cultural capital – Mrs Nash having admitted that 'there's some things you don't under-stand' which have 'caught us out' when trying to help with homework. One evening, for example, Zoe has to write down the definition of words ending with –cial and use them in a sentence. She tells her mother, who is cooking in the kitchen, that she is stuck on a word ('beneficial'), to which Mrs Nash, delving into various cupboards for ingredients, does not respond at first. After Zoe repeats that she is stuck, Mrs Nash replies: 'You obviously learnt them in school.' She then reads the sheet of paper explaining what Zoe has to do and tells her daughter to use the children's dictionary from the other room. Zoe does so, and when she looks up the word she says it 'means "helpful"', to which Mrs Nash replies, '"Means helpful"? I am, very.' Another word, which Zoe has difficulty pronouncing, is 'artificial'. 'It's like an artificial plant or flowers,' says Mrs Nash, giving a *practical example* rather than an abstract definition. Zoe says 'thank you' and writes down 'plant' as the definition, with Mrs Nash, ripping open a bag of pasta, struggling to articulate the usually unarticulated with a 'Well, it, it, that's what it is.' Next is 'financial', which Zoe has looked up in the dictionary. As an example of a sentence using the word, she says: 'Going to spend some financial.' Mrs Nash says, 'That doesn't make sense'; but when Zoe asks 'What can I say?', in reply Mrs Nash, attending to the pan of pasta beginning to boil on the hob, does not respond. Zoe keeps asking, 'What does that mean? What does that mean?' and her mother, who appears to be agitated by her inability to answer her daughter's constant questions, responds, 'I don't know. Look in the dictionary.' Zoe starts playing with a pink mobile phone and says, 'Can't think of it. Will leave it and go back to it.' Mrs Nash does not encourage her otherwise and continues cooking.

Later on in the evening, the meal finished, Mrs Nash and her daughters are sitting in the front room, where Charlotte is using a laptop computer to play a simple word game (meanings are given of three-letter words – bed, fox, etc. – and the player has to guess the word). Zoe returns to her homework and the word 'financial'. This time Zoe suggests it means 'money matters' and asks her mother if she should put that down, to which her mother, watching Charlotte, responds 'Can do.' While it might appear that she is uninterested in Zoe's homework, this is only insofar as she feels she cannot be of much use, so instead she pays close attention to Charlotte's game. Zoe returns to the word 'artificial', saying she has put 'A plant is artificial, but not all plants', but Mrs Nash does not respond as she watches Charlotte complete the word game, congratulating her on correct answers and laughing at the accompanying animations. Zoe points to a word on the homework sheet and asks what it means; Mrs Nash gives an abrupt 'I don't know, love.' Zoe wants to look it up on the internet, but Mrs Nash does not see how that will help and does not want to disturb Charlotte's game. The final word attempted is 'official'. Zoe reads it out and Mrs Nash hesitantly replies, 'Think it means being on time.' Zoe, trying to put it in a sentence, says: 'My granddad, official over time' before then asking if her mother can think of a sentence. Despite obviously hearing her eldest, Mrs Nash, unable to answer and perhaps trying to deflect the discomfort of the situation, gives no response and instead sings along with a tune on Charlotte's game. Zoe reads from the dictionary 'public authority and duties' and then turns 'My mum went on duty' into 'My mum went on official' as an example, but is unsure of herself:

ZOE: I don't know. What can I put, Mummy? Got no idea.
MRS NASH: Don't know, [Zoe].

Not only has Mrs Nash been unable to *directly* instil symbolic mastery through pedagogy, then, but, crucially, this tension and lack of attention flowing from her uneasiness at her incapacity to do so may well be just one instance among many which together unintentionally nurture, over time, the impression that schoolwork (at this level) *works against affective recognition*, or at least does not secure it, especially *vis-à-vis* other activities. In any case, at this point Zoe gives up on her homework, joins in with Charlotte's word game and finally manages to gain the cheerful attention of her mother with her commentary on it.

Uncertainty and tensions in the middle

There are many families whose stocks of cultural and economic capital are more 'middling' and among whom, therefore, links between parental desires, libido channelling and accumulation or not of cultural capital – quite apart from any pressures from other fields or hysteresis effects – are not quite so clear-cut. A quirk of the sample exacerbates this opacity: most of the families taking part in the study who might be described as closer to the intermediate zone of the social space had very young children only just beginning on their journeys through the education system. Libido-shaping is yet to take on sharper form, masteries are yet to condense, the degree of 'fit' with schooling is yet to fully emerge and so typifications of the children, and parental perceptions of and desires for the future – the subjective field of possibles, in other words – were somewhat less precise, studded with caveats along the lines of 'who knows?', 'it might change', etc. and more open than they might be by the time their children are the same age as the Newcombe/Olivers', or even the Greens', whose eldest child was a few years into his schooling.

Trajectory effects, moreover, appeared to infuse the family spirit in a number of cases, since many believed they were in a position to offer 'better' than they had as children – whether in relation to advice, help with schoolwork or money – and that their children may well do 'better' than they have, continuing an intergenerational upwards thrust. The Greens too wanted better for their children, of course, but the difference here is that parents see themselves as instrumental in realising that future through mobilisation and investment of their acquired resources, at least up to a certain point. They also made it clear that they did not wish to be (categorised as) 'pushy parents', perhaps as a means of distancing themselves from the perceived (including caricatured or stereotyped) practices of sections of the dominant class, or as a defence against a label commonly pinned on those who feel they have to actively intervene rather than rely on children's 'gifts' to see them through – the phrase is semantically mobile, being harnessed by different people in different ways depending on their social position to assert or protect their symbolic worth (see Beauvais, 2015).[4]

Take, for example, Ms Floyd. She declares she wants to 'have a lot more influence than I was given, which was none', in relation to her children's schooling so as to avoid them being 'lost for many, many years […] career-wise and stuff', as she believes she was. Being relatively rich in cultural capital (she has taught classes on English as a second language), this will involve her intervening in her eldest son's learning:

> I just want to be helpful and facilitate him and…he loves… so far he loves nursery and he's bright and I don't think we'll have much trouble – well, not until he goes to secondary; it might change then, mightn't it? But… and I'll enjoy helping him, I think, like I enjoy teaching and teaching literacy and stuff at a very basic level. I think I'll really enjoy helping him. I've got loads of books, you know, and the…. the pre-school books and stuff. I did buy those for students – I was teaching kids. But erm…[eldest son]'s had a look at a few, you know, and how to form letters, and he likes copying and… […] Yeah, I'll make sure I'm quite involved.

Clearly there is a desire for her sons to develop the masteries necessary for scholastic success to some degree – laying the foundations for a class-inflected familial orthodoxy insofar as she indicates elsewhere this is shared with their father – and she demonstrates a disposition to actively foster them. Yet this is not only tempered by lack of certainty about the future ('it might change') given by young age, but also perhaps indicates less assurance and fixation on educational success than those richer in capital might typically have. Notice too that, in line with her middling cultural capital stocks – she has acquired a degree in art, but has little inherited cultural capital (her father was a barber and her mother a shop worker) – the confidence and self-perceived likely enjoyment is confined to the early years (the 'very basic level'). Ms Floyd is, furthermore, adamant that 'I don't want to be really pushy, though, about his career or anything', admitting that is 'probably quite a difficult balance'.

Mr Hughes and Ms Barnes talk in parallel terms about their five-year-old daughter, with Ms Barnes saying she wants to actively 'guide her to getting qualifications' and 'make her a lot more aware of just how much education you need in order to get whatever job it is that you want to do, and help her to get there, more than we were helped, I think'. Mr Hughes concurs, adding that 'I see it as our job to put together the building blocks to enable her and to support her to achieve more' – a task facilitated by their cultural capital more than anything else – but Ms Hughes also adds that she does not want to become a dreaded 'pushy parent'. Another, Mrs Buchanan, distanced herself from what she called 'helicopter parenting', where parents metaphorically hover over the shoulder of their children, regulating and directing their behaviour, their friends and their interests, though it is interesting that Mr and Mrs Buchanan also felt that they should be 'doing more' (reading, music practice, etc.) and be more 'consistent' with their children despite being 'so busy doing other things' – indicating, ultimately, misrecognition of the dominant style of parenting as legitimate.

There are, however, a couple of families where the children are older, and so themes comparable with those teased out among the dominant and dominated classes are more detectable. The Kings, whom we have met several times already, are one such, though it must be made clear that their particular experience bears the distinct trace of their specific conditions of existence given by their volume and composition of capital, characterised as they are by reasonable economic capital (household income of around £68,000) but only relatively modest cultural capital (A levels). Thus they too want to help their children get to university and provide opportunities they themselves did not have, primarily on the grounds that they believe education is instrumental to getting 'good jobs' nowadays (rather than self-enlightenment or discovery), but this appears to be through financial support more than anything else:

> [We] want to get the kids through school as far as they want to go, and I'd like to be in a position to…if one of them says, 'I want to go to university, can you help me out?' I want to be in a position to say yes, i.e. give them the opportunities that my parents couldn't give me in terms of saying, 'Yeah, we can help you out on that. Don't expect to not do anything and not have a part-time job yourself, but we can help you out.' (Mr King)

This also plays out in their current investment of resources. They do not necessarily have the symbolic mastery to consistently intervene in their children's pedagogy, but they can at least convert economic capital into objectified cultural capital in the form of reference works (encyclopaedias, history books, etc.) that can be consulted – or 'activated', as Lareau (2003) would say – with some prompting (itself telling, of course):

> I may not know the answers on some of the homework but, you know, I can attempt to help them with homework or point them in the right direction. You know, we've got lots of resources upstairs: you know, reference books. I mean, you quite often get [their son] come to you and say, 'I don't know how to do this.' 'Well, have you looked in the encyclopaedias?' 'Oh no, I haven't looked in there.' (Mr King)

Yet this is only half the story. As we know by now, the complex of exchanges and practices adding up to what would be described as intergenerational 'reproduction' of social position, or deviation therefrom, is saturated with and complicated by specifically *familial* forms of symbolic power and misrecognition. In the Kings' case, the rub appears to lie in the play of different forms of capital within the family, or, more specifically, the domestic sub-field thereof. In short, while completion of schoolwork seems to be policed by Mr and Mrs King overtly using the symbolic power attached to a cluster of heteronomous properties – age, economic capital, physical capital, etc., wrapped up in a construction of 'parental authority' – only dimly paired in their children's perception with care (even if entwining with it in driving parental practice), the capital of affective recognition flows more readily from class practices only loosely connected to educational advance. The result is that schoolwork is seen as something that 'has to be done' ('or else!'), rather than something the children expressly and consistently desire to do, while other activities draw their libido. Thus the Kings have the following to say when talking about their son's homework:

MR KING: We've always had quite a pragmatic approach to homework, I think, i.e. we continually hassle him. He doesn't like it, and I don't care, we will hassle him to make sure he does homework at a sensible time, a sensible hour, not sort of eight o'clock on a Sunday night.

MRS KING: If he doesn't do it, he gets his PlayStation games confiscated.

MR KING: Yeah, basically.

MRS KING: And his laptop will go unless he needs to use it to do his homework, you know.

MR KING: Yeah, and that sort of stuff. And, you know, frankly, if he doesn't like it, I don't care.

Evidently the young King is no fan of doing homework – otherwise his parents would not have to 'hassle' him to do it, as he would do it of his own accord – indicating already something of his emergent, conditioned libido. Although it is not clear whether it is the hassling or the homework that Mr King says his son 'doesn't like', he signals plainly enough ('I don't care') that this practice is not about bonding via sharing enjoyment, i.e. about exchange of affective recognition, even if Mr and Mrs King are ultimately hassling him only because they care enough about him to want him to acquire the prime means to symbolic worth in the contemporary misrecognition order. It is, instead, a strategy oriented around the mobilisation of other capitals securing familial symbolic power – the power to confiscate cherished items (the parents perhaps bought them, or have the physical capital to prevent resistance) – the end of which is to secure alignment to the dominant familial construction of what must be done. Such extreme measures were never observed *in situ*, though the Kings were indeed observed asking their children whether they were getting on with their homework or revision (as their son was studying for his GCSE exams) on the evenings. One assumes their effect is, in fact, to render them less necessary insofar as they instil a sense of the likely future inscribed in specific practices or resistances, and, since this bears on sources of pleasure, on desirable futures too, even if in a negative sense (the children do homework to avoid sanction, recognising parental authority, more than to win recognition).

Affective capital, meanwhile, seems to revolve more readily around other practices, chiefly sporting ones. Football – watching it at the local stadium or on television together, or watching the Kings' son practise in the evening – appears to be particularly salient, regularly acting as a springboard for affectionate, bonding banter between Mr King and his son regarding the latter's skill and knowledge, as does swimming. Regarding the latter, Mr and Mrs King have invested economic capital, as well as their own time, in paying for both their son and daughter to be in a club and to drive them to Cardiff every weekend for training and competitions, but they have also actively taken an *interest*, learning the technical vocabulary of the sport so they can converse competently with them – which Mrs King sees as easy enough since it is 'a little bit common sense' and can be picked up from watching swimming on television – congratulating performances, 'giving them the boost when they need it and just telling them that it doesn't matter when it doesn't go so well' (Mrs King), 'chivvy[ing] them along' (Mr King), acting as a 'psychological soundboard' in relation to it (Mrs King) and turning it into a phenomenon of positive familial togetherness: 'All four of us will be together, so it's all the point to me of doing this sort of stuff' (Mr King).

So invested in their children's swimming performance are they, in fact, that it seems to almost trump schooling. They emphasise how 'hectic' their life is because of the constant trips to Cardiff and wryly observe that their son is 'managing to fit schoolwork into his busy swimming life', indicating the secondary nature of the former in their son's eyes at least, but stress that they are 'prepared to do [it] for the kids' because 'our kids are very important to us so we give them opportunities, and it's very important'. For his part, their son pithily summarises the (im)balance of his libido between accumulation of cultural capital and his sport – which is, at one and the same time, a position-taking in the symbolic space and a potential means of accumulating a sublimated form of physical capital: 'Like school, argghh, that's rubbish; sport, like swimming, I'm really committed.'

Yet football and swimming do not altogether displace schoolwork, as might be found in families with a much bleaker intuition of the likely future available to them through the education system given their economic and cultural capital. Instead, the Kings' son has been encouraged to marry his taste for physical prowess with at least some degree of school-sanctioned capital accumulation via a GCSE in physical education, at which he excels (he won an award for best pupil in the school, and the school specialises in sports) and which he wishes to study further – furnishing a mixture of technical and cultural capital with some, albeit limited, currency in the misrecognition order. Nevertheless, as befits their middling position within the social space, especially in terms of their possession of cultural capital, the Kings locate him – and have told him this – somewhere in the middle of the scale of worth revolving around symbolic mastery: he is 'not stupid by any means', they believe, and is 'perfectly capable of achieving Cs in his GCSEs', thus distinguishing him from those deemed to be below him, but he is 'not the sharpest knife in the drawer' so 'anything over and above that would be fantastic'. For this reason, returning to their protention and desire in relation to higher education, university, while possible *economically*, is hardly definite, necessitating a projection of alternative plans grounded in their class ethos and trajectory:

We've given him the commitment, that said, as long as he's [i.e. their son] in full-time education, then we will subsidise him in terms of not doing anything daft like charging him rent on his room; but at the point when he stops full-time education, then he's got to start earning because he's not sitting on his bum. Because, I mean, we do know some other parents who let their kids give up school, give up education, not do anything and they're quite happy to subsidise them. And we've already informed [him] that that will not happen, 'So don't get any bright ideas about giving up stuff and then sitting on your bum and not doing anything.' Because I wasn't allowed, [Mrs King] wasn't allowed, and him sure as hell is not going to be allowed to do that. And I don't care if it's going out working in McDonald's, he will be out earning some money somehow, some way; he's not sitting on his backside. […] Because, you know, when it comes down to it, they have to earn money. At some point they need a job of some sort. So both of them will have the commitment while they're in full-time education, then we will subsidise them to the best of our abilities. But after that, 'Go out and earn, whether you like it or not.' (Mr King)

Others with a middling stock of capital, but weighted toward the cultural variety in composition, also spoke more even-handedly of non-university futures than the dominant, though usually in the form of developing 'artistic' talents instead (Mr Geoffrey), 'finding oneself' (Ms Floyd) or travelling (Mr Hughes) – all of which recalls the desire for liberation and expression Bourdieu (1984) saw as characteristic of the cultural intermediaries. For the Kings, however, the ethos feeding into the perception of the future appears to blend elements from the upper dominated, from whence they came ('I wasn't allowed'), and the economically rich intermediate class: honest graft, paying one's way, getting nothing for nothing and striving above all for money, or accumulation of economic capital – cultural capital can be a means to this end, but not so much an end in itself. The same generic class disposition toward the forthcoming given by height in social space may well be, therefore, specified by composition of capital and trajectory effects.

Conclusion

If I have tried to bring out the emotional investments, bitter disappointments and moments of joy woven into the practices through which cultural capital is fostered or not among children, it is not simply to make for more lively cases and interesting stories, but to demonstrate the utility of particular concepts and a certain mode of analysis. Specifically, we have seen that what is generally called social reproduction – gauged statistically in Chapter 2 by the relationship between parental position and one's own position in social space – is achieved through, but also complicated by, implication in a space of relationships other than that of class. Struggles in the familial field for love, care, affection, attention, praise and so on, or simply to avoid sanction, discomfort and tension – in other words, struggles revolving around specifically familial forms of capital – interweave with the capitals definitive of class to mould individual desires and set in motion unique trajectories. Intra-familial practices and exchanges are multiple plays, yielding effects in more than one web of relations, and are loaded with multiple pertinences, being practically perceived at once – thanks to the world horizon – as bearing on present and likely future position in social space (not doing well at school) and in the familial or domestic space (drawing anger and disappointment). Only by turning our attention to lifeworlds can we unpick that.

Let me be absolutely crystal clear to avoid any confusion, however, that this is not an argument that some, particularly those in the dominated class, do not care enough about their children, do not try hard enough to help them or do not aspire highly enough for them. All the families we studied want their children to flourish and 'do well', which in the UK, as we have seen, is measured by educational performance and monetary riches. Yet, once again entwining class and familial forces, expectations and desires for the future are premised on a feel for the game – a practical, subjective sense of what is objectively possible given their recognised resources and their children's emergent masteries – and thus what is taken for granted or rewarded, what is pushed or surprising, what breeds togetherness or tension – together with the class *tastes* developed in adaptation to conditions of existence – depends on the unequal distribution of class capitals. Pernicious political and social scientific claims that people only need to raise their 'aspirations' and 'aim higher' for their children to be successful, without any meaningful change in material conditions or the ethos of the educational system, let alone the dismantling of the scales of value defining the misrecognition order that would enable those changes, only serve to jam that practical sense and breed struggle, discomfort and 'failure', and, with that, lifelong regret and meagre self-worth.[5]

Notes

1 In so doing the analysis broadly harmonises with, but at the same time integrates and throws fresh light on, findings from a plethora of other studies hampered by their partial nature (focussing only on the middle classes, or on parental aspirations, for example, or relying solely on interviews) and/or their limited conceptual framework, including in relation to the model of class adopted (e.g. NS-SEC) but also apropos the construction of family affect and its relationship to class (on this see further Atkinson, 2016). I have in mind studies like those of Reay (2000, 2004), Walkerdine *et al.* (2001), Devine (2004) and Irwin and Elley (2011, 2013).

2 In this chapter, unlike the others, the constant to-and-fro contained within the observational data necessitates the use of pseudonyms for children.

3 Of course, the possible effect of the researcher has to be factored in. It could be that the children are striving for recognition in his eyes too, putting on 'a show', but the Samuels give no indication that this type of activity is unusual (and they *do* openly say the children are being better behaved than usual), and that would still indicate the channelling of the libido toward symbolic mastery anyway.

4 Recall the Richards family's opposition to 'pushy' parents in their area from Chapter 6 too: despite being vastly richer in economic capital than the families from the intermediate class, their cultural capital stocks are less dissimilar, and this might facilitate use of the same label to categorise and distance themselves from a common 'other' (those very rich in cultural capital), even if the meanings are likely to be slightly different with their slight difference of relative position.

5 On this 'Icarus effect', see Atkinson (2012).

References

Atkinson, W. (2012) 'Reproduction Revisited' *The Sociological Review*, 60(4): 734–52.

Atkinson, W. (2016) *Beyond Bourdieu*. Cambridge: Polity Press.

Ball, S. (2003) *Class Strategies and the Education Market*. London: RoutledgeFalmer.

Beauvais, C. (2015) 'An Exploration of the 'Pushy Parent' Label in Educational Discourse' *Discourse*, DOI: 10.1080/01596306.2015.1064098.

Bourdieu, P. (1984) *Distinction*. London: Routledge.

Bourdieu, P. (2000) *Pascalian Meditations*. Cambridge: Polity Press.

Chodorow, N. (1978) *The Reproduction of Mothering*. Berkeley: University of California Press.

Devine, F. (2004) *Class Practices*. Cambridge: Cambridge University Press.

Hoggart, R. (1957) *The Uses of Literacy*. Harmondsworth: Penguin.

Irwin, S. and Elley, S. (2011) 'Concerted Cultivation? Parenting Values, Education and Class Diversity' *Sociology*, 45(3): 480–95.

Irwin, S. and Elley, S. (2013) 'Parents' Hopes and Expectations for Their Children's Future Occupations' *The Sociological Review*, 61(1): 111–30.

James, W. (1950) *The Principles of Psychology* (Vol. 1). New York: Dover.

Lareau, A. (2003) *Unequal Childhoods*. Berkeley: University of California Press.

Reay, D. (2000) 'A Useful Extension of Bourdieu's Conceptual Framework?' *The Sociological Review*, 48(4): 568–85.

Reay, D. (2004) 'Gendering Bourdieu's Concepts of Capitals?' *The Sociological Review*, 52(s2): 57–74.

Stefansen, K. and Aarseth, H. (2011) 'Enriching Intimacy' *British Journal of Sociology of Education*, 32(3): 389–405.

Vincent, C. and Ball, S. (2007) "Making up' the Middle-Class Child' *Sociology*, 41(6): 1061–77.

Walkerdine, V., Lucey, H. and Melody, J. (2001) *Growing Up Girl*. Basingstoke: Palgrave.

10 Conclusion

Britain and beyond

Class has been around for millennia – cross-cut and offset it may have been by gender and other relatively autonomous forms of contention in different ways at different times, but it is still true, in a sense, that the history of all hitherto existing society is the history of class struggle. The principles of that struggle, however, the forms of misrecognition defining classes, and the capitals shaping the local, regional or – latterly – national social spaces have differed radically. From the physical capital of early civilisations through to the courtly symbolic capital and religious capital pervading feudal society, the properties and possessions arbitrarily defined and imposed as legitimate have altered dramatically, but the very fact that some properties and possessions are defined as legitimate and, *ipso facto*, others defined as inferior, and that these definitions are subject to greater or lesser struggle, contestation, mutation and, at times, revolution, is a constant throughout human history. The United Kingdom at the start of the third millennium BCE is no different. It bears a misrecognition order, it hosts a multidimensional social space, and it has detectable classes and class fractions – in the sense of more or less distinct clusters of individuals – characterised by their place within this. These classes are not what they were one hundred years ago (let alone one thousand) and they will no doubt be very different in another hundred years. Indeed, they are not entirely the same from one year to the next, never mind one decade to the next, since time, and the declines, ascents and stasis it reveals, is an inextricable constituent of classes, their style of life and their political-ethical outlooks. Yet class there is, and its general structures are ceaselessly reproduced and modified through individual human beings going about their daily business of working, consuming and raising children.

We have seen that the key axes of the social space in contemporary Britain – if not necessarily the precise distribution of jobs along them – are essentially the same as Bourdieu detected in 1960s and 1970s France. In the UK today, as in France almost fifty years ago, the two major principles defining a person's worth are economic capital – money, wealth, property, and so on, all displayed in luxurious lifestyles – and cultural capital – being 'intelligent' and, with that, 'cultured', 'sophisticated', 'knowing' and so on. They may well compete with all manner of other principles of misrecognition in smaller-scale, specific fields – whether those within the field of power or local social spaces – but these are the fundamental measures of value underpinning and specifying all else. More particularly, the prime dimension of difference is *volume* of capital in both forms (including by virtue of social capital), with *composition* of capital playing a crucial secondary role, distinguishing fault lines amongst those otherwise positioned high, low or 'in between' in terms of capital volume.

From our exploration of the British social space we distilled a set of analytical classes, convertible into a usable measure, to help us chart its homologies. There is a dominant class, an intermediate class and a dominated class, each with four internal fractions possessing different relative quantities and balances of capital. Analysing morphological changes over the last couple of decades, moreover, we saw that the feminine, 'cultural' pole of the social space is, generally, on the rise, while portions of the masculine right-hand side, particularly skilled workers, are declining. Shifts in the industrial constitution of the UK's economy wrought by neoliberal politics, i.e. the turn from heavy industry to services and from production of goods to provision of knowledge, are largely responsible for this, coupled with feminisation of the workforce and an expansion of the higher education system aimed at fostering 'human capital', though at least one effect of the latter has been simply to relocate class differences to a new site. Neoliberalism is also held to be responsible for increased employment insecurity across the board, but close inspection reveals that fate to be distributed somewhat unequally and, what is more, in a manner that has not changed all that much, at least in recent times.

As to those homologies, the symbolic space and the space of political position-takings in Britain display correspondences with class fractions remarkably similar to those unveiled by Bourdieu in France. Whether in relation to sports, clothes, home decor, restaurants, cultural events and producers, television programmes or body modifications, the exclusive lifestyles of the dominant stand opposed to the 'common' or practical tastes of the dominated, with the intermediate class sitting in between, but this principal division is cross-cut by the opposition between those richer in cultural capital than economic capital and those with the reverse fortune. Omnivorousness is not particularly salient, nor is the 'voraciousness' posited by Bennett *et al.* (2009), especially when mode of consumption is factored in. The entwinement of capital composition with *gender*, as well as age, cannot be ignored, however. The cultural poles of both the social space and the symbolic space are populated disproportionately by women, and this may have the effect of casting cultural capital and its lifestyle manifestations as feminine, opposed to the masculine right-hand side of the social and symbolic spaces, thus shaping the perception of the possible and modes of differentiation and symbolic violence in relation to both class and gender. Certain jobs and practices may be perceived as 'effeminate', 'gay', 'macho', 'manly' and so on whether they are attached to a man or a woman in a specific instance, but also as what 'men' and 'women' – and thus oneself – can and should do, manifest in so many calls to order, depending on the position of the perceiver (see further Atkinson, 2016).

When it comes to politics, meanwhile, the split between left-wing and right-wing orientations toward material matters and the split between liberal and authoritarian stances, mixed with pro- or anti-welfare attitudes, cut through the social space at diagonals. Possession of cultural capital corresponds with liberalism and its lack with a more 'authoritarian personality', while possession of economic capital seems to incline one toward the political right on material issues and its lack with the political left, arraying class fractions according to their respective volumes and balances of each capital. Yet just as fundamental to understanding the contemporary political landscape of the UK is the opposition between, on the one hand, those who feel entitled to, interested in and fully capable of forming opinions on all manner of issues, and, on the other, those who do not. The latter tendency, a disposition of the dominated class in particular, has been exacerbated by transformations in the political field, specifically the decline of trade union power and the rightwards turn of the parliamentary Labour Party in the 1990s.

Position in the social space and its various homologies, however, do not exhaust the determinants of experience. Fundamental they may be, but the people, places, events and objects of our individual lifeworlds sit within multitudinous circuits of symbolic power laid out by those in fields we do not contend within, and harmonise or clash with practices and pertinences emanating from other fields we are positioned in. Thus we explored the specification of classed experience by spatial location and movement at the national and the urban levels, the local milieus and symbolic struggles differentiating the perceptual schemes and practices of people otherwise sited in similar positions in social space and the home as the hub of forces and relevances from a multitude of fields, including the social space, indeed, but also those fields relating to paid employment and the family. Unpicking the phenomenology of domestic experience also revealed that objects, practices and places are often alloys, with pertinences in multiple fields embedded within the horizons of perception, ultimately being integrated into the *world* horizon as the sense of potentialities – the subjective field of possibles – across myriad spaces of struggle inscribed in one action, utterance or project.

This insight also allows us to nuance the model of social reproduction first proffered by Bourdieu a half-century ago. For the process through which children develop masteries and tastes of different worth within the education system and within the symbolic space, and which sets the course for their trajectories through the social space, implicates more than one relatively autonomous structural space, more than one struggle for recognition, more than one source of symbolic power. It is a class process, yes, but – as well as being moulded and offset by schooling, locale and so on – it is driven by, saturated with and even complicated by familial significances. To put it briefly, struggles for specifically familial forms of recognition – love, care, attention and so on – are fundamental to channelling the child's libido toward accumulation of cultural capital and its symbols or, alternatively, to practices and pastimes accorded rather less value in the education system and beyond. Metaphors of 'transmission' or 'inheritance' of cultural capital may thus be economical at the global level, when looking at general patterns of origins and destinations in the social space, but when the actual process through which children develop the masteries and tastes celebrated or not within the education system is examined they no longer quite fit the bill.

The variant and the invariant

Research in other Western nations has steadily begun to unearth the same distribution of worth – the same general structures of the misrecognition order – as that documented here (Prieur *et al.*, 2008; Rosenlund, 2009; Coulangeon and Duval, 2014). It may reasonably be conjectured, therefore, that this is a commonality of all democratic capitalist societies with expansive education systems, whatever the differences might be in the industries, typical jobs and welfare regimes across countries. Yet just as intriguing are the *variations* within that similarity, and indeed the next major task facing Bourdieusian research into class – the task which both Goldthorpe and Wright took up once their initial studies of their home nations were complete – may be systematic cross-national comparison. How do social spaces arranged according to otherwise similar principles differ in their rates of dispersion, their balance of the axes, the most suitable proxy occupations, the entwinement with gender and so on? How are these bound up with national political-economic histories, worldwide circuits of symbolic power (trade, cultural exchange, supranational politics, etc.) and migration flows, themselves revealing something of the structure of the *global* social space (or perhaps, more loosely, global universe) in which nation-level social spaces are situated, and what are the specifying effects on national spaces of lifestyles and political position-takings?[1] Do national social spaces and their homologies in the capitalist West appear to be becoming more homogenous under the influence of neoliberalism, as Bourdieu (2005) seemed to believe, or do differential rates of deindustrialisation, privatisation, deregulation and financialisation of the economy, varying degrees of workforce feminisation, immigration into and emigration out of certain sections of national social spaces and differential emphases upon academic and technical education still make a difference to the size, shape, stability, distribution and demographic composition of, and thus influence of and alliances between, different class fractions? Piecemeal assessment of similarities and differences, at least as they pertain to symbolic spaces, there may have been (see e.g. Prieur and Savage, 2011, 2013; Purhonen and Wright, 2013), but methodical investigation of these questions has hitherto been precluded by a lack of appropriate tools: few have tried to derive a measure of social space position that can be applied across datasets, let alone across nations. Perhaps, then, the schema developed here can offer a starting point – not simply as something to be imposed on other nations *a priori*, without testing its degree of fit, but as a mode of proceeding, or a spur to creating homologous measures which can then yield properly comparable data.

The need for cross-national comparison extends to lifeworld analysis too, particularly as it relates to the balance or conflict between employment-related fields and the familial field for time, space, attention and desire and its inflection by both class fraction and gender. Rates of feminisation of the workforce, themselves linked to different welfare regimes favouring or discouraging female engagement in paid labour, are likely to play a significant role (Crompton and Lyonette, 2006), though how that differs within and across different nations by class fraction – whether, for example, the cultural fraction of the dominant class, predisposed to question traditional gender roles, is most likely to advocate parity of gender in the labour market – is yet to be determined. Then again, it may well be that specific social forces have operated to transform and homogenise lifeworld experiences and struggles across nations, including neoliberal pressures on employment policy and ethos (efficiency drives, 'long hours culture', flexible working, etc.), technological change (internet, social media, air travel) and so on (see Southerton and Tomlinson, 2005).

In any case, the road ahead is clear. We know class is still crucial in shaping people's life paths and decisions – that reports of its death, whether from prophets of postmodernity or the heralds of high modernity, are greatly exaggerated – and we now have some insight into its precise structure, effects and place in everyday experience in the UK. Only via comparison across nations will we advance toward fuller understanding of the variant and invariant, the particular and the universal, that Bourdieu's famed epistle to anglophone readers of *Distinction* hinted at, at least across Western nations, and take first steps toward a sketch of the world system determining the situation of not only national social spaces but, with that, the individuals – their singular biographies, their specific possibilities, their unique passions and particular desires – comprising them.

Note

1 On the difference between a social space or field and a universe, see Atkinson (2016).

References

Atkinson, W. (2016) *Beyond Bourdieu*. Cambridge: Polity Press.

Bennett, T., Savage, M., Silva, E., Warde, A., Gayo-Cal, M. and Wright, D. (2009) *Culture, Class, Distinction*. London: Routledge.

Bourdieu, P. (2005) *The Social Structures of the Economy*. Cambridge: Polity Press.

Coulangeon, P. and Duval, J. (eds.) (2014) *The Routledge Companion to Bourdieu's Distinction*. London: Routledge.

Crompton, R. and Lyonette, C. (2006) 'Work-Life 'Balance' in Europe' *Acta Sociologica*, 49(4): 379–93.

Prieur, A. and Savage, M. (2011) 'Updating Cultural Capital Theory' *Poetics*, 39(6): 566–80.

Prieur, A. and Savage, M. (2013) 'Emerging Forms of Cultural Capital' *European Societies*, 15(2): 246–67.

Prieur, A., Rosenlund, L. and Skjott-Larsen, J. (2008) 'Cultural Capital Today: A Case Study from Denmark' *Poetics*, 36(1): 45–71.

Purhonen, S. and Wright, D. (2013) 'Methodological Issues in National-Comparative Research on Cultural Tastes' *Cultural Sociology*, 7(2): 257–73.

Rosenlund, L. (2009) *Exploring the City with Bourdieu*. Saarbrücken: VDM Verlag Dr Müller.

Southerton, D. and Tomlinson, M. (2005) '"Pressed for Time'- the Differential Impacts of the 'Time Squeeze' *The Sociological Review*, 53(2): 215–39.

Appendices

Appendix I: Codes for deriving the class scheme

The construction of the social space is premised on aggregation of the Standard Occupational Classification (SOC) codes provided by the Office for National Statistics, in particular the SOC2000 variable. The only omission is the category 'sports players', since (a) they do not often appear in government datasets and (b) when they do they throw up quite divergent results in different datasets since they are so heterogeneous as a category, depending upon their position within the field of their particular sport and its position within the field of sports. A case could be made for including them in the cultural intermediary category alongside sports coaches – though the latter category is a far more widespread job and routinised – but I decided not to do so on the grounds that the field of professional sports is about as heterogeneous as the social space itself. One can well imagine many professional sports players (including top-flight football players, boxers and so on) being situated in the top right of social space, following an individual upwards trajectory, but beyond that – the humdrum reality of professional life for the full variety of sports – it is harder to pin down. Only a study of the sporting field itself would have resolved the issue.

For the last few decades the ONS has revised its SOC codes every ten years to account for occupational change, producing three different versions: the SOC90 applies to data gathered in the 1990s, the SOC2000 to data collected in the first decade of the millennium and the SOC2010 to data gathered since 2010. The SOC2000 variable was initially selected to facilitate comparison between the main datasets used, as they all used it, and because the ONS provided both the SOC2000 and SOC2010 codes in the 2011 Labour Force Surveys. A version of the scheme for the SOC2010 variable was later constructed. The ONS's algorithm for converting between SOC2000 and SOC2010 contains many discrepancies, mainly due to a tighter definition of 'managers', which have an effect on any aggregation (including their own), so that if versions of the class scheme are constructed using the two variables in the *same* dataset there are discordances between them – most notably, business executives reduce by about 3 per cent and white-collar workers increase by the same amount in the SOC2010 version (cf. Elias and Birch, 2010). A further particularity of the 2010 codes compared to the 2000 codes is the conflation of the chief executives from the economic field with senior officials from the bureaucratic field in one category, which, though it remains largely composed of those in the private sector and can thus be categorised with the business executives, blunts analysis somewhat.

To explore historical data using the SOC90 codes, it was necessary to repeat the method of construction for 1991, exploring the income and educational profiles of unit codes and aggregating them accordingly. There have also been some shifts of particular occupations, e.g. civil engineers from engineers to professions, in part due to the content of the occupational categories but also due to changing capital possession, and it is notable that the SOC90 codes make less space for the kinds of occupations that fall into the cultural intermediary category, testifying to this class fraction's rise and relative social youth. In any case, some caution should be exercised when interpreting historical trends since the constitutive categories of the different measures are not exactly the same. Of course, the same caveats apply just as much to any other SOC-based scheme, including the NS-SEC.

The construction of the social space is not considered definite and unassailable, but simply the best working solution for the task at hand. In the hope that other researchers may be encouraged to use, refine or assess the model, from the distribution of individual occupations to the relative positioning of fractions, I have therefore provided below the allocation of unit codes for the successive generations of the SOC codes and a comparison with the NS-SEC. Given that, in the latter, the two managerial-professional categories together comprise the 'service class', the intermediate and own-account workers the 'intermediate class' and the rest the 'working class', some key sources of deviation include: (i) the subsuming of many of what would here be called the intermediate class within the service class, mainly due to the 'lower managerial and professional' category; and (ii) the subsuming of many of what would here be called the dominated class within the intermediate class, along with administrators. The three-class NS-SEC scheme could thus be said to overestimate the size of the dominant class, incorporating most of the higher tracts of the middle section of social space, while its intermediate class category underestimates the relative position of the so-called intermediate. In turn, since some skilled workers (and some manual workers, sales services and caring services too) are categorised as intermediate or small employers in the NS-SEC, the size and dispersion of the dominated class is also underestimated.

This is, perhaps, enough to caution against halfway-house solutions when it comes to class analysis, like that of Flemmen (2014), who tries to blend a Bourdieusian methodology with use of the NS-SEC category of service class. Such a move is logically questionable anyway, since it capitulates to the Weberian reasoning that differences in employment contracts form the key boundary between classes – premised on differences in life chances for Goldthorpe rather than misrecognition – and thus fudges the real objective and subjective barriers in social space, and, just maybe, represents a failure to fully break with the substantialist vision of classes enshrined in existing classifications. Not only that, but it is contradicted by Flemmen's commitment elsewhere to a class scheme for Norway grounded in wholly Bourdieusian assumptions, not unlike the one constructed here, and dispensing with the notion of the service class under the implicit assumption that it must not be analytically acute enough. This sharpens the impression that reliance on the service class classification in his 2014 research was in fact as much a practical decision based on what is readily available in datasets as anything else. The trouble is, Flemmen then tried to use it to boldly call for a synthesis of Bourdieusian and Weberian insights, the latter of which were either already accommodated by Bourdieu or thoroughly at odds with the logic of his approach.

Table A1.1 Unit codes for construction of the class scheme

Class fraction	1990 SOC codes	2000 SOC codes	SOC 2010 codes
Business executives	101, 110–11, 113–24, 126, 131, 139, 199	1112, 1114, 1121–37, 1151, 3532, 2131	1115, 1121–50, 3532, 2133–2134, 2150
Professions	220, 222–4, 240–62, 312–13, 330–32	2121, 2211, 2215–16, 2411–34, 2311–13	2121, 2211, 2215–16, 2412–34, 3511–13
White-collar workers	350–64, 390–2, 394–9, 700–19	2132, 3520–31, 3533–44, 3561–8,	2135–9, 2435–6, 2461–2, 3520–31, 3533–46, 3561–7
Cultural dominant	100, 102–3, 132, 150–5, 190–1, 221, 232, 233–9, 270, 292–3, 371, 600–1, 200–9, 230, 231, 290–1, 271, 380–6	1111, 1113, 1171–3, 1181–4, 2111–13, 2212–14, 2311–19, 2321–9, 2441–52, 3214–15, 3221–9, 3411–22	1116, 1171–84, 1241, 2111–19, 2141–2, 2212–14, 2217–29, 2311–9, 2451–2, 2463, 3411–22
Lower managers/proprietors	112, 125, 140–2, 160–79	1174, 1185, 1211–39, 1141–2, 1161–3	1161–2, 1190–226, 1242–59
Technicians	210–19, 300–11, 320, 610–13	2122–9, 3111–32, 3311–19	2122–9, 3111–32, 3311–19
Administrative	127, 130, 400–40, 450–91	1152, 4111–50, 4211–17	4112–62, 4211–17
Cultural intermediaries	340–49, 371	3211–13, 3216–18, 3231–2, 3431–4, 3442–9, 3551–2	2231–2, 2471–3, 3213–39, 3442–3, 3550
Skilled trades	500–52, 500–52, 554–99, 620	5111–499	5111–449
Sales workers	720–92	3514, 7111–212	7111–220
Manual workers	393, 441, 553, 614–19, 621–22, 800–999	8111–9259	8111–9279
Caring services	370, 630–99	6111–292	6121–240

Table A1.2 Proportion of class fractions in NS-SEC categories (%)

Class fraction	NS-SEC major group (SOC2010 based)							
	Higher managerial and professional	Lower managerial and professional	Intermediate occupations	Small employers and own-account workers	Lower supervisory and technical	Semi-routine occupations	Routine occupations	Total
Business executives	69.6	20.3	0.0	10.1	0.0	0.0	0.0	100.0
Professions	92.2	7.8	0.0	0.0	0.0	0.0	0.0	100.0
White-collar	30.7	67.5	1.6	0.1	0.0	0.0	0.0	100.0
Cultural dominant	28.2	60.5	4.9	6.4	0.0	0.0	0.0	100.0
LMPs	4.3	64.9	0.0	30.7	0.0	0.0	0.0	100.0
Technicians	26.4	54.5	15.5	0.5	1.7	1.3	0.0	100.0
Administrators	0.0	13.5	71.4	4.3	1.0	9.7	0.0	100.0
Cultural intermediaries	0.0	91.5	4.2	2.9	0.3	1.0	0.0	100.0
Skilled trades	0.0	3.7	5.0	34.6	36.7	8.1	11.9	100.0
Sales workers	0.0	14.1	23.0	4.1	7.8	50.4	0.7	100.0
Manual workers	0.0	0.0	0.0	12.5	14.1	25.0	48.5	100.0
Caring services	0.1	5.4	28.6	10.9	8.4	40.2	6.5	100.0

Source: LFS 2015

Table A1.3 Proportion of NS-SEC categories in the class fractions (%)

Class fraction	NS-SEC						
	Higher managerial and professional	Lower managerial and professional	Intermediate occupations	Small employers and own account workers	Lower supervisory and technical	Semi-routine occupations	Routine occupations
Business executives	27.8	4.6	0.0	6.0	0.0	0.0	0.0
Professions	26.4	1.3	0.0	0.0	0.0	0.0	0.0
White-collar	19.2	24.1	1.1	0.1	0.0	0.0	0.0
Cultural dominant	18.3	22.6	3.6	6.1	0.0	0.0	0.0
LMPs	1.3	11.5	0.0	14.1	0.0	0.0	0.0
Technicians	6.8	8.1	4.5	0.2	0.9	0.4	0.0
Administrators	0.0	5.4	55.4	4.5	1.3	7.9	0.0
Cultural intermediaries	0.0	15.6	1.4	1.3	0.2	0.3	0.0
Skilled trades	0.0	1.5	3.9	36.1	51.5	6.8	13.2
Sales workers	0.0	3.5	11.2	2.6	6.7	25.8	0.5
Manual workers	0.0	0.0	0.0	19.5	29.5	31.0	80.4
Caring services	0.0	1.8	18.8	9.5	9.8	27.9	6.0
Total	100.0	100.0	100.0	100.0	100.0	100.0	100.0

Source: LFS 2015

Appendix II: Data tables and sources

Table A2.1 Eigenvalues and variance explained by the axes in the model of the symbolic space

Axis	Eigenvalue	Percentage	Cumulated percentage	Modified eigenvalue★	Modified percentage	Cumulated modified percentage
1	0.270	5.65	5.65	0.02731	56.5	56.5
2	0.208	4.35	10.00	0.00893	18.5	75.0
3	0.176	3.69	13.69	0.00345	7.1	82.1

★ Modified eigenvalues and percentages are calculated to rectify the underestimation of explained variance in MCA.

Table A2.2 Contributions of active categories to the model of the symbolic space★

Label	Relative weight (%)	Squared distance to origin	Axis 1	Axis 2	Axis 3
No. artists known					
0–2 artists	1.5	7.409	**5.833**	**3.754**	0.666
3–5 artists	7.6	0.655	1.725	1.363	0.061
6 artists	2.7	3.669	**9.691**	0.208	0.939
7 artists	0.6	18.550	**3.701**	**4.003**	0.031
TOTAL	12.4		20.950	9.328	1.698
Favourite sport					
Exclusive	0.9	12.964	**4.650**	**6.604**	**13.573**
Keep fit	1.0	11.512	0.291	**6.656**	**3.988**
Self-cultivation	1.2	9.861	1.983	**3.129**	0.148
Swimming	0.8	15.463	0.660	**2.791**	**3.332**
Walking	1.2	9.639	1.631	0.000	0.853
TOTAL	5.0		9.215	19.181	21.893
Ideal home					
Clean & tidy	4.7	1.642	**3.194**	0.438	0.188
Comfy	3.0	3.116	0.603	1.627	0.662
Distinctive/imaginative/ uncluttered	1.0	11.031	**2.512**	0.794	0.029
Easy to maintain	0.7	16.977	0.011	0.158	1.077
Elegant/well-designed	0.8	15.638	0.993	0.592	1.036
Lived-in	0.8	15.638	0.386	0.325	0.680
TOTAL	11.0		7.699	3.933	3.672
Style of dress					
Casual	3.7	2.335	0.073	0.617	1.163
Comfy	4.9	1.547	0.035	0.482	**6.303**
Easy/cheap/designer	0.9	12.600	0.006	0.607	1.888
Fashionable	1.5	7.104	0.046	**6.992**	**9.326**
Smart/traditional	1.3	8.310	0.138	0.780	0.714

continued

Table A2.2 (cont.)

Label	Relative weight (%)	Squared distance to origin	Axis 1	Axis 2	Axis 3
TOTAL	12.5		0.299	9.478	19.394
Newspaper					
Guardian/Independent	0.7	17.400	**5.644**	**2.873**	3.185
Mirror	1.1	10.252	1.052	0.388	0.004
No news	3.1	2.980	0.076	0.743	1.332
Other red top	2.8	3.507	**6.664**	1.555	2.206
Regional	1.3	8.654	0.421	0.146	0.293
Times/Financial Times/ Telegraph	1.1	10.252	**6.801**	1.511	0.605
Tabloid	2.3	4.393	1.603	**2.942**	0.365
TOTAL	12.4		22.261	10.159	7.989
Favourite sport to watch					
Athletics/gymnastics	1.1	10.171	0.038	**3.731**	0.623
Boxing/speedway	0.7	16.378	1.189	0.939	0.004
Formula 1	0.9	12.841	0.634	0.142	0.049
Golf/cricket/horse-racing	1.2	9.156	0.312	**9.450**	**3.459**
Rugby Union	0.9	13.218	1.037	0.213	0.012
Tennis	1.2	9.497	1.692	0.032	1.562
Snooker/darts	1.1	9.937	**2.530**	0.005	**2.927**
TOTAL	7.2		7.433	14.512	8.636
Reason like sport					
Buzz/competition	1.0	11.512	0.295	0.009	**9.355**
Fitness	2.1	4.858	0.429	**9.366**	0.080
Mental element	2.5	4.078	**6.675**	0.267	**2.405**
No sport	5.7	1.212	**7.204**	2.710	**3.408**
Sociability	0.8	14.039	0.823	2.584	**11.034**
TOTAL	12.1		15.426	14.937	26.282
Type of art liked most					
Landscapes	6.0	1.099	0.140	**7.262**	0.000
Modern art	1.0	11.031	0.039	**6.827**	**5.165**
None	1.1	10.416	**5.093**	0.044	0.550
Performance art	1.0	11.715	0.122	**2.584**	1.377
Renaissance/Impressionism	1.7	6.377	**10.187**	0.128	**3.287**
Still life/portrait	1.7	6.343	1.135	1.627	0.058
TOTAL	12.5		16.716	18.472	10.437

* Above-average contributions to the axes are shown in bold.

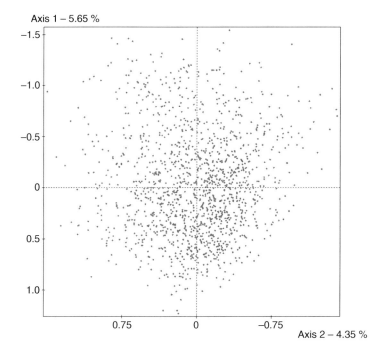

Figure A2.1 Individuals within the model of the symbolic space, axes 1 and 2

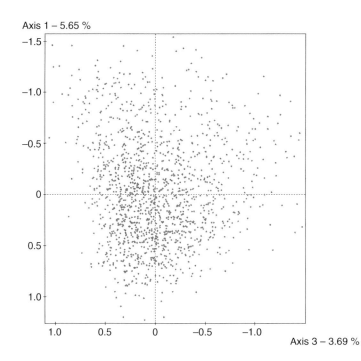

Figure A2.2 Individuals within the model of the symbolic space, axes 1 and 3

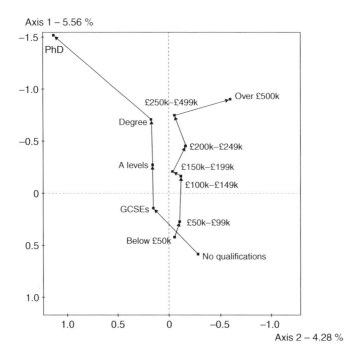

Figure A2.3 Respondent's highest qualification (cultural capital) and house value (economic capital) in the model of symbolic space, axes 1 and 2

Table A2.3 Eigenvalues and percentage of variance explained by the axes in the model of the space of political position-takings

Axis	Eigenvalue	Percentage	Cumulated Percentage	Modified Eigenvalue	Modified Percentage	Modified Cumulated Percentage
1	0.221	9.5	9.5	0.02269	36.2	36.2
2	0.209	9.0	18.5	0.01888	30.2	66.4
3	0.194	8.3	26.8	0.01458	23.3	89.7

Table A2.4 Contributions of active modalities to the axes in the model of the space of political position-takings⋆

Label	Relative Weight (%)	Squared distance to origin	Axis 1	Axis 2	Axis 3
Party identity					
Conservative	2.4	2.496	**3.984**	**2.734**	0.090
Labour	2.6	2.261	**2.827**	0.370	0.033
Liberal Democrat	1.0	7.022	0.168	0.000	1.222
None	1.3	5.197	0.007	0.825	0.356
Other/don't know/ refused	0.5	15.241	0.096	0.251	0.195
TOTAL	7.8		7.082	4.181	1.897
redist					
redist yes	2.5	2.294	**8.663**	0.069	0.176
redist neither	1.9	3.338	1.240	**5.524**	0.184
redist no	2.5	2.371	**4.500**	**6.297**	0.071
TOTAL	6.9		14.402	11.890	0.431
wealth					
wealth yes	4.0	1.072	**5.877**	0.114	1.874
wealth neither	1.9	3.443	**5.174**	**3.047**	1.583
wealth no	1.0	7.263	**3.680**	**10.920**	1.718
TOTAL	6.9		14.730	14.082	5.175
richlaw					
one law yes	4.0	1.059	**4.909**	0.217	2.992
one law neither	1.6	4.217	**3.290**	**3.980**	1.520
one law no	1.3	5.516	**4.230**	**10.831**	**3.877**
TOTAL	6.9		12.430	15.028	8.389
boss					
boss yes	3.6	1.327	**3.712**	0.000	**3.929**
boss neither	1.9	3.327	1.825	**5.186**	1.102
boss no	1.4	4.984	**2.739**	**8.321**	**4.850**
TOTAL	6.9		8.277	13.508	9.880
death					
death yes	3.8	1.176	0.002	0.121	**5.294**
death neither	1.1	6.888	1.114	**3.247**	0.352
death no	2.0	3.116	0.458	1.111	**8.627**
TOTAL	6.9		1.575	4.479	14.272
wronglaw					
wrong law yes	2.9	1.895	0.036	0.666	1.359
wrong law neither	2.4	2.452	0.976	**3.019**	0.333
wrong law no	1.6	4.176	1.765	1.643	1.152
TOTAL	6.9		2.777	5.329	2.844
censor					
censor yes	4.3	0.927	0.012	0.113	1.594
censor neither	1.5	4.560	0.658	**2.963**	0.292
censor no	1.1	6.685	0.958	2.616	**4.683**
TOTAL	6.9		1.628	5.693	6.568

continued

Label	Relative Weight (%)	Squared distance to origin	Axis 1	Axis 2	Axis 3
morewelf					
morewelf yes	2.2	2.847	**6.612**	0.004	0.051
morewelf neither	2.2	2.874	0.669	**4.143**	0.659
morewelf no	2.6	2.204	**2.984**	**3.827**	0.557
TOTAL	6.9		10.265	7.975	1.267
unempjob					
unempjob yes	3.8	1.219	1.444	1.516	**4.788**
unempjob neither	1.7	3.936	0.706	**3.992**	**2.698**
unempjob no	1.5	4.684	**6.988**	0.182	**4.059**
TOTAL	6.9		9.138	5.690	11.545
sochelp					
sochelp yes	2.5	2.347	0.975	2.006	**9.169**
sochelp neither	2.4	2.485	2.059	**4.426**	0.708
sochelp no	2.0	3.132	**6.391**	0.819	**7.185**
TOTAL	6.9		9.424	7.251	17.062
dole fiddle					
dole fiddle yes	2.4	2.463	0.346	1.232	**10.923**
dole fiddle neither	2.4	2.420	**2.706**	**2.900**	0.504
dole fiddle no	2.1	3.060	**5.221**	0.764	**9.241**
TOTAL	6.9		8.273	4.896	20.669

* Above-average contributions to the axes are shown in bold.

Table A2.5 Coordinates of some supplementary variables in the model of the space of political position-takings

Supplementary variable	Axis 1	Axis 2	Axis 3
Sex			
Male	−0.025	−0.069	0.049
Female	0.020	0.053	−0.038
Age			
18–24	0.051	0.093	−0.010
25–34	0.110	0.036	−0.020
35–44	0.064	0.021	−0.067
45–54	−0.029	0.056	−0.158
55–64	−0.139	−0.048	−0.085
65–97	−0.014	−0.061	0.219
Religion			
Buddhist	−0.624	−0.024	0.014
Christian (no denomination)	0.096	−0.011	−0.053
Church of England	0.174	−0.079	0.119
Hindu	0.184	0.019	0.513

continued

Table A2.5 *(cont.)*

Supplementary variable	Axis 1	Axis 2	Axis 3
Jewish	0.224	−0.340	−0.135
Muslim	−0.085	0.214	0.148
No religion	−0.057	0.010	−0.052
Presbyterian	−0.367	0.014	0.022
Roman Catholic	−0.054	0.089	0.047
Racial origin			
Asian – Bangladeshi	0.007	0.064	0.292
Asian – Chinese	0.407	−0.055	−0.305
Asian – Indian	0.269	0.200	0.251
Asian – Pakistani	0.088	0.040	−0.280
Asian – other	−0.006	−0.010	0.292
Black – African	−0.084	0.316	0.174
Black – Caribbean	−0.213	0.381	0.067
Black – other	−0.527	0.708	1.030
White	0.005	−0.016	−0.005
Mixed origin	−0.292	0.262	0.012

Axis 1: positive values = right wing; negative values = left wing
Axis 2: positive values = disengagement; negative values = engagement
Axis 3: positive values = authoritarianism/individualism; negative values = liberalism/pro–welfare

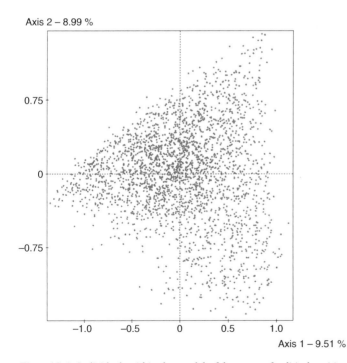

Figure A2.4 Individuals within the model of the space of political position-takings, axes 1 and 2

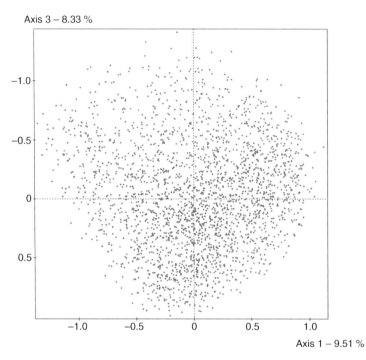

Axis 3 − 8.33 %

Axis 1 − 9.51 %

Figure A2.5 Individuals within the model of the space of political position-takings, axes 1 and 3

Table A2.6 Data sources

Name	Survey	Data collector	Sample size★
BCS 2009	The British Cohort Study, 2009 wave	Centre for Longitudinal Studies, Institute of Education	8,874
BCS 2012	The British Cohort Study, 2012 wave	Centre for Longitudinal Studies, Institute of Education	7,650
BSA 1991	British Social Attitudes Survey 1991	Social and Community Planning research	2,918
BSA 2005	British Social Attitudes Survey 2005	National Centre for Social Research	4,268
BSA 2008	British Social Attitudes Survey 2008	National Centre for Social Research	4,486
BSA 2010	British Social Attitudes Survey 2010	National Centre for Social Research	3,297
CCSE 2003	Cultural Capital and Social Exclusion survey 2003	Bennett *et al.* (2009)	1,564
GHS 1991	The General Household Survey 1991–2	ONS	27,944

continued

Table A2.6 (cont.)

Name	Survey	Data collector	Sample size★
LCFS 2010	Living Costs and Food Survey 2010	ONS	12,178
LFS 1995	Labour Force Survey (April-June) 1995	ONS	155,965
LFS 2000	Labour Force Survey (April-June) 2000	ONS	142,484
LFS 2005	Labour Force Survey (April-June) 2005	ONS	126,587
LFS 2010	Labour Force Survey (April-June) 2010	ONS	114,970
LFS 2013	Labour Force Survey (April-June) 2013	ONS	97,274
LFS 2015	Labour Force Survey (April-June) 2015	ONS	95,359
WAS 2006/8	Wealth and Assets Survey 2006/8	ONS	46,293
WER	Workplace Employee Relations Survey 2011	Dept. of Business, Innovation and Skills	21,981

★ All datasets were weighted. The LFS was usually weighted for population estimates, but when calculating incomes the income weight was used.

Appendix III: The Ordinary Lives project

The Ordinary Lives project, from which all qualitative material in this book is taken, took place between 2010 and 2012. Led by Harriet Bradley and myself, with the assistance of a dedicated fieldworker, it was conceived as a means to grasp the everyday experience of class to rival the famous 'community studies' of years gone by. For my part, the interest lay in documenting precisely how class fits into lifeworlds – the mundane tensions and struggles, the way in which social reproduction is achieved through countless exchanges, *in situ* perceptions and judgements rather than just rationalisations in an interview, and so on. The majority of respondents were recruited through a mail-out to the three selected areas chosen on account of their class composition as revealed by the 2001 Census and neighbourhood statistics: Lockleaze, Southville/Bedminster and Redland. Three hundred letters of invitation were sent out to each zone using names selected at random (excluding student halls of residence, sheltered housing and so on) from the electoral register. The missive explained the broad purpose of the project and made clear that as we were interested in parent–child relations and schooling, we were looking for families with at least one resident school-aged child to take part. If families expressed interest, one of the research team visited them to collect basic information (ages, number of children, occupation) and assess the suitability of the family for participation – a task which was necessary to guard against the possible ethical pitfalls of offering a monetary incentive, since we paid each participating family £100.

The response from Redland was ample, with far more families (or, more accurately, the women in the families) registering their interest in taking part than we were able to include in the final sample. From Southville, the mixed area, there was enough of a turnout to fill up the dominant and intermediate quotas, plus a few within the upper reaches of the dominated class. From Lockleaze, however, we had a frustratingly low response, despite being equipped with the expectation that those living in this area would be less inclined to take part in university research due to suspicions of state institutions, an ingrained sense of being 'nothing special', a proud privatism and so on. Furthermore, those we did manage to get hold of from the area were generally within the upper reaches of the dominant, a fraction whose particular orientation, combining in complex ways the dispositions of the petite bourgeoisie and the taste for the necessary of the dominant *per se*, became particularly salient only when compared to the few 'middle dominated' we did recruit. This was, of course, if they were not actually at the lower end of the intermediate class, as with those who lived in the comparatively more affluent and secure areas surrounding the deprived core of the Lockleaze ward.

The task remained, therefore, of recruiting several more families within the dominated class. This proved to be an exceptionally hard feat, if only because we set ourselves the demanding assignment of trying to avoid recruiting only the aspirational upper dominated – the tradespeople, the college-educated, the certified who wanted to 'get on' and 'strive', to invest what meagre resources they had in their children, as opposed to those who resign themselves to the objectively likely future. The array of strategies we adopted to do this was messy, with some tactics being planned and toiled over whilst others were improvised and opportunistic. The lines of action included snowballing, trudging almost every street and block of flats to pass on information to residents, visiting multiple parent-toddler groups, speaking at community meetings and being put in touch with prospective participants by a debt advice agency.

Though variations, accommodations, concessions, improvisations and curtailments were common, for most participating households the research involved eight consecutive days of activity, running from one Sunday to the next. For the first three days, from Sunday morning through to Tuesday evening, members of each family – adults and, if they were old enough and willing, dependants – completed a qualitative time-diary, recording their activities in time chunks of their own choosing. They were asked to state the main activity, where they were, any significant secondary activities occurring in the time frame, who they were with, how typical the activity was and any reflections they may have had. A camera was also provided for them to take pictures of objects and events from their everyday lives. The open-ended nature of this first task meant that the length of diaries and numbers of photographs varied considerably between individuals and families, with those high in cultural capital frequently requiring extra pages to elaborate their reflections in a playful and often very revealing manner and snapping up to a hundred pictures, while others, disproportionately the dominated, were much more concise, almost list-like in their accounts, and took only a couple of photos. In some cases, moreover, men from the dominated class refused to fill in the diaries at all ('I'm not writing things down,' said one) and the women, perhaps because they are more used to dealing with agents of the state and self-documentation on account of their childcare responsibilities, not to mention their gendered dispositions and position in the family field, were compelled to complete them on their behalf. Consequently the diaries were identified as one of the barriers to recruitment of dominated families, and so we renamed them 'time records' and modified their presentation so as to make them appear less demanding, though to little overall effect.

The second phase of the research comprised three separate occasions of observation: the Wednesday evening, entering the field before preparation of the evening meal and leaving at a time negotiated with the family (usually just before they prepared for bed), the Thursday evening for the same or similar time period and the Saturday daytime, ranging from morning until the evening meal or just a few hours in the day. Though times varied significantly between families, generally the stretches spent with participants were thus considerable to say the least. In some instances the fieldworker would enter the field at 5.30pm and leave at 10.30pm, or spend a Saturday from 9am to 5.30pm with the family, generating a barely manageable yet incredibly rich mountain of notes and data on all that occurred within that time frame – filtered only by memory and, inevitably, sociological schemes of perception.

'Participation' when doing observational research operates on a scale rather than categorically, and we shifted along it depending on the proclivities of the observed and the solicitations of the situation, but these observations were intended to cluster toward the non-participatory pole in order to let the flow of family life carry on as uninterrupted as possible. Fieldworkers did not eat with the families, as tempting as the aroma of the food might be, and generally, apart from questions of clarification, tried to keep 'out of the way', in the background, so as to disturb the current of conduct as little as possible and maximise the richness of our notes (made on the spot). More often than not, the urge to talk and to self-present, so as to assuage the peculiarity of the situation, would be most pronounced on the first evening, but over the course of the observations this would ebb.

Though the time-diaries and the observations covered the bulk of the week, they were complemented by several extra methods. The first of these was a 'home tour', that is to say, a participant-led and audio-recorded tour of the rooms in the house and the garden. Our guides were encouraged to talk about the uses of, and objects of significance in, the different rooms, as well as the decor, in order to grasp regionalisations, artefacts of family doxa and classed and gendered aesthetic orientations, but in many instances the talk turned to other themes – family history, mobility, travel – of significance. Again, however, the character of the home tour differed dramatically between the classes. Those rich in cultural capital, for whom reflection and abstraction are par for the course in life, and who were confident in their abode, were keen to elaborate the narratives woven around certain objects and rooms with minimal prompting, to the point where they – including, most strikingly, the children – very much 'took charge' and led the tour. Those without such capital and confidence, however, were more nervous, unsure of what to say, apologetic about what they perceived as 'mess', ashamed of the size of their dwelling ('it won't take long') and likely to give shorter, more concrete explanations. Ultimately, in opposition to the dominant, they expected to be led by us – representatives of the dominant class, of probing professionals – i.e. to be asked questions to which they could give answers ('I don't know what you want me to say', 'what do you want to know?').

The next complementary method was what has been dubbed a 'go-along' interview, which essentially took the form of accompanying family members on a routine time-space path, taking photos and asking questions aimed at deciphering the phenomenology of the journey (cf. Kusenbach, 2003). Usually this occurred in the course of the observations, if family members were going somewhere, and the fieldworker would switch out of observation mode and into interviewer mode (sometimes with an audio recorder, sometimes without). In reality, the data yielded by this method was much more complex and heterogeneous than anticipated. There would be insight into the perception of space, the shared and contested labelling and meaning of local objects and sites and the layers of familiarity within lifeworlds, but sometimes the interactions between family members would overwhelm the interview and it would slip more into an observation – in many cases reaping abundant conversational data – and sometimes the topics of the interview would, as with the home tour, wander on to broader themes.

Finally, the fieldworker conducted, on the second Sunday, a formal 'sit-down' interview with as many family members as possible – adults were always present, but sometimes children, especially if a little older, would participate and be asked questions too. The point of this last exercise was to gather extra information on facets of life not seen in the observations or the diaries – such as holidays, weekday routines, the broader family constellation etc. – and to probe some of the practices witnessed in the week, soliciting rationalisations, perceptions and expectations. The interview also collected information on the resources and trajectories of the parents (and indeed of their parents and grandparents, in order to approximate the direction and velocity of intergenerational movements in social space) so as to 'place' them, however roughly, within the space of classes. They were not classified using the class scheme developed in Part I of this book, and not only because the Ordinary Lives project antedated the scheme's construction. The scheme is designed to approximate social space position for statistical data analysis when a full range of indicators may not be available, and it may act as a practical preliminary orienting device in some instances insofar as it signposts where the average person in a certain type of job more or less sits in the social space – as well as the kinds of jobs a certain amount and type of capital are usually associated with – and the structure of the space as a whole. At the individual level, however, there is too much dispersion for it to be the be-all and end-all, and the scheme cannot substitute for the rich information on capitals and trajectories, revealing the nuances of positioning distinct from occupational title (which is only a proxy, after all), that qualitative research, particularly when it has a biographical component, is able to gather. When participants are situated in the dominant, intermediate or dominated sections of the social space in the text, therefore, this is done not simply on the basis of occupation (as an indicator of field effects, and sometimes a proxy for economic capital) or income and educational level as the fundamental gauges of capital, as efficient as these often are, but home ownership and likely value, type of school attended, subject studied at university, the type of university attended, parents' and grandparents' occupations and educational levels, friendship networks and suchlike too. Not all of these, however, can be systematically presented to readers if participant anonymity and confidentiality are to be properly safeguarded.

Table A3.1 Participants in the Ordinary Lives project

Family name	Parents' occupations and ages	Children (ages) and other household members*	Highest educational qualification**	Household income (per annum)	Area of residence
Allen	Mr: Telecommunications engineer (43) Mrs: Sales representative for a publishing house (37)	B (12), G (10)	Mr: HND Mrs: A levels	Unknown	Redland
Anderson/Braithwaite	Mr A: Freelance meteorologist (42) Ms B: Primary school teacher/educational consultant (part-time) (43)	B (8)	Mr: PhD Ms: Degree	£23,000	Southville
Arnold/Jeffers	Mr A: Construction site engineer (52) Ms J: PA, cleaner, administrative worker (all part-time) (44)	B1 (13), B2 (11)	Mr: HNC Mrs: CSEs and one GCE	£65,000	Kingswood (via Lockleaze)
Atwell	Mrs A: Homemaker	B1, B2, B3, B4, B5, B6, G	Ms: No qualifications	Unknown (benefits only)	Lockleaze
Buchanan	Mr B: Electronic designer (self-employed) (46) Mrs B: Medical receptionist (44)	B1 (9), B2 (7)	Mr: HND Mrs: Degree	£62,000	Lockleaze
Carlisle	Mr C: General practitioner (50) Mrs: Administrator	B1 (15), B2 (14), G1 (20), G2 (17) (plus L1, 17, and L2, 21)	Mr: Medical degree Mrs: Nurse training	£102,000	Redland
Cavendish/Burton	Mr C: Self-employed landscape gardener/builder Ms B: Hospital auxiliary	G (11)	Mr: O levels Ms: NVQ	£25,000	Lockleaze
Collins/Taylor	Miss C: Student (22) Mr T: Barman (assistant manager) (22)	B (5), G (2)	Mr: GCSEs Ms: GCSEs	£13,000	Brislington
Daniels	Mr D: Electrical engineer (42) Mrs D: Primary school teacher (38)	B1 (4), B2 (10 months)	Mr: HND Mrs: PGCE	£51,000	Redland
Duncan	Mr D: long-term unemployed due to disability, former lorry-driver (48) Mrs D: Part-time cleaner (44)	B1 (20), Ba (16), Bb (16)	Mr: CSEs, O level Mrs: GCSEs	£19,000	Lockleaze

continued

Table A3.1 (cont.)

Family name	Parents' occupations and ages	Children (ages) and other household members★	Highest educational qualification★★	Household income (per annum)	Area of residence
Evans/Francis	Mr E: Nursery teacher (40) Ms F: Hospital consultant (39)	B1 (5), B2 (2), G (8)	Mr: Degree Ms: Medical degree	£97,000	Southville
Floyd/Babinski	Mr B: Design technician (33) Ms F: Part-time English teacher and barmaid (44)	B1 (4), B2 (2) (plus L)	Mr: Master's degree Mrs: Degree	£32,000	Southville
Geoffrey	Mr G: Policeman (42) Mrs G: Housewife, former restaurant manager (45)	G1 (4), G2 (3), G3 (2) (plus 3 lodgers)	Mr: A levels Mrs: HND	£44,000	Southville
Green	Mr G: Plasterer's mate (27) Mrs G: Housewife (26)	B1 (7), B2 (3), B3 (16 months)	Mr: GCSEs Mrs: GCSEs	£15,000	Lockleaze
Hughes/Barnes	Mr H: Freelance copywriter, part-time childcare assistant (43) Ms B: Part-time self-employed childcare provider, part-time assistant bank manager (42)	G (5)	Mr: HND Mrs: Degree	£57,000	Southville
Illsley/James	Mr I: International tax lawyer (54) Ms J: Postgraduate student (45)	Ga (12), Gb (12) (twins)	Mr: LLM Ms: Master's degree	c. £235,000	Redland
Johnson/Kent	Mr J: Self-employed personal trainer and doorman (44) Ms K: Housewife (41)	G1 (9), G2 (6)	Mr: City and Guilds Ms: Degree	£39,000	Fishponds (via Lockleaze)
King	Mr K: Business analyst (41) Mrs K: Project analyst (40)	G (10), B (15)	Mr: A levels Mrs: BTEC	£68,000	Southville
Lewis	Mr L: Estate agent (45) Mrs L: Part-time occupational therapist (42)	B (13), G (11)	Mr: Diploma Mrs: Diploma	£62,000	Southville
Lyon	Mr L: Self-employed painter-decorator (thirties) Mrs L: Nursery nurse (twenties)	G1, G2 (2)	Mr: NVQ Mrs: NVQ	£18,000	Southville

Family	Parents	Children	Qualifications	Income	Area
Michaels	Mr M: Senior support worker (43) Mrs M: Social worker (42)	B (14), G1(16), G2 (8)	Mr: Degree Mrs: Master's degree	£51,000	Lockleaze
Morgan	Ms M: Shop worker (37)	G1 (10), G2 (7)	Ms: Nursery nurse training	£7,000	Totterdown (via Southville)
Nash	Mr N: Delivery-driver (38) Mrs N: Part-time cleaner (36)	G1 (8), G2 (4)	Mr: No qualifications Mrs: CSEs	£20,000	Lockleaze
Newcombe/Oliver	Mr N: Self-employed policy consultant (63) Ms O: Self-employed third-sector management advisor (52)	B (15), G (10)	Mr: Master's degree Ms: Master's degree	£45,000	Redland
Patrick	Mr P: Barrister (44) Mrs P: Social worker; self-employed businesswoman (40)	G1 (14), G2 (12), G3 (5), G4 (4) (plus L, 24)	Mr: LLB Mrs: Degree	Unknown	Redland
Quinn	Mr Q: Accountant (45) Mrs Q: Further education teacher (43)	B (14), G (5)	Mr: Degree Mrs: PGCE	£96,000	Southville
Richards	Mr R: International Tax Accountant Mrs R: Occupational Therapist (part-time)	G (15), B (13)	Mr: Degree Mrs: Diploma	c. £116,000	Redland
Samuels	Mr S: Human resources advisor (42) Mrs S: Manager in a publishing house (40)	B (10), G (10) (twins)	Mr: Postgraduate diploma Mrs: Degree	£68,000	Southville
Tanner/Upson	Mr T: Housing association manager (54) Ms U: Events manager (49)	B (10)	Mr: Degree Ms: Degree	£67,000	Redland
Williams	Mr W: Area manager (43) Mrs W: Housewife (39)	B (2), G (5)	Mr: Degree Mrs: Degree	£65,000	Redland
Yates	Mr Y: Physiotherapist (40) Mrs Y: Part-time physiotherapist (38)	B1 (11), B2 (8), B3 (5)	Mr: Degree Mrs: Postgraduate diploma	£64,000	Redland

* B = boy, G = girl, L = lodger, B1 = eldest boy, B2 = next boy down etc.; Ga and Gb and Ba and Bb refer to same-sex twins. The decision was made early on to use these rather impersonal pseudonyms for practical purposes, i.e. to avoid having to conjure a gigantic and possibly confusing catalogue of pseudonyms.

** For those not familiar with British educational qualifications, CSEs, GCEs, GCSEs and O levels are qualifications usually gained at 16; A levels are academic qualifications usually gained at 18; NVQs, BTECs and City and Guilds are lower-tier vocational qualifications; HNCs, HNDs and diplomas are higher-level vocational qualifications; PGCEs and postgraduate diplomas are vocational qualifications requiring a prior degree.

References

Elias, P. and Birch, M. (2010) 'SOC2010: Revision of the Standard Occupational Classification' *Economic and Labour Market Review*, 4(7): 48–55.

Flemmen, M. (2014) 'The Politics of the Service Class' *European Societies*, 16(4): 543–69.

Kusenbach, M. (2003) 'Street Phenomenology: The Go-Along as Ethnographic Research Tool' *Ethnography*, 4(3): 455–85.

Index

Taylor & Francis eBooks

Helping you to choose the right eBooks for your Library

Add Routledge titles to your library's digital collection today. Taylor and Francis ebooks contains over 50,000 titles in the Humanities, Social Sciences, Behavioural Sciences, Built Environment and Law.

Choose from a range of subject packages or create your own!

Benefits for you

» Free MARC records
» COUNTER-compliant usage statistics
» Flexible purchase and pricing options
» All titles DRM-free.

Benefits for your user

» Off-site, anytime access via Athens or referring URL
» Print or copy pages or chapters
» Full content search
» Bookmark, highlight and annotate text
» Access to thousands of pages of quality research at the click of a button.

REQUEST YOUR **FREE** INSTITUTIONAL TRIAL TODAY	**Free Trials Available** We offer free trials to qualifying academic, corporate and government customers.

eCollections – Choose from over 30 subject eCollections, including:

Archaeology	Language Learning
Architecture	Law
Asian Studies	Literature
Business & Management	Media & Communication
Classical Studies	Middle East Studies
Construction	Music
Creative & Media Arts	Philosophy
Criminology & Criminal Justice	Planning
Economics	Politics
Education	Psychology & Mental Health
Energy	Religion
Engineering	Security
English Language & Linguistics	Social Work
Environment & Sustainability	Sociology
Geography	Sport
Health Studies	Theatre & Performance
History	Tourism, Hospitality & Events

For more information, pricing enquiries or to order a free trial, please contact your local sales team:
www.tandfebooks.com/page/sales

 Routledge
Taylor & Francis Group

The home of Routledge books

www.tandfebooks.com